SWCA Anthropological Research Paper Number 9

Prehistory in West Prescott, Arizona

Prepared by Richard A. Anduze, Thomas N. Motsinger, and James M. Potter

With contributions by
Andrew L. Christenson
Linda Scott Cummings
John D. Goodman II
Dawn M. Greenwald
Dee A. Jones
Paul V. Long
Thomas E. Moutoux
Kathryn Puseman
Mary-Ellen Walsh

SWCA®
ENVIRONMENTAL CONSULTANTS
Phoenix _ 2003

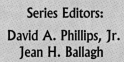

Series Editors:
David A. Phillips, Jr.
Jean H. Ballagh

TABLE OF CONTENTS

List of Figures

List of Tables

Acknowledgments

The Hassayampa Country Club project represents a collaborative effort among a smorgasbord of strange bedfellows: private developers and public agencies, archaeologists and Native Americans, and professionals and paraprofessionals. On the developer end, Desert Troon Companies and their affiliate, Hassayampa Village Community, L.L.C., could scarcely have been more supportive or responsible with regard to the management of archaeological resources on their property. At times when clients usually ask, "How much do we have to do?" Troon asked, "What else can we do?" In funding this project and choosing to preserve and stabilize the Hassayampa Ruin, they made a lasting contribution to local and regional archaeology and set a standard for others in the private sector. Phil Ordway, David Blouin, and David Gulino of Troon and HVC were particularly supportive, and Tom Weiskopf of Tom Weiskopf Designs was agreeable to integrating preserved sites into his golf course design.

Carol Heathington of the Arizona SHPO, Larry Flatau of the Corps of Engineers, and Nancy Burgess and Ramona Mattix of the City of Prescott provided a healthy dose of common-sense agency oversight that kept the project on track. Tribal Archaeologist Linda Blan and para-archaeologist Stan Rice, Sr., of the Yavapai-Prescott Indian Tribe assisted with removal of human remains and other aspects of the fieldwork.

Thomas N. Motsinger of SWCA's Tucson office managed the project. Richard A. Anduze of the Flagstaff office directed the fieldwork, with the assistance of Stewart Deats, also from Flagstaff. The field crew included Andy Arias of SWCA and Virginia Johnson, Paul Long (who also contributed most of the material for the Culture History section of the report), Mary Spall, and Charlie Steger of the Arizona Archaeological Society's Yavapai Chapter. Several people, including David H. Greenwald, Richard V. N. Ahlstrom, and Andrew L. Christenson, volunteered all or part of a weekend to complete the stabilization work at the Hassayampa Ruin under the direction of Lynn A. Neal.

For SWCA, Mary-Ellen Walsh oversaw analysis of the ceramics assemblage, Dawn Greenwald carried out the lithic artifact analyses, and Dee A. Jones conducted the study of human osteological remains. Other SWCA personnel undertook supplementary studies: Tom Motsinger reported on the ceramic figurines; Dee Jones, Rick Anduze, John D. Goodman II, and James M. Potter studied the faunal assemblage; and John Goodman analyzed the shell artifacts. Consultants who contributed key portions of the studies were Andrew Christenson, who assisted with the ceramics analysis and wrote sections of that report; Linda Scott Cummings, Kathryn Puseman, and Thomas E. Moutoux of PaleoResearch, who analyzed the archaeobotanical remains; and the staff of Beta Analytic Inc., who conducted the analysis of radiocarbon samples. Mary-Ellen Walsh was the laboratory director, assisted by Laura James.

Maps were prepared by Jill Caouette, Aron Hauser, and Lisa Kearsley. Lisa was also responsible for the lithic artifact illustrations; John Goodman drew the bone and shell artifacts. Jean Ballagh edited the technical report, and Serena Roseke produced that document. In preparing this Anthropological Research Paper, Robert C. Euler, Jean Ballagh, and David A. Phillips, Jr., were the editors, and Heidi Hill prepared the graphics for publication. Michelle Weigmann, Heidi Hill, and David Phillips are responsible for the new design of these volumes.

As always, more individuals had a hand in creating the final product than we have space to acknowledge. We extend our thanks to all, named and unnamed.

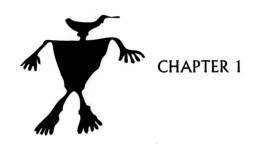

CHAPTER 1

Introduction

Thomas N. Motsinger, Richard A. Anduze, and Paul V. Long

In 1995 SWCA completed an archaeological survey of a property in Prescott, Arizona, owned by the Desert Troon Companies, the location chosen for the new Hassayampa Country Club (Terzis and Motsinger 1995) (Figure 1.1). Later that year and in 1996, SWCA undertook archaeological excavations at 10 sites (Anduze et al. 1999). This monograph focuses on the seven sites with Prescott Culture components (Figure 1.2).

Although the project was begun to ensure compliance with City of Prescott guidelines (Amended Ordinance No. 3267), it was carried out in accordance with federal historic preservation standards. When the Army Corps of Engineers became involved in the project late in 1995 in connection with wetlands permitting, the cultural resource compliance work could have become entangled in costly and time-consuming bureaucratic review of the sort that often sours private developers on the "Section 106 process." Instead, the Corps of Engineers, the Arizona State Historic Preservation Office, the City of Prescott, and Native American tribes agreed to a streamlined (yet no less stringent) review process that allowed the archaeology to move forward without undue delay. In doing so, these agencies provided a model of how privately funded archaeological projects can benefit all the "publics" the National Historic Preservation Act is intended to serve. In a reciprocal demonstration of responsible development, Desert Troon elected to sponsor stabilization and preservation of the Hassayampa Ruin, a two-room masonry structure.

Natural Setting

Prescott is 63 miles northwest of Phoenix, on the edge of the Prescott National Forest. The project area is in west Prescott, at elevations of 5,499 to 5,884 feet (1,676 to 1,793 m). The east half of the Hassayampa property consists of gently rolling hills and includes the original nine-hole golf course and clubhouse buildings of the old Hassayampa Country Club. This portion of the project area is Petran Montane Conifer Forest, dominated by ponderosa pine (Brown and Lowe 1980). The topography of the western half is more extreme, with steep hills, numerous rock outcrops, and deep washes. Brown and Lowe (1980) place this portion in the interior chaparral biome, which mixes scrub oak, manzanita, mountain mahogany, and cliffrose with ponderosa.

Butte Creek and its tributaries flow through the north half of the project area, and Aspen Creek flows along the southeast boundary of the property. Although both creeks are seasonal, bedrock pools in the creek beds contain water almost year-round.

Cultural Setting

The sites on the Hassayampa Country Club property reflect use of the area by Archaic period hunters and gatherers, by the Formative period Prescott Culture, and by Historic period Euroamericans. Sources on local culture history include overviews by Jeter (1977), Stone (1986, 1987), Macnider et al. (1989), Horton and Logan (1993, 1994), and Logan and Horton (1994). Our synopsis of the prehistory and history of the region reflects the paucity of available information on the Prescott Culture.

Paleoindian (pre–9000 B.C.)

Paleoindian remains in the region are sparse, which may be due more to lack of intensive surveys than to an

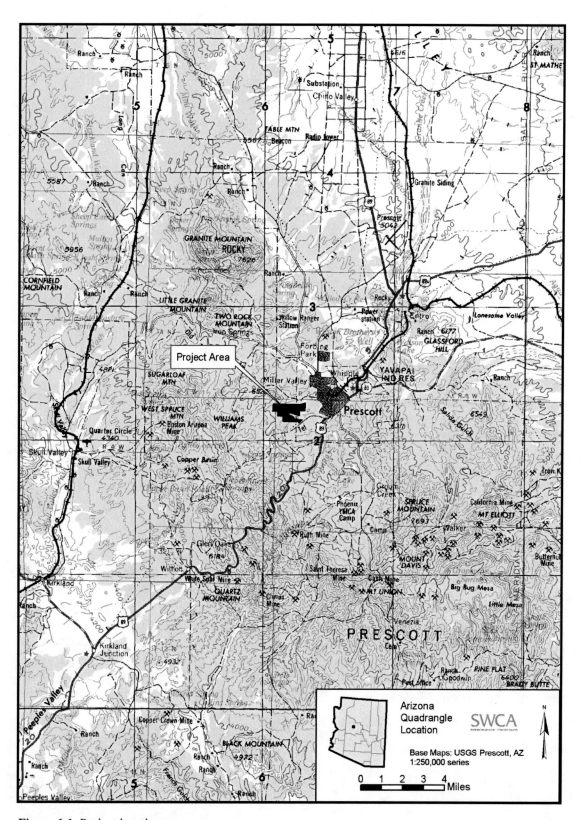

Figure 1.1. Project location.

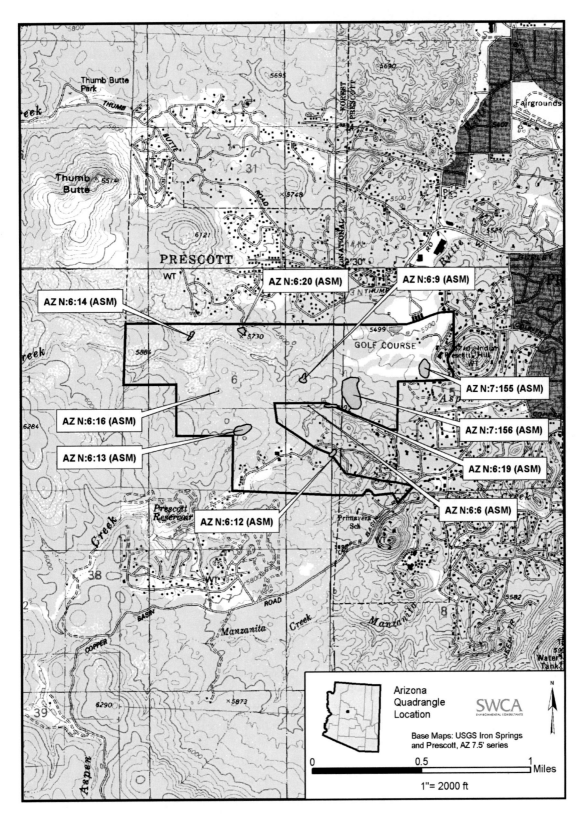

Figure 1.2. Project area boundary and sites.

absence of evidence for this period. Until recently the only evidence for these early hunters and gatherers came from the extreme western slope of the Juniper Mountains and a basal portion of a Clovis point recorded in the Upper Verde River area. However, recent surveys conducted on the Prescott National Forest, in the eastern Juniper Mountains, recorded two Paleoindian projectile points. One was an Eden point made from black rhyolite, the other a basal fragment of a Folsom point made from Government Mountain obsidian. The Eden point is the westernmost occurrence of this type in Arizona (Ryan 1992).

Archaic (9000 B.C.–A.D. 1)

In the Prescott area, Archaic remains are rare but widespread. Excavators of the Glassford Hill site, on the banks of the Agua Fria River, documented a temporary Archaic camp for resource procurement and processing. Considerably more is known about the Archaic presence in the Juniper Mountains, where such remains have been recorded over a wide area (with concentrations along Chino Wash and the upper Verde drainage). Surveys along Big Chino Wash east of the Juniper Mountains have identified sites dated to the Middle Archaic (4500–2000 B.C.), with a minor Late Archaic (2000 B.C.–A.D. 1) component also present (Ryan 1992). Archaic-style points have been found in the southwestern Juniper Mountains (Macnider et al. 1989), and Formby (1986) has documented numerous Archaic projectile points from the vicinity of Chino Valley, north of the Stone Ridge project area. The local Archaic remains may be a blending of the Amargosa and Cochise traditions, as occurs in other parts of west-central and southern Arizona (Formby 1986:99–127; Stone 1986:91). The paucity of documented Archaic sites in the Prescott region may be due to the lack of intensive surveys and past failures to recognize Archaic technology in aceramic artifact assemblages. Recent archaeological projects (e.g., Mitchell et al. 2000; Motsinger and Mitchell 1994; Shepard and Bruder 1996, 1997) have demonstrated that Archaic peoples made frequent forays—some associated with short-term habitation—into the Black Hills east of Chino Valley. Similar Archaic period use of the lower reaches of the Bradshaw Mountains around Prescott is likely.

Formative (A.D. 1–1540)

The local transition from a hunter-gatherer subsistence strategy to a sedentary lifeway is not well documented. Wood (1980) suggested that the transition would be identified by the presence of "small, more or less autonomous pit house villages close to agricultural land, plain and possibly simply decorated pottery, [and] limited exchange of material goods with unrelated populations." The available records suggest a hiatus, however, not a gradual transition. Following this break in the local archaeological record, a late Pioneer or early Colonial Hohokam intrusion is indicated by large rancheria-style villages along the upper Agua Fria River and by Colonial period habitations in the Peeples Valley and Kirkland Creek areas (Macnider et al. 1989:111). These early Hohokam colonists must have subsisted on a mix of hunting, wild-plant collecting, and farming. Wood (1978) suggested that large groups along the Agua Fria and its tributaries practiced both irrigation and dry farming. A particularly important example, the Henderson Site near Dewey, is a large pit house village intensively occupied by people who may have had their origins in the Salt-Gila Basin. The Henderson Site dated to the Santa Cruz phase (A.D. 700–900) (Weed and Ward 1970).

Three hundred meters northwest of the Henderson Site is the Dewey Site, excavated in 1990. Radiocarbon samples from this large site yielded dates of A.D. 630, 790, and 1030. The two earlier dates suggest that the Dewey Site is the earliest pit house site in the Prescott region (D. Weaver, personal communication 1994). Unfortunately, a final report on this site and others excavated during the project has not been completed. Weaver (personal communication 1995) indicates that only 10 percent of the sherds from the Dewey Site are Hohokam. Recent projects along State Route 69, completed with funds from the Arizona Department of Transportation, have yielded convincing evidence of an early version of the Prescott Culture that may have developed directly out of in situ Archaic populations along the Agua Fria River and Big Bug Creek (Punzmann 2000; Punzmann et al. 1998; Weaver 1996). This period is characterized by small pit house settlements, increased reliance on maize and other domesticated plants, and the appearance of a plainware ceramic industry.

During this period, the Hohokam or Hohokam-like groups practiced dry farming and irrigation agriculture at large pit house villages such as the Henderson (Weed and Ward 1970) and Dewey (Rodgers and Weaver 1990; Weaver 1996) sites, and at sites along Big Bug Creek near Mayer (Punzmann 2000; Punzmann et al. 1998). Increasing representation of Hohokam pottery and architectural styles during this time suggests an influx of Hohokam immigrants from the south; in at least one case, Hohokam and Prescott Culture architecture appear to be contemporaneous on the same site (Weaver 1996).

By A.D. 900 a distinctive Prescott Culture had emerged in the grassland and chaparral zones near Prescott (Macnider et al. 1989). One Prescott Culture site in the Williamson Valley is reported to date as early as A.D. 620 (Barnett 1970, 1981). The Prescott Culture area, first defined by the distribution of Prescott Black-on-gray pottery, the dominant ceramic tradition of the region, encompasses more than 25,000 square miles (65,000 km²). In 1936 Edward Spicer drew on Gila Pueblo surveys to argue that Prescott Black-on-gray pottery is found in an area bounded "on the northeast by the headwaters of Oak Creek, on the southeast by the headwaters of New River, on the southwest by the Plomosa Mountains, and on the northeast by the Hualapai Mountains" (Spicer 1936:8–9). In other words, typical Prescott Culture sites occur west and northwest of Prescott. According to Spicer and Caywood (1936), Prescott Gray Ware accounted for about 10 percent of the pottery on the periphery of the culture area, becoming more common from the Big Sandy River eastward into the Agua Fria drainage—where Prescott ware was mixed with Alameda Brown Ware and Hohokam wares. In the Verde Valley Spicer and Caywood (1936) found Prescott Black-on-gray in association with local plain, black-on-white, and black-on-yellow pottery (the latter two wares suggesting a "down the line exchange" relationship with the Anasazi and later with the Hopi to the northeast).

Stone (1987:59) identified the environmental core of the Prescott Branch as a cluster of grassland valleys surrounded by mountains with piñon, juniper, and ponderosa pine. Within this zone are the Kirkland, Chino, and Peeples Valleys to the southwest and the Bradshaw, Juniper, and Sierra Prieta mountain ranges to the north-

west. Euler and Dobyns (1962:79) indicated that the Yolo Ranch Site is on the western "frontier" between the Prescott and Cerbat branches and shows a mixing, temper-wise, between Prescott Gray Ware and Tizon Brown Ware. This evidence suggests that Bozarth Mesa marks the western border of the Prescott Branch heartland.

For more than 100 years, scientific investigations have accepted that the prehistoric culture in west-central Arizona differed from contemporary cultures in the surrounding areas. In his early survey of Walnut Creek, Fewkes (1912:181–221) reported similarities with the puebloan area to the northeast and recognized the existence of "forts" in the area. Thirty years later Gladwin and Gladwin (1930a) conducted surveys in the area to search for the Hohokam. Their results prompted them to include west-central Arizona in their Yuman root (Gladwin 1934:14, Figure 1). Considerable discussion ensued, as one result of which Colton (1939a:22–23, 30–32) suggested a new designation: the Prescott Branch. Colton tentatively assigned the Prescott Branch to the Patayan Root, suggested a Yuman linguistic affiliation, and described two foci (phases) separated by a 25-year hiatus: The Prescott (A.D. 900–1000) and the Chino A.D. (1025–1200). Subsequent research has modified the chronology only slightly. On the basis of revised tree-ring dates, Gumerman et al. (1973) extended the time spans for the two suggested phases to A.D. 850–1025 for the Prescott phase and A.D. 1025–1310 for the Chino phase. Work by Jeter (1977) supported the general A.D. 900–1200 range for the Prescott Branch in Copper Basin. Several reports (Barnett 1970, 1973a, 1975, 1978; Cline and Cline 1983; Ward 1975) on excavations in the Prescott area have relied on these ceramic dates only, without questioning the existing chronologies.

Recent data recovery projects have added to our understanding of the chronology of the Prescott Branch. In addition to the five dates derived from Jeter's Copper Basin project (Jeter 1977:24), radiocarbon dates have been obtained from projects near Iron Springs (Dosh and Halbirt 1985:22, 41) and Lynx Creek (Logan and Horton 1993:40, 1994:72). With the exception of two late dates from the Campground Site (a small site near Granite Mountain Lake, northwest of Prescott) and one from NA18451 (at Iron Springs), all of the radiocarbon dates fall into the accepted range for the Prescott Branch (A.D. 850–1310). Most researchers therefore continue to use the phase designation described by Colton (1939a) and modified by Gumerman et al. (1973), although even these are of questionable validity. The Prescott phase (ca. A.D. 900–1000) was characterized by shallow, rectangular pit houses in hamlet-like settlements. During the Chino phase (ca. A.D. 1000–1300) local populations shifted into somewhat larger pueblos, although pit houses did not disappear. According to Jeter (1977), these groups constructed small agricultural field houses away from the permanently occupied pueblos and used them seasonally during the growing season. Jeter (1977) further observed that in Copper Basin, shallow pit houses were the rule before A.D. 1000, whereas rock-lined and masonry-walled pit houses and pueblos were common between A.D. 1000 and 1200 (Macnider et al. 1989:84). Pit houses with partial rock linings appear to be a transitional style that appeared about A.D. 1050 and continued into the 1200s, while one-room and two-room masonry structures and multi-roomed pueblos dated to the A.D. 1100s and 1200s (Macnider et. al 1989:84).

The largest Prescott Culture pueblo sites are small compared to those of the Middle Verde, such as the nearly 100 room Tuzigoot Ruin. "Large" excavated Prescott Culture sites include King's Ruin, with 12 rooms, and Rattlesnake Ruin, with 8 rooms. Fitzmaurice Ruin, the largest excavated site in the Prescott area, had 27 rooms within the pueblo proper and another 20 to 25 rooms outside (Caywood 1936:88). Other prominent sites subject to at least some professional and paraprofessional investigation include the PC Ruin (Ward 1975), the Yolo Site (Euler and Dobyns 1962), Lonesome Valley Ruin (Barnett 1973a), the Matli Ranch Ruins (Barnett 1970), Las Vegas Ranch Ruins East and West (Barnett 1978), and the Storm Site (Cline and Cline 1983).

Wood (1980) suggested that the reason for the Prescott phase–Chino phase shift in architectural styles was an aggregation of local population into larger subsistence groups. As multi-roomed pueblos grew larger and more common, fewer dispersed hamlets were built, although they did not disappear (Stone 1986:93). Wood's assessment is in agreement with Ward's (1975:160) analysis that "between A.D. 1025 and 1200 in the Prescott home-

land, there were apparently two basic residence patterns in vogue ... some people chose to remain in small scattered hamlets ... in the more traditional pit house mode of their ancestors [while] nearby were other families living in large masonry pueblos" (i.e., Fitzmaurice Ruin).

No complementary shift is evident in subsistence activities and material culture, probably due to the lack of research in the Prescott Culture region. In light of this lack of strong evidence for an overall shift in cultural patterns, Macnider et al. (1989:84) suggested that for the time being, it might be prudent not to assign a phase designation to sites associated with the Prescott Culture.

At present, subsistence and settlement pattern data for the Prescott Culture are available from only a few sources (Barnett 1973a, 1978; Bayham 1977; Gasser 1977; Jeter 1977; Ward 1975; see also Macnider et al. 1989:87). Ward (1975:159) suggested that the subsistence base depended equally on agriculture and on hunting and gathering. Past Copper Basin research has indicated a tendency for habitation sites to be located near arable land, particularly near the Lynx series of loams and clay loams. Besides exploiting the agricultural potential of this soil series, the inhabitants could have roamed surrounding areas in search of wild resources. Analysis of botanical remains has been so limited, however, that extrapolations from existing results could overlook a broader and more complex system of food gathering. Plant products are abundant in the region today, and there is no reason to doubt that they were exploited in prehistoric times, as was the case among the historic Yavapai (Gifford 1936:254–255). Jeter (1977:235) further posited use of secondary agricultural zones with semi-permanent field houses at these locations. Such a pattern would suggest maintenance of agricultural fields during the summer growing season and a less sedentary lifeway away from the fields after the harvest. Given the sometimes erratic rainfall in the Prescott region, hunting and gathering would have had a high priority in any year (Jeter 1977:237). Analysis of faunal remains from Prescott Culture sites indicates that deer, antelope, cottontail rabbit, jackrabbit, and prairie dog complemented the agricultural products and wild-plant foods in the aboriginal diet (Macnider et al. 1989:87).

Perhaps the most impressive feature of the Prescott Culture settlement system is the type of structure known as a "fort." These sites occur on the tops of mountains and mesas and usually are distinguished by massive surrounding walls. Fewkes (1912:207) noted that "one rarely loses sight of one of these hill forts before another can be seen." He suggested that they were used to communicate warnings across a large area by means of smoke signals. Austin (1977:9–10) also proposed that these sites could have been used as a line-of-sight communication system to warn of attackers, and Spoerl et al. (1984:276) suggested that they were defensive in nature as well. Page (1970:49, 54) agreed that use for defense was a possibility but offered an alternate explanation: the hilltop sites could have had religious significance or might have functioned as an extended family's power base over the surrounding area. Weed (1973) implied that they could have served as redistribution or trade centers, and Rodgers (1977:129) thought that a "fort" near Cave Creek might have been a manifestation of "agricultural ceremonialism." Whatever these "forts" were, positive functional identification will require a more focused and theoretically oriented approach than has been used in the past.

Prior studies have yielded limited information on trade and other external contacts. Analysis of the Fitzmaurice Ruin pottery suggests that it was a locally produced variety of Tuzigoot Plain, intimating a close relationship with the Sinagua of the Verde Valley. Prior to this time, Prescott Gray Ware was abundant in the Verde (and was considered by Fish and Fish [1977] as the dominant utility ware for the Middle and Upper Verde Valley between A.D. 1125 and 1300; Macnider et al. 1989:88). Concurrent with the exchange of pottery—and possibly forming the contents of the vessels—obsidian, marine shell, and turquoise have been recovered from Prescott sites, indicating strong trade links with other areas. Marine shell came from the Pacific or Gulf coasts and turquoise also came from outside the area, but obsidian was available near Mt. Floyd and Ash Fork to the north and in the San Francisco Mountain volcanic field to the east.

Materials that could have been exported include argillite, malachite, and other copper ores. Argillite quarries occur in neighboring areas, particularly at Perkinsville and in the Chino Valley. Although no local source of turquoise is known, the trail along Walnut Creek may have served as a route to the turquoise quarries in the Kingman area and southern Nevada (Macnider et al. 1989:88–89). The export of raw materials or finished products of turquoise, shell, and argillite may have provided a buffer against failures of crops and wild foods. Comprehensive subsistence data are lacking in the Prescott area, however, and this interpretation must remain conjectural (Macnider et al. 1989:89).

After A.D. 1300 evidence of possible occupation of the Juniper Mountains area includes post–A.D. 1300 Jeddito pottery "at sites near springs south and north of Walnut Canyon" (Macnider et al. 1989:89) and at the Neural Site (Grossman 2000). These remains may have been early Yavapai sites. Otherwise, the next 200 years form an archaeological hiatus (Stone 1986:94). It is not clear whether there was an actual abandonment of the region or a shift from sedentary settlements back to a mobile lifeway emphasizing hunting and gathering (which would have left few archaeological remains).

Protohistoric Period (A.D. 1540–1865)

When the Spanish first visited the Prescott region in the 1500s and 1600s, the Yavapai and Pai peoples were well established there—the former in the south half of the Juniper Mountains and the latter in the north half (Macnider et al. 1989:90). The Yavapai were organized into regional bands that in turn consisted of subgroups roaming a particular territory in their quest for food. Gifford (1936:250) noted that the Northeastern Yavapai comprised two bands, the *Wikutepa* and the *Wikenichapa*, with overlapping territories. The domain of the *Wikutepa* or Granite Peak band included the area around Prescott, the grasslands of Chino Valley and the south end of Williamson Valley, the high grasslands east of Prescott, the Sierra Prieta Mountains, and the northern Bradshaw Mountains. The *Wikenichapa* or Crown King band roamed from the southern Bradshaw Mountains south to Wickenburg and east across the Agua Fria River (Gifford 1936:250).

All of the bands of the Yavapai were welcome in each other's territories (Gifford 1936:249). Buffer zones of uninhabited land separated the Yavapai from the Pima and Maricopa on the south and the Pai to the north and west. While the Yavapai avoided the Pai, Maricopa, and Pima, they were friendly with the Tonto Apache (Gifford 1936:253).

The Yavapai and other historical groups in the area were hunters and gatherers who also practiced limited agriculture (Gifford 1936:254). They utilized most plants in some way, but agave was a critical staple that could be stored against times of drought (Macnider et al. 1989:90). A southeastern Yavapai informant described agave as the "essential" food (Gifford 1936:206). During the summer these groups exploited desert regions for mesquite and paloverde pods and saguaro fruit and visited uplands in search of piñon nuts, acorns, and walnuts. Sunflower seeds, yucca pods, prickly pear fruits, and other plant foods helped round out the diet of these people. Animals supplied food, clothing, and tools; the Yavapai hunted deer, antelope, rabbits and hares, rodents, birds, and lizards.

From the seasonal round reported by Gifford (1936:254–255), it is obvious that the Yavapai lifeway revolved around wild foods. Their material culture, in particular, had to be portable and reusable. Milling stones were used with manos and mortars with pestles to grind and crush piñon nuts, mesquite pods, acorns, yucca pods, and all manner of berries. Previously made bedrock mortars were used when possible. Milling stones were usually stones of approximately the right shape that were selected locally and left for use during subsequent visits to the area (Gifford 1936:280). Pottery vessels included globular water jars, shallow dishes, and deep cooking bowls (Gifford 1936:280). Coiled and twined baskets and yucca-fiber cordage provided water bottles, burden baskets, winnowing trays, and parching trays. Obsidian and chert were the primary materials for serrated triangular projectile points with concave bases; occasionally the points were side-notched. The Yavapai produced stone knives and scrapers themselves and obtained metal knives from the Colorado River tribes and the Navajo or made them by pounding metal between stones (Gifford 1936:279–280).

Agriculture may have been more important to Yavapai subsistence than Gifford suspected (1936:254). He reported that the northeastern Yavapai prepared small circular areas in which they planted seed corn but that

they practiced only limited cultivation of the growing plants. After the plants had grown to a height of 18 inches or so, the Yavapai left the area to harvest saguaro and paloverde, returning when the corn ripened (Gifford 1936:254–255, 262–263). However, the areas where farming might have been more intensively pursued were around springs and seeps and in places where arable land was present—just the places that Euroamerican settlers would have selected for their own settlements, forcing the Yavapai to give up these choice pieces of territory (Stone 1986:94).

Caves, rock shelters, and domed structures provided shelter for the Yavapai. The huts had frameworks of mesquite, willow, or ocotillo branches set in a ring and thatched with juniper bark or beargrass. Small boulders were embedded in the ground next to the bottom of each branch, to act as a brace when the poles were bent to form the dome-shaped structure. The Yavapai seldom reused old huts, building new ones instead (Gifford 1936:271).

Historic Period (A.D. 1865–1920)

Hispanic colonization of the Southwest apparently had little effect on the Yavapai. In 1583 Antonio de Espejo led a small party of Spaniards and a larger contingent of American Indian guides through the region, reaching the vicinity of Jerome. In the early 1600s Juan Marcos Farfán de los Godos, under the direction of Don Juan de Oñate, explored across Arizona in search of the "fabulous" wealth in the region. On their treks both adventurers either encountered or were guided by Yavapai. No other Yavapai contacts with Spanish explorers are recorded.

The final chapter in local history was the arrival of Euroamericans as explorers or entrepreneurs. Mountain men must have trapped Granite Creek, Lynx Creek, and the streams issuing from the Juniper and Santa Maria mountains. U.S. military expeditions in search of railroad routes also found their way into the area. In 1863 prospectors discovered gold along the Hassayampa River, 5 miles (8 km) south of present-day Prescott. In the same year Prescott became the territorial capital of Arizona. The Prescott-Mohave Toll Road (Hardyville Toll Road) was in operation by 1864.

In 1870 Cienega Springs accidentally became part of local history. In 1868 a father and son named Buckman settled at what is now Fort Rock. While trailing a group of natives who had stolen most of their horses, they found the springs. A surveyor named Henry Marion (or Mehren; the sources do not agree) then filed a claim at Cienega Springs and with his partner (an ex-soldier named Otto Weber) presumably began a ranching operation (Granger 1960:338). For the next 20 years the homestead operated as an isolated, almost self-sufficient farm and ranch. An orchard and a field were developed at the springs, and a ditch carried water to Lower Corral Tank (Ruskin 1993). Thus, Cienega Ranch was part of the earliest years of cattle ranching in Yavapai County.

Development of Euroamerican ranches and mining activities in the prime hunting, gathering, and farming areas of the Yavapai eventually led to open conflict between the two groups. Ranches were raided, livestock was stolen, and lives were lost on both sides. Military intervention came in the form of military posts and armed patrols. During the late 1860s and early 1870s, there were numerous encounters between the Yavapai and the soldiers and settlers. Loss of life was minor, but the losses in livestock grew with each succeeding year. In response to the open hostilities the Army established Fort Whipple, Camp Hualapai, and a number of temporary posts along the Hardyville Road. By 1875 the military had pressured the Yavapai into moving onto a reservation—first at Date Creek, then at Camp Verde on the Verde River.

When the Army arrived in the area, the resulting demand for beef led to an expansion of the local cattle industry. Later, the need to feed the several thousand Yavapai on the reservation increased the demand. By March 1870, 27 ranches were in operation in Williamson Valley (Granger 1960:363). Yavapai County was considered one of the best ranching areas in Arizona, but overgrazing left the herds vulnerable. In 1894 a drought destroyed nearly 75 percent of the cattle on local ranges; half the cattle that had survived died in the following year (Macnider et al. 1989:92). Meanwhile, uncontrolled lumbering in the mountains around Prescott had denuded vast areas. One result of this poor land management was establishment of the Prescott Forest Reserve (later Prescott National Forest) in 1889. The

Walnut Creek Ranger District was formed in the Juniper Mountains between 1908 and 1911 (Macnider et al. 1989:92). During the mid 1930s the Civilian Conservation Corps occupied camps at Camp Wood and the Walnut Creek Ranger Station, developing fire trails and cutting firewood (for public sale) in both the Santa Maria and Juniper mountains (Macnider et al. 1989:92–93). In 1980 the Walnut Ranger District became part of the Chino Valley Ranger District.

Previous Research and Nearby Sites

Based on a review of the archaeological literature and project files at the Arizona State Museum, Museum of Northern Arizona, and Prescott National Forest, no surveys had been conducted in or adjacent to the project area, and no archaeological or historical sites had been recorded in the project area prior to SWCA's 1995 survey. However, two archaeological sites had been recorded near the property boundaries, and SWCA field-checked these resources.

AZ N:7:63 (ASM) is a prehistoric Prescott Culture habitation site within the City of Prescott's Stricklin Park, south of Thumb Butte Drive and adjacent to the northern boundary of the property. The site consists of at least one two-room masonry structure and associated domestic trash, with buried and partly buried architecture. The artifacts described on the ASM site card include Prescott Gray Ware sherds and a scatter of flaked stone. Cultural remains at the south edge of the site extended to within 2 m of the north edge of the Hassayampa property, but the site appeared to be within Stricklin Park. A number of horse and bike trails have impacted the area.

NA 13240 is atop Indian Hill, a volcanic butte at the center of Country Club Circle, about 150 m east of the project area. This prehistoric Prescott Culture "fort" once included extensive walls and flaked stone artifacts (see Austin 1977 and Christenson 1992:19). The site was visited and described by Jesse Walter Fewkes (1912:215), who reported that it had large, well-preserved walls. According to Jack Ogg (1973a), these walls were still standing at a height of 3 feet (1 m) as late as 1926. The site has since been damaged by the leveling of the hilltop, the erection of two large water tanks, and construction of an associated access road.

Short segments of the walls and a few artifacts are on the north side of a fence that surrounds the water tanks. The site is outside the Hassayampa property but in all likelihood was directly associated with the prehistoric community that surrounds this prominent hill. The site affords an outstanding view of the entire Hassayampa property to the west and of other hilltops with prehistoric forts to the east (Austin 1977).

Research Design

In their overview of cultural resources on the Prescott National Forest, Macnider et al. (1989) developed a historic context and 10 themes for evaluating archaeological sites. In his overview of archaeology within the City of Prescott, Christenson (1992) adapted seven of the themes as relevant to prehistoric sites within the city: Demography, Social-Political-Ideological Systems, Technology, Exchange and Trade, Subsistence, Warfare, and Transportation and Communication. SWCA's researchers thought that all of these themes could be addressed by investigations at the Hassayampa sites. The excavation project's research design (Motsinger 1995) identified five specific problem domains that either coincide with or crosscut these seven themes: Site Function, Community Patterning and Regional Interaction, Subsistence, Chronology, and Historic Use of the Project Area. The research design and project methods can be found in the CRM report for the project (Anduze et al. 1999).

CHAPTER 2

Site Descriptions

Richard A. Anduze and James M. Potter

The seven excavated Prescott Culture sites described here represent three site types: resource procurement and processing camps (3), possible agricultural sites with limited habitation (2), and multiple-activity habitation sites (2). The Hassayampa Ruin, a two-room masonry structure at the most complex site, AZ N:7:155 (ASM), has been stabilized and preserved.

AZ N:6:9 (ASM)

Site Type: resource procurement and processing
Size: 3,025 m²
Elevation: 5,650 feet (1,720 m)

This amorphous site was on a small saddle on a ridge in the center of the project area. Granitic rock outcropped in the northwest, southeast, and central portions of the site (Figure 2.1). The local sediments were decomposed granitic rock, ranging up to the size of boulders but generally forming an unconsolidated tan sandy loam. The site drained to both the east and the west. In spots with dense vegetation an A soil horizon was developing. Across the site, roots had disturbed the sediments down to bedrock. The site had an overstory of ponderosa pine, piñon, and juniper and an understory of scrub oak, mountain mahogany, manzanita, and grasses.

Excavations

Site studies consisted of surface collections and subsurface excavations. The site surface was divided into 92 grid units, each 5 by 5 m, and all artifacts within each unit were collected. This strategy permitted systematic inspection of the entire site and provided in-field artifact density data that assisted in the placement of excavation units. Nearly 60 percent of the 396 artifacts collected were sherds and 40 percent were flaked stone; two items were ground stone tools. The southeast portion of the site contained most of the artifacts, including all but four of the flaked stone tools and cores and one piece of ground stone. The remainder of the artifact scatter extended north from this concentration. A small, low-density concentration in the northwest corner of the site contained one core.

To investigate Features 1, 2 and 3, field crews excavated a control unit over each one. Feature 1, in the northeast portion of the site, was an oval arrangement of stones measuring 2.6 by 2.0 m. At its western end was an associated milling stone. The excavators suspected that the stones were a foundation or support for a brush structure and excavated Control Unit 1 over the northern portion of the feature in an attempt to locate an interior floor, a wall, or an exterior occupation surface. The three arbitrary levels of the unit exposed a homogeneous fine brown loam with pockets of decomposed gray organic matter. The upper 10 cm were loosely compacted and contained rootlets that extended into Level 2. With depth, compaction increased, roots increased in size, and cobbles of decomposed granite increased in frequency. Granitic bedrock encountered near the bottom of Level 2 was present across the unit in Level 3 (at 17–26 cm below the ground surface), with small pockets of sediments on the west side of the unit. The unit yielded one core and five sherds, all from Level 1, but contained no subsurface evidence of a structure.

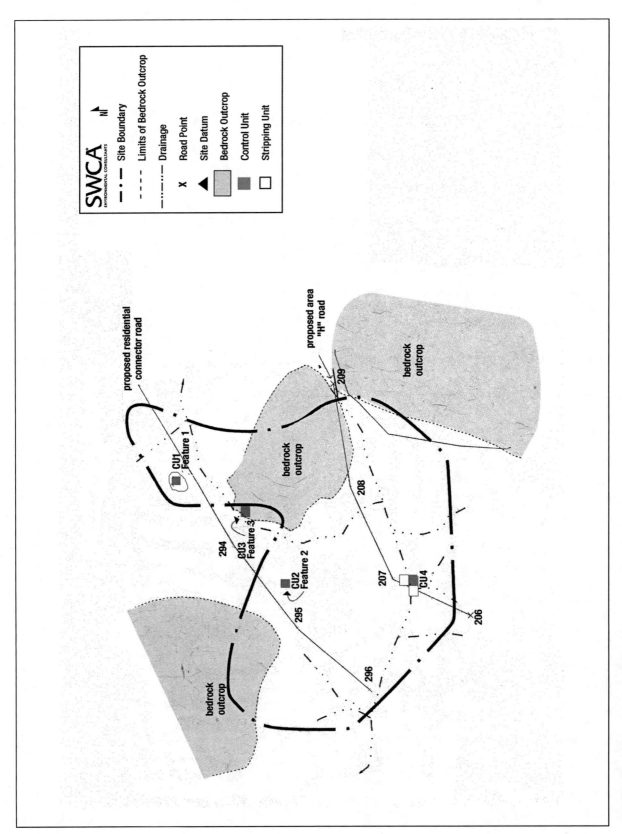

Figure 2.1. AZ N:6:9 (ASM) site map.

Feature 2 was a possible pit feature consisting of a semi-circular concentration of granitic cobbles and boulders that measured 90 by 55 cm. Control Unit 2, excavated in three arbitrary levels, completely encompassed the rock concentration (Figure 2.2). The sediment was a homogeneous tan loamy sand with small rocks in all levels and roots in Level 3. Excavation ended at decomposing granitic bedrock between 20 cm and 25 cm below the ground surface, although small pockets of sediments continued deeper. Four Prescott Gray sherds collected from Level 2 were the only cultural materials found. No evidence indicated that Feature 2 was anything other than a natural distribution of rocks and artifacts.

Feature 3 was a 70-cm-long alignment of granitic boulders thought to be a wall segment. Control Unit 3, excavated to better define the possible wall and locate any associated occupation surfaces, extended down three arbitrary levels to decomposed granitic bedrock (Figure 2.2). The sediment was a homogeneous, somewhat compact sandy loam with grass roots in the upper two levels and larger roots in Level 3. Rocks ranging from pebbles to boulders derived from weathering of bedrock were common in Levels 2 and 3. The decomposing bedrock occurred between 25 cm and 31 cm below the ground surface. The only cultural materials present were three sherds of Prescott Gray collected from Level 1. The field crew determined that the alignment was in situ eroded bedrock remnants.

The crews excavated two 1 by 1 m units (Control Units 4 and 5) in the southeastern portion of the site, where surface artifact density was high and sediments appeared to be thickest. This area was on a north-facing ridge slope in a drainage. The concentration contained 84 percent of the flaked stone tools and one of the two ground stone tools collected from the surface of this site. Erosion, including sheetwash, had probably concentrated artifacts in the drainage. The fill of Control Unit 4, excavated in four arbitrary levels, was tan granitic loamy sand with little compaction in the upper two levels, grading into a more compact, medium gray sandy loam in Levels 3 and 4. Rocks first appeared at the bottom of Level 3. At the bottom of Level 3 and the top of Level 4, the crew encountered gray staining and a deposit of charcoal. Although there was no evidence that the charcoal was cultural, it was collected as sample

BN 99 and submitted to the Laboratory of Tree-Ring Research at the University of Arizona. The sample was juniper but was undatable because of "very difficult doubles," that is, false-ring problems. Decomposing granitic bedrock was 31–43 cm below the ground surface in this unit.

Two 1 by 1 m units stripped next to the north and west edges of Control Unit 4, without screening or vertical controls, exposed the surface where the charcoal originated. No additional charcoal or cultural features were visible in the excavation. The control unit and the additional units contained 20 artifacts, all sherds and flaked stone.

Control Unit 5, excavated in two arbitrary levels, ended at granitic bedrock 17–20 cm below the ground surface. The unit fill consisted of moderately compacted tan sandy loam containing rocks (ranging from pebbles to cobbles) derived from the decomposing bedrock. All but one of the 35 artifacts from this unit were sherds.

Discussion

Eighty percent of the flaked stone from AZ N:6:9 (ASM) was debitage, but the assemblage also included used flakes, cores, core/hammerstones, and hammerstones. The high frequency of core/hammerstones and hammerstones, the small number of used flakes, and the presence of ground stone tools suggest that the site was a processing camp, primarily for plant resources such as piñon nuts, acorns, and grass seeds that required pounding. Many whole flakes were relatively large, suggesting little trampling and thus short-term use of the site.

Ninety-five percent of the sherds from the site were Prescott Gray, indicating affiliation with the Prescott Culture. The rest of the sherds were Wingfield Plain. The lack of temporally diagnostic ceramics and chronometric samples makes dating the site impossible, other than to the recognized date for the culture, circa A.D. 700 to 1350 (or A.D. 850 to 1310; see Gumerman et al. 1973). The lack of decorated sherds at this site could be the result of several factors: an early, pre-decoration occupation; site function (decorated vessels were not used for certain activities); or chance (no decorated vessels were broken).

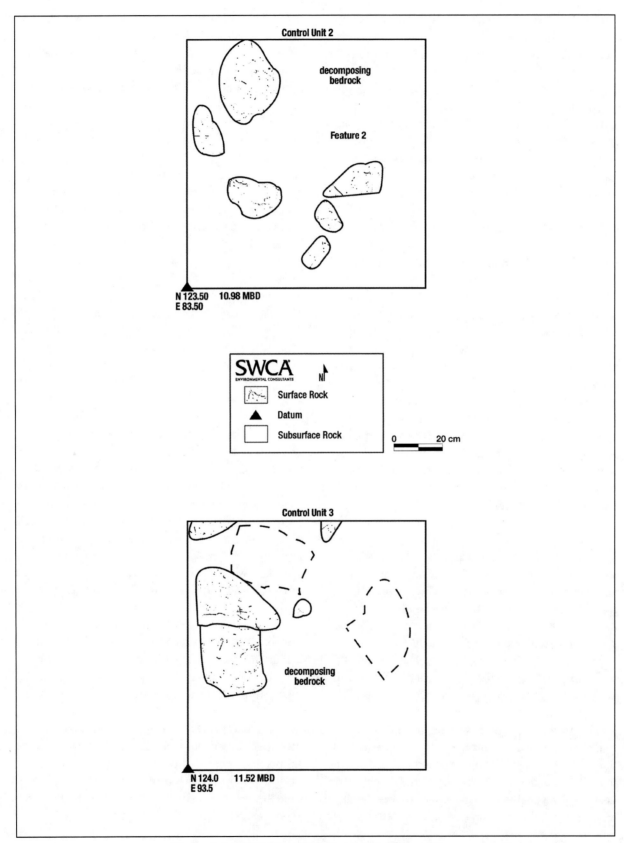

Figure 2.2. AZ N:6:9 (ASM), Control Units 2 and 3.

The excavations did not yield any evidence of intact subsurface cultural deposits or features. The stones in Feature 1, in the northeast corner of the site, may have been foundation or supporting stones for a temporary brush structure. The presence of a metate at the west edge of the concentration suggests a cultural origin for this feature. The site had probably experienced both deposition and erosion, along with disturbance from plant growth, so the patterning used to identify Feature 1 may have been natural. In summary, AZ N:6:9 (ASM) was a Prescott Culture short-term seasonal camp used during the procurement and processing of plant resources, probably nuts and seeds.

AZ N:6:13 (ASM)

Site Type: resource procurement and processing
Size: 6,600 m²
Elevation: 5,800 feet (1,768 m)

AZ N:16:13 (ASM) was on the upper flanks of a ridge in the southwest portion of the property. Sediments derived from decomposed granite ranged to boulder size but generally formed an unconsolidated tan sandy loam. The site had an overstory of ponderosa pine, piñon, and juniper and an understory of scrub oak, mountain mahogany, manzanita, and grasses. Trails used by hikers, bicyclists, and equestrians crossed the site and the surrounding area. Archaeological survey crews located three prehistoric artifact concentrations and several possible rock concentrations and identified three features (Terzis and Motsinger 1995).

Excavations

Data recovery crews defined an additional five artifact concentrations, including one with historical remains (Figure 2.3). Six of the loci (A–D, F, and H), clustered in the southwest portion of the site along the ridge crest, were defined as separate areas based on topography, vegetation, and differences in the artifact assemblages. Loci A, B, and D represented the three artifact concentrations defined during survey. Loci E and G were north and northeast of the main cluster.

Data recovery at AZ N:6:13 (ASM) did not involve excavation, and work at most of the site consisted of

instrument mapping (establishing horizontal and vertical control values), photographing features, and collecting all observed surface artifacts by locus. The exception was Locus H, which contained the historical artifacts and a few prehistoric artifacts; the crew identified the historical artifacts in the field but collected only one of them (see Anduze et al. 1999) and point provenienced items recognized as tools or cores. Of the 752 artifacts collected, nearly 85 percent were sherds and 15 percent were flaked stone, with a few ground stone items.

The data recovery investigations revealed that Features 1 and 3 were probably recent. Moreover, they were completely deflated and thus lacked excavation potential. Feature 2 proved to be a historical check dam built for erosion control. Otherwise, the rocks on the site appeared to be the remnants of decomposing bedrock, and any clustering was either natural or the result of recent trail clearing. On the site as a whole, the sediments were shallow and eroding, with little possibility for subsurface cultural deposits.

Locus A covered 115 m² and contained Feature 1, a 4-m-long discontinuous alignment of cobbles and small boulders extending across a drainage or trail. This area was deflated, and the rocks were scattered. No direct evidence indicated the cultural or temporal affiliation of the feature. The over 200 artifacts from Locus A consisted of sherds, flaked stone, and one tabular tool.

Locus B, a 25-m² area, contained 11 artifacts, one of them another tabular tool. Locus C was 50 m² in area and contained over 80 sherds and flaked stone artifacts and one handstone/scraper. Seven of the flaked stone artifacts were tools. The pottery assemblage included Prescott Red, Prescott Black-on-gray, and an unidentified ware. Locus C yielded the most ceramic types of any locus at this site, as well as the largest number of lithic tools.

Locus D was the largest prehistoric locus, at 245 m², and contained Feature 3, a rock pile adjacent to the main trail through the site. Feature 3 was 1 m in diameter and 40 cm high and consisted of about a dozen granite boulders piled three high. Additional boulders were present immediately to the northwest and west. The pile did not

Richard A. Anduze and James M. Potter

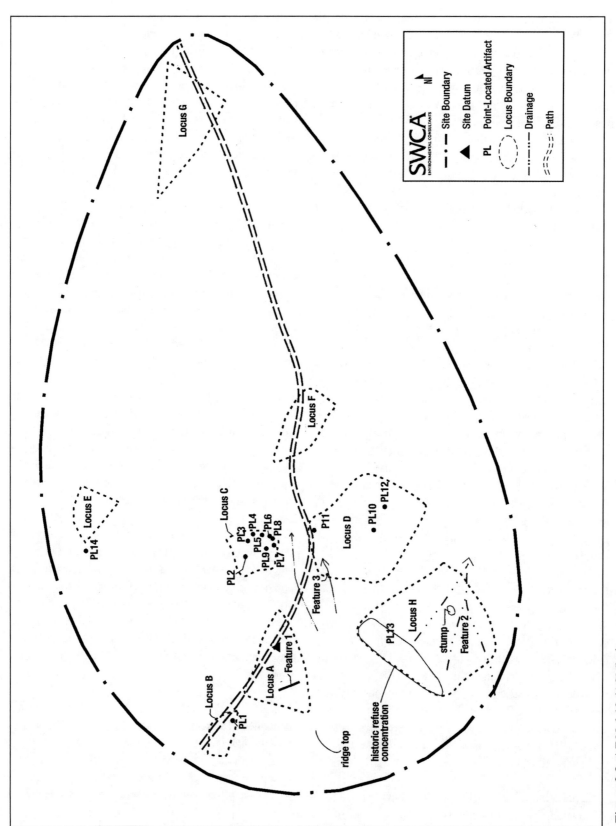

Figure 2.3. AZ N:6:13 (ASM) site map.

appear to be very old and was most likely rocks that had been removed from the trail. Locus D yielded over 200 sherds, including Prescott Red, Prescott Gray, and Prescott Black-on-gray, as well as the second-largest lithic tool assemblage at this site.

Locus E, one of the two outlying loci, covered 40 m². This locus contained fewer than 30 ceramic and lithic artifacts, including a tabular tool. Locus F was 70 m² in area and yielded nearly 50 sherds and pieces of flaked stone debitage. This was one of two loci that did not contain any tools. Locus G, the second outlying locus, was 120 m² in area. Most of the nearly 120 sherds were Prescott Gray. However, it was one of three loci that contained decorated sherds and was the only locus with no flaked stone artifacts.

Locus H, at 320 m² the largest of the loci, was primarily historical. The field crew collected a core/hammerstone and a core but not the few undecorated sherds that were present. Feature 2, a check dam 8 m from the concentration of historical refuse, consisted of two alignments of granitic boulders totaling 9 m in length and ranging from 40 to 50 cm high. The western segment was 5 m long and consisted of one course of large boulders; the eastern segment was one to two courses of small to large boulders and was 4 m long. The two alignments were separated by a 3-m gap containing a very large stump. The stump did not appear to have displaced any rocks and was probably present when the check dam was built, suggesting construction in historical times. The area just upslope from the check dam had partly filled with sediment. At the time of data recovery two drainages were flowing over the dam segments to join a third, larger drainage. The few prehistoric sherds at Locus H were found at Feature 2 but probably had washed down from the ridge crest. A historical to recent fence through Locus H was removed prior to data recovery; where it had been was not clear.

Discussion

The dominance of Prescott Gray Ware sherds on the prehistoric loci of AZ N:6:13 (ASM) indicates an affili-

ation with the Prescott Culture, which has been dated to circa A.D. 700 to 1300 (though a range of A.D. 850 to 1310 has also been suggested; see Gumerman et al. 1973). Prescott Black-on-gray ceramics date to about A.D. 900 to 1350 (Wood 1982:41), but Breternitz (1966:101) used tree-ring samples to argue for a narrower date range of A.D. 1050 to 1200. The presence of decorated sherds at some loci but not others suggests two possibilities: that there were at least two episodes of site use, one during the production span of Prescott Black-on-gray; or that decorated vessels were used in a restricted portion of the site. Only 23 percent of the 628 sherds recovered from the site were large enough for analysis, suggesting breakage by trampling; the assemblage may have represented only a few vessels. The small number of sherds and the low frequency of decorated sherds indicate that AZ N:6:13 (ASM) was a limited-activity site, even allowing for skewing of the average sherd size and the ratio of plain to decorated sherds by casual collecting.

The tool assemblage indicates that the inhabitants of AZ N:6:13 (ASM), like those at AZ N:6:9 (ASM), used the site to process plant resources. The lithic assemblage included tabular tools, which are associated with agave processing. Furthermore, some researchers (Fish, Fish, and Madsen 1985; Fish et al. 1985) consider rock concentrations and piles to be prehistoric agricultural features used primarily to support production of agave. The argument for agave production at this site would have been strengthened had Features 1 and 3 proved to be prehistoric.

The concentration of tools at Locus C suggests that this was the primary processing area on the site. The remainder of the tools were spread across the site; no more than one tabular tool was present at any given locus, and only one passive grinding stone, a slab metate, was found. This distribution might indicate that processing, and a variety of other activities, were conducted at specific loci. The lack of tools at Loci F and G supports this hypothesis. However, the artifact distribution could also represent site formation over time, with each locus representing a discrete use of the area.

AZ N:6:16 (ASM)

Site Type: habitation; resource procurement and processing
Size: 553 m²
Elevation: 5,760 feet (1,756 m)

The field investigators identified AZ N:6:16 (ASM) at the proposed location of the new clubhouse after completion of data recovery; to protect the resource, the developers chose to move the clubhouse. AZ N:6:16 (ASM) is on a high ridge in the west-central portion of the project area, overlooking an unnamed drainage to the west at a point southeast of its junction with Butte Creek. The ridge consists of granitic outcrops and derivative sediments ranging up to boulder size. At the time of fieldwork the area had an overstory of ponderosa pine, piñon, alligator juniper, and Emory oak, with an understory of manzanita and scrub oak.

The site consists of an amorphous pile of stone rubble, a collapsed stone wall, a stone alignment, and two possible bedrock mortars (Figure 2.4). The rubble and wall are most likely remnants of one or two seasonally occupied habitations or shelters. The alignment may have been related to limited agricultural production, and the mortars would have been used for resource processing.

Most of Feature 1, an amorphous pile of granite cobbles and boulders 3 m in diameter, is on a bedrock outcrop. This feature may represent a temporary masonry structure with the entry oriented to the northeast, as the quantity of rubble is smaller there and extends onto sediment.

Feature 2 is a segment of collapsed wall 3 m long, oriented northeast-southwest. Three to four courses of granitic cobbles and boulders are evident, suggesting an original wall height of 1 m. The rocks are partly covered by recent sediments, suggesting the possibility of buried remains.

Feature 3 consists of 10 granitic boulders in a crescent-shaped alignment about 4 m long, oriented 80 to 260 degrees east/north with the ends curving slightly to the north. The rocks were partly buried; while not within an obvious drainage, the feature could have trapped mois-

ture, and the investigators interpreted it as a small agricultural feature.

Features 4 and 5 are two possible bedrock mortars on an irregular granitic boulder measuring 95 by 70 cm. Feature 4 is 22 by 17 cm across and 1 to 8 cm deep. Feature 5, just north of Feature 4, is 13 cm in diameter and 1 to 5 cm deep (the depths vary due to the slope on the upper surface of the boulder). No evidence was observed to indicate that Features 4 and 5 were cultural.

Artifacts on the site were collected but not analyzed. Ten Prescott Gray sherds were scattered across the northern portion of the site, and a well-shaped mano of vesicular basalt was found at the northwest corner of the collapsed wall. The mano was plano-convex in cross section, with use wear on the planar surface only.

AZ N:6:19 (ASM)

Site Type: resource procurement and processing
Size: 1,600 m²
Elevation: 5,590 feet (1,704 m)

AZ N:6:19 (ASM), previously recorded as AZ N:7:164 (ASM), included Archaic (6000 B.C.–A.D. 500), Prescott Culture (A.D. 700–1350), possible Yavapai (A.D. 1300–1900), and historical Euroamerican (ca. 1860–1945) components. The site was on a bench in the granitic exposures that form the easternmost ridges and hills in the project area, most of it in an alcove bounded by bedrock to the south, west, and north (Figure 2.5). Sediments at the site were shallow and derived from decomposed granitic rock. The local overstory consisted of ponderosa pine, piñon, and juniper, with an understory of manzanita, scrub oak, and grasses. Several well-used recreational trails met in the site area.

AZ N:6:19 (ASM) straddled the property line between the Hassayampa Country Club (Desert Troon) property and the church camp immediately to the south. The cultural resource survey crew found a petroglyph (Feature 1) on the church camp property in the rocks above "The Tubs," a series of water-eroded bedrock depressions in the bed of Aspen Creek. Data recovery personnel identified three Prescott Gray sherds and a large boulder with

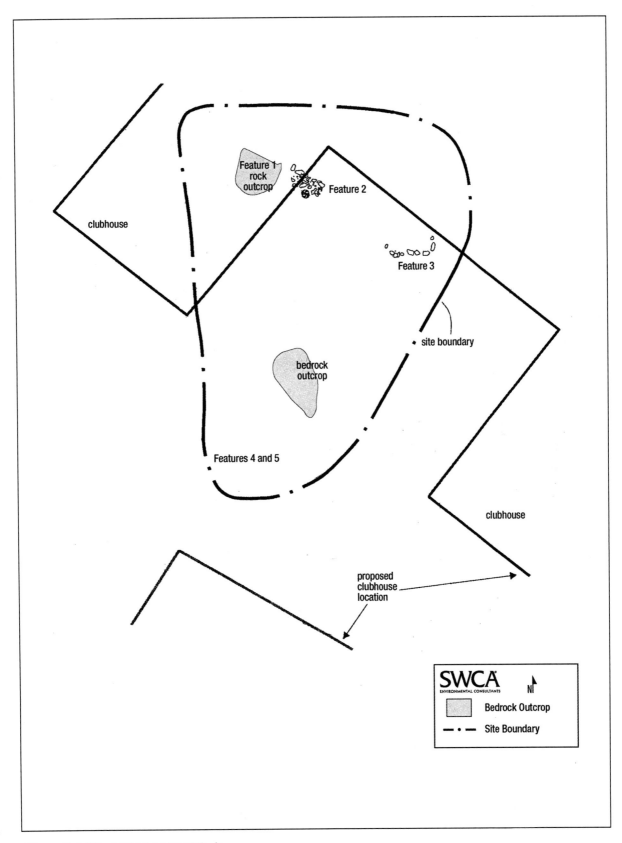

Figure 2.4. Site AZ N:6:16 (ASM) site map.

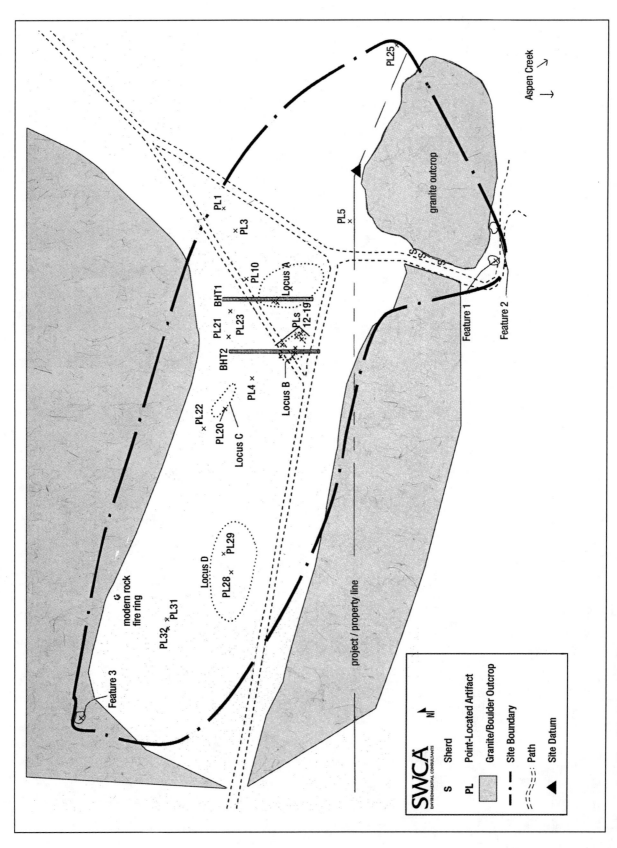

Figure 2.5. Site AZ N:6:19 (ASM) site map.

a grinding slick and two possible mortars (Feature 2) on the church camp property, and a second grinding slick (Feature 3), the remainder of the very dispersed artifact scatter, and a deposit of ashy sediment on the Hassayampa property.

Excavations

The site consisted of four small artifact concentrations, designated Loci A–D, and three features, none of them within the loci. Features 1 and 2 were outside of the Hassayampa County Club property. Data recovery fieldwork on the entire site included instrument mapping, point proveniencing of all recognized tools and cores, and detailed recording of the bedrock features. The field crews collected surface artifacts and excavated two 10-m-long backhoe trenches on the Hassayampa property.

One-third of the 78 prehistoric artifacts collected from the site surface were sherds, 44 percent were flaked stone, and 23 percent were ground stone. One of the sherds was Tizon Wiped, the only example of this pottery from the project area and an indication of possible Yavapai use of the site. The flaked stone assemblage included the only drill recovered during the project. The debitage represented eight material types, a considerable variety given the few specimens found. One .22-short cartridge case was also collected.

Locus A, at the trail junction in the area of the ashy sediments, covered 23 m² and contained 20 ceramic, flaked stone, and ground stone artifacts. The field crew excavated Backhoe Trench 1 through the locus, exposing bedrock between 20 cm and 30 cm below the ground surface, but found no intact subsurface cultural materials. Trench fill was a homogeneous sandy loam with rocks of various sizes and some roots. The ashy dark gray sediments, evident at the center of the trench, graded into the sterile loam at each end.

Locus B was about 4 m west of Locus A, also at the trail junction, and also within the area of ashy sediments. Locus B was 11 m² in area and contained five ground stone tools, three other artifacts, and multiple pieces of rock that had been burned and cracked by exposure to heat. Backhoe Trench 2, excavated at this locus, again

exposed bedrock within 20 to 30 cm of the ground surface and failed to locate intact subsurface cultural materials. Trench fill was a homogeneous sandy loam with rocks of various sizes and some roots. Within the locus the sediments were ashy and dark gray, grading into sterile loam at each end of the trench.

Locus C, the smallest of the four loci at 4 m², was north of the trails, near exposed bedrock. This locus contained few artifacts, among them the Tizon Wiped sherd.

Locus D, the westernmost of the four concentrations, was the largest, at 40 m². The artifact assemblage consisted of just 11 prehistoric items and the cartridge case.

The petroglyph, Feature 1, was lightly pecked into the south face of a large granitic boulder immediately above Aspen Creek. The glyph was an indistinct group of geometrical and possibly zoomorphic elements, measuring 35 cm high by 30 cm wide (Figure 2.6).

Feature 2, about 2 m west of Feature 1, consisted of an eroded bedrock boulder with a grinding slick and two depressions that may have been mortars. The slick was a smoothed patch of the rock surface measuring 45 by 30 cm, with some erosion evident. The possible mortars had highly eroded interior surfaces with no evidence of grinding or pecking. The smaller depression measured 22 by 12 cm across and 5 cm deep. The second depression was somewhat trough-like, with a circular depression near one end, and measured 37 by 18 cm across and 8 cm deep at the bottom of the inner depression.

Feature 3 was a well-smoothed grinding slick, 50 cm long by 19 cm wide, on an eroded bedrock boulder in the extreme northwest corner of the site. About 10 m east of Feature 3 was a recent fire ring of granitic rocks with a diameter of 50 cm. A scatter of recent burned refuse was in this area as well.

The sparse artifact scatter across the site contained, in addition to the three sherds on the church camp property, 11 artifacts that were point located and 12 sherds and flaked stone items that were collected from the general site.

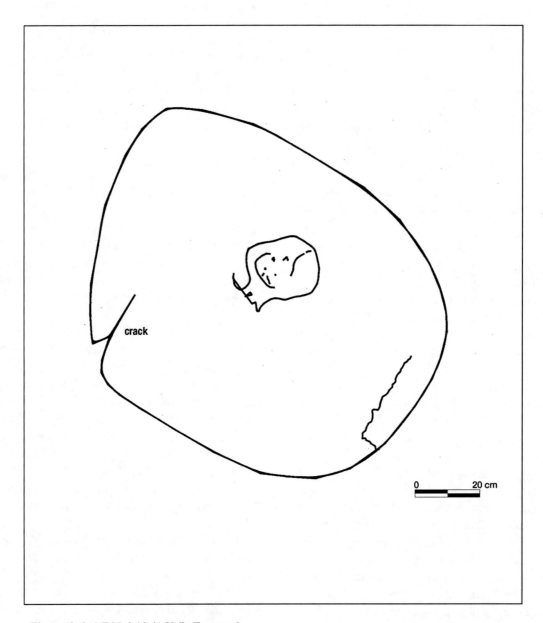

Figure 2.6. AZ N:6:19 (ASM), Feature 1.

A low rock wall crossing AZ N:6:19 (ASM) was probably a historical Euroamerican feature. The wall intersected a quarter-section corner marker outside the site.

Discussion

The 78 artifacts from AZ N:6:19 (ASM) constituted the smallest of the site assemblages studied during this project, but the assemblage was unique in several aspects. This site had the highest ratio of lithic tools to other lithic artifacts (0.54:1), yielded the only drill recovered, had the most varied assemblage of flaked stone material types relative to the number of artifacts (8 materials among 34 artifacts), had the most bedrock grinding features, and was the only site with a Tizon Brown Ware sherd. It was also one of the two sites with petroglyphs. The total number of stone tools, including cores, the bedrock grinding slicks, and possible mortars, was 32. The character of the assemblage strongly indicates that the site was a locus for resource processing, an assumption supported by the presence of the ashy sediments (although no formal cooking features were identified). The location of the site immediately above Aspen Creek further supports this interpretation, as an ample supply of water would have been available during much of the year.

AZ N:6:19 (ASM) may have been related to AZ N:7:156 (ASM), also above Aspen Creek, a short distance to the east (see below). These were the only sites with petroglyphs and bedrock grinding features. However, casual collectors had probably removed many of the surface artifacts on both sites, and the investigators could not determine a definite relationship from the surviving evidence. The association of bedrock grinding features with petroglyphs in two of three instances suggests contemporaneity of these sites. Peter Pilles, Coconino National Forest Archaeologist, believes that the petroglyphs are Archaic (personal communication 1996), and SWCA field personnel defined an Archaic component at Site N:7:156 (ASM) based on bifacial reduction technology and material type in portions of the flaked stone assemblage (Chapter 5). The erosion evident on the bedrock grinding features and the faintness of the petroglyphs are supporting evidence for a possible Archaic affiliation for these features, and an association between the sites.

AZ N:6:19 (ASM) was a multi-component site with evidence of art, resource processing, and ranching or homesteading. The site appeared to have been repeatedly used over the last 8,000 years, primarily by the Prescott Culture but also during the Archaic, Yavapai, and historic Euroamerican periods.

AZ N:6:20 (ASM)

Site Type: habitation; resource procurement and processing
Size: 3,150 m²
Elevation: 5,725 feet (1,745 m)

AZ N:6:20 (ASM) was on Stoney Ridge, which extends southeast from the base of Thumb Butte along the north-central portion of the project boundary, immediately north of Butte Creek. The ridge consists of outcropping granitic bedrock and derivative materials up to the size of boulders. The site had an overstory of ponderosa pine and piñon, alligator juniper, and oak, with an understory of manzanita, mountain mahogany, buckthorn, shrub oak, prickly pear and hedgehog cacti, and grasses. Drainage was downslope in all directions.

The site was immediately south of the Country Club Park neighborhood and had been used extensively for recreation, especially by the local residents. The general lack of diagnostic artifacts on the ground surface was at least partly due to casual collecting. One resident commented that he had collected sherds from the site, including a ceramic disc and "Hohokam sherds."

AZ N:6:20 (ASM) consisted of nine features (Figure 2.7): three structures, three middens, a check dam/terraced area, a possible second check dam, and a bedrock grinding slick. At first glance, two rock concentrations at the east end of the site appeared to be cultural and were designated Features 4 and 11. After clearing brush from the concentrations and inspecting them more closely, the field investigators determined that they were natural rock outcrops. "Feature 4" was within the site boundary as defined by the distribution of surface artifacts, but "Feature 11" was outside that boundary. Two cores were collected from the "Feature 4" outcrop.

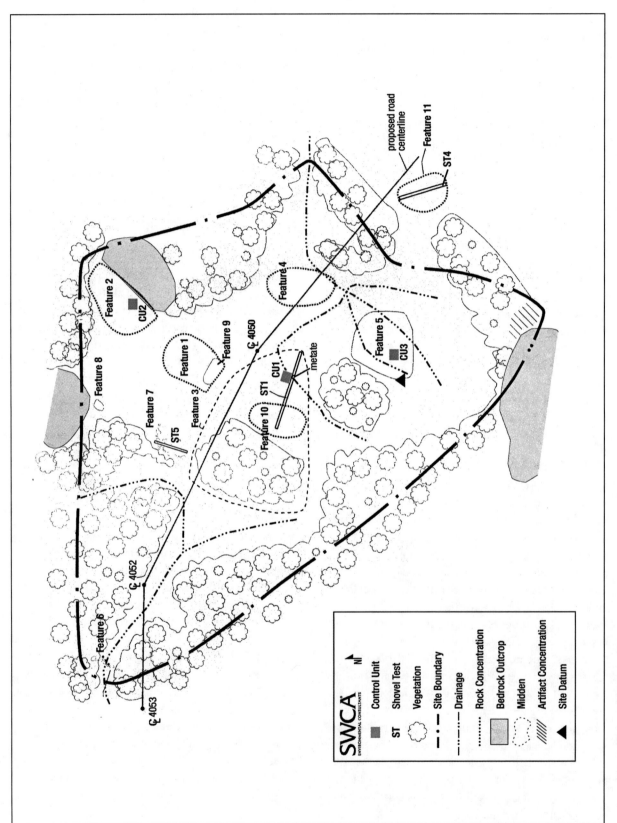

Figure 2.7. Site AZ N:6:20 (ASM) site map.

Excavations

Field personnel photographed all features, drew individual plan views of the structures and check dams, and added the middens and grinding slick to the general site plan, then excavated the structural features in their entirety and conducted limited excavations in the middens and check dam/terrace. All observed lithic tools, a partial ceramic figurine, a rim sherd, a mineral specimen, and a piece of heat-altered rock were point provenienced on the site map, and all except the heat-altered rock were collected. Sixty-one percent of the 540 artifacts from this site were sherds, 34 percent were flaked stone artifacts, and 5 percent were ground stone. Two ceramic figurine fragments were recovered as well (see Chapter 4).

Feature 1 was a large, oval pit structure outlined with rocks, with maximum exterior dimensions of 7.7 by 6.0 m, maximum interior dimensions of 7.1 by 4.9 m, and a depth of 20 to 25 cm below ground surface (Figure 2.8). Two shovel trenches excavated through the feature along the long and short axes exposed its extent. Shovel Trench 2 revealed the north and south walls of the structure, as well as a concentration of rocks later determined to be the north wall of Feature 9 (a smaller structure superimposed on the south end of Feature 1). Excavation of the feature was in quarters, with the fill in the upper 10 cm designated feature fill and the lower 10 cm removed as floor fill. Crew members screened all of the fill in the northwest quarter of the structure but only the floor fill in the other quarters.

The feature fill matrix was a light brown residual sandy silt containing roots and granite pebbles and cobbles. Wall fall consisted of granite slabs and boulders; the fill contained no clay or daub. The floor fill matrix was a silty sand similar to the upper fill.

The floor itself consisted of granite bedrock with a decomposing pebble/cobble mixture filling the interstices. An uneven surface of bedrock sloped downward to the southeast across the feature; some fill appeared to have been placed over the bedrock to level the floor. A single burned red patch on the granite surface in the approximate center of the pit structure indicated a hearth area. This subfeature was oval and measured 58 cm north-south by 74 cm east-west. One of three upright tabular stones was set in a hole dug into the bedrock in the southeast corner of the structure. The other two were set in fill, with no discernible footing holes.

The basal walls of Feature 1 were granite boulders and slabs, with up to three courses preserved in places, but most of the surviving wall was a single course. No plaster or other wall facing was apparent. The upper walls probably were of wattle work or upright branches held in place by the boulders and slabs. No post holes or formal entryway were present; a gap in the wall suggested entry through the southeast side of the structure.

Seven of eight artifacts in the floor assemblage were ground stone. Seventy percent of the nearly 240 artifacts in the fill were sherds; the ground stone included a tabular tool.

Economic taxa identified in pollen and flotation samples from the floor of Feature 1 included corn, other monocots, mountain mahogany, and oak. Calibrated results from a radiocarbon sample from the floor fill indicated a date of A.D. 1045 to 1105 or A.D. 1115 to 1415.

Feature 2 was a midden 5 m northeast of Feature 1, measuring 9.3 m northeast/southwest by 5.4 m northwest/southeast and 42 cm deep. The field crew surface collected all artifacts from this feature and excavated a 1 by 1 m control unit in 20-cm arbitrary levels. The fill was a slightly dark gray sandy loam with many leaves, needles, and twigs close to the modern ground surface and large amounts of decomposed material farther down. This dark, highly organic fill rested directly on a C horizon. Artifact density throughout the feature was fairly high; the assemblage totaled 137 sherds and flaked stone items, and one mano. Economic taxa observed in botanical samples from the control unit were corn, Cheno-ams, purslane, manzanita, saltbush, oak, pine, juniper, and mountain mahogany.

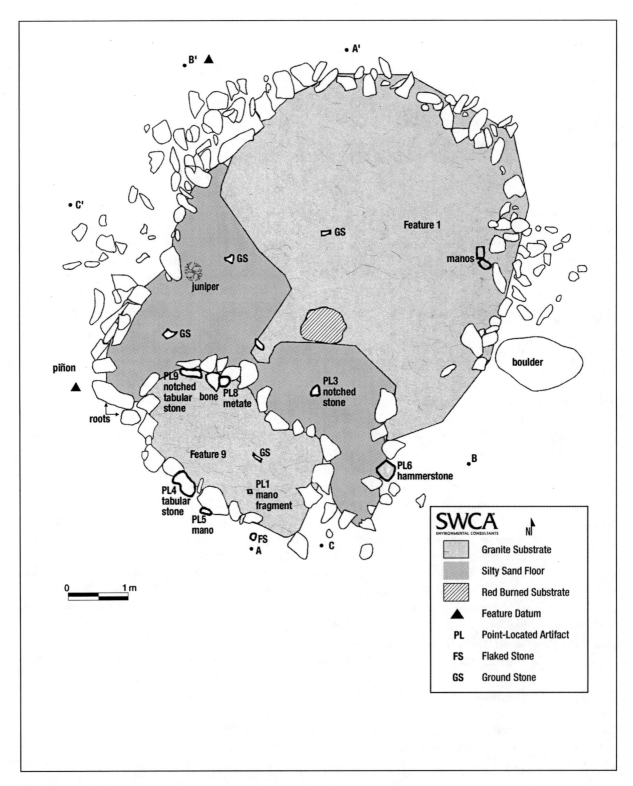

Figure 2.8. AZ N:6:20 (ASM), Features 1 and 9 plan view.

Feature 3, a midden 2 m southwest of Feature 1, measured 19.2 m east-west by 4.5 m north-south and was 70 cm deep. Data recovery work consisted of surface collection of artifacts, shovel trenching, and excavation of a 2 by 1 m control unit in 20-cm arbitrary levels. The midden fill was a dark gray sandy loam with pebbles and cobbles of granite, sparse flecks of charcoal, and rootlets. The 97 artifacts recovered consisted of nearly equal numbers of sherds and flaked stone items (including a core, a hammerstone, and a projectile point), with a few pieces of ground stone. The test trench exposed Feature 10, a pit structure. Possible economic taxa identified in composite pollen and flotation samples were corn, prickly pear, rose family, juniper, oak, pine, and mountain mahogany.

Sixteen meters south of Feature 1 was the third midden, Feature 5. This midden measured 8.6 m northeast/southwest by 8.1 m northwest/southeast and was 32 cm deep. Investigations consisted of surface collection and excavation of a 1 by 1 m control unit in 20-cm arbitrary levels. The fill was a moderately compact tan sandy silt loam with granitic inclusions that became more common with depth. Forty sherds and flaked stone artifacts were collected from this feature; densities were highest in the upper 10 cm.

Feature 6 consisted of nine granite boulders in a 4-m-long straight line across a drainage, 35 m northwest of Feature 1. The northern three or four rocks were part of a bedrock outcrop, but the other rocks appeared to have been placed there. No excavations were conducted at this feature, and no artifacts were recovered.

Feature 7, a rock alignment 10 m northwest of Feature 1, may have been a check dam or a terrace retaining wall. The feature consisted of a 6-m-long arc of 13 granite cobbles and boulders; the largest rock was 60 cm across. A shovel trench excavated along the interior of the arc exposed a fill of sandy loam derived from decomposed granite, changing in color from dark gray to orange with depth. The sediment was moderately compacted and contained a few granitic cobbles, some rootlets, and one core/hammerstone. Sediments extended below the rocks. Given its proximity to Feature 1, Feature 7 most likely provided erosion control for Feature 1 or for a garden plot next to Feature 1.

Feature 8 was a series of possible grinding spots on a boulder 8 m north of Feature 1. The top of the boulder was flat and up to 30 cm higher than the adjacent ground surface. Smooth spots within an area of the boulder measuring 135 by 90 cm might have been created by limited grinding, but no other evidence supported this interpretation. No artifacts were visible in the vicinity.

Feature 9, at the southwest end of Feature 1, was a subrectangular feature, 3.8 m long by 1.5 m wide, outlined with rocks. The builders reused part of the wall of Feature 1 as the southwest wall of Feature 9. The fill, generally similar to that of Feature 1, was a light brown sandy silt with granitic pebbles and cobbles throughout. Wall fall consisted of granite slabs and boulders; the fill contained no clay or daub. The floor fill was a silty sand.

The floor of Feature 9 was granite bedrock, with no formal floor apparent, although fill had been used to level the floor surface in the northwest portion of the feature. No floor features were present. The walls consisted of granite boulders and slabs, most preserved to a height of one course, although two courses were present in spots. No formal entryway was evident, but a 60-cm gap in the southeast wall may have provided access.

Feature 9 may have been a storage space or a temporary shelter, or it may have represented remodeling and reuse of a portion of Feature 1 as a smaller structure or a freestanding storage unit. Five artifacts and two pieces of human bone were collected from this feature. Corn and little barley grass were the only possible economic botanical remains observed.

Feature 10 was a large, oval pit structure indicated by an alignment of large granite boulders along the perimeter of a shallow pit (Figure 2.9). Field personnel found this structure within Feature 3 during mechanical stripping of the midden to search for human remains. The interior of Feature 10 measured 6 m north-south by 3.9 m east-west and extended about 10 to 20 cm below the adjacent ground surface.

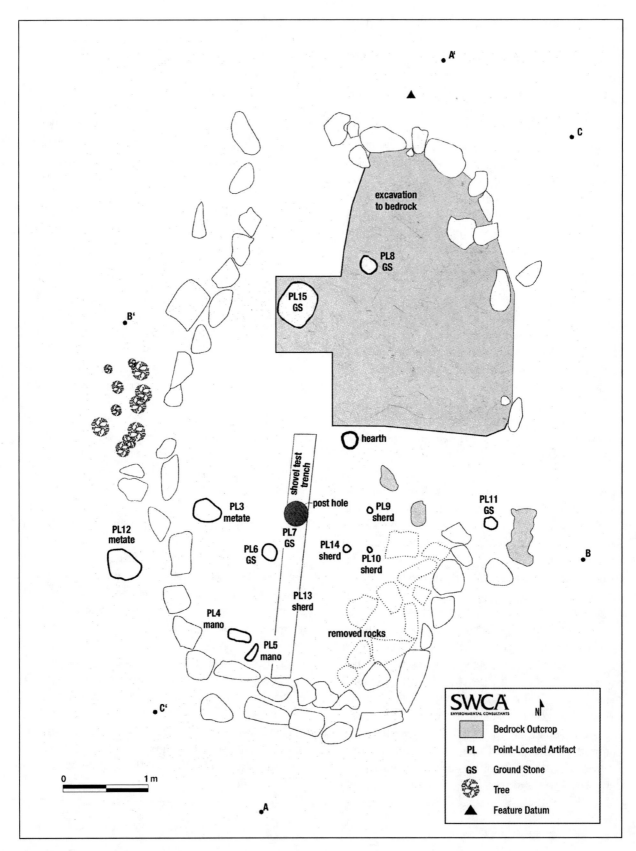

Figure 2.9. AZ N:6:20 (ASM), Feature 10 plan view.

The pit structure fill was a homogeneous dark brown sandy loam with many roots and rootlets throughout. A very small amount of charcoal was present. Some wall fall was in the fill close to the edges of the pit, and sherds and flaked stone were in the upper fill. The floor was distinguishable from the floor fill only by the hearth and several flat-lying sherds and ground stone artifacts. The subfloor matrix was similar to the floor fill and upper fill but with more clay close to the bedrock, which was about 10 cm below the floor.

Feature 10 had two floor features. The hearth, Subfeature 10.01, was a more or less circular pit excavated into the granite bedrock at the approximate center of the structure. The hearth measured 19 cm across and 20 cm deep and was clay lined from the top of the pit to 8 cm below the floor. The clay also extended 3 to 5 cm out from the rim of the pit, forming a collar. Reddish-orange discoloration due to oxidation was apparent around the edge of the feature and 8 to 10 cm to the southwest. The fill was a homogeneous dark brown sandy loam with many rootlets and pencil-thick roots.

Subfeature 10.02 was a post hole, 40 cm deep and 25 cm in diameter, 1 m southwest of Subfeature 10.01. The feature extended through the subfloor matrix and into the granite bedrock. The fill was a homogeneous dark brown sandy loam with weathered granite pebbles. The lower portion consisted of a single course of boulders placed on the occupation surface next to the post hole; parts of the perimeter may once have consisted of two courses of rocks. No plaster or adobe was apparent. The boulders probably were bracing for poles that bent or curved from one side of the structure to the other. No formal entry was observed, but a gap in the rock alignment on the east side of the structure may have provided access.

Discussion

AZ N:6:20 (ASM) may have been a long-term or reoccupied habitation site, or both. Creation of a midden (Feature 3) over a pit structure (Feature 10) and the remodeling of a pit structure (Features 1 and 9) indicate prolonged use of the site. The most likely site history

begins with construction of Feature 10 early in the occupation sequence. The refuse from use of Feature 10 became Feature 5 and part of Feature 3. Feature 1 may have been built either before or after abandonment of Feature 10, but refuse from the use of Feature 1, deposited at Feature 3, covered Feature 10. Feature 1 was subsequently remodeled into a smaller, less permanent structure, Feature 9, prior to final site abandonment.

The site appeared to have been a locus of core reduction. The flaked stone assemblage included 19 hammerstones or core/hammerstones, as well as high proportions of cores and debitage. The abundance and diversity of ground stone tools indicate intensive plant processing and suggest long-term, possibly year-round occupation of the site. Corn remains were found in all sampled features. The formality of the structures and the amount of trash at the site support the notion of long-term occupation. The radiocarbon date from Feature 1 is consistent with occupation within the traditional span of the Prescott Culture, but with an occupation after the traditional dates for that culture as well.

AZ N:7:155 (ASM)

Site Type: habitation
Size: 11,200 m²
Elevation: 5,515 feet (1,680 m)

AZ N:7:155 (ASM) was the most substantial prehistoric habitation site in the project area, with two pit houses, one two-room masonry structure, three trash middens, seven human burial features (two additional burials were identified in the laboratory), a rock alignment, and several associated features in an area measuring 140 m north-south by 80 m east-west (Figure 2.10; Table 2.1).

The site was on a low rise. A granitic outcrop south of the architectural features undoubtedly supplied raw material for the rock alignment and the masonry structure. The vegetation overstory in the area is ponderosa pine, piñon, alligator juniper, and oak, with an understory of manzanita, mountain mahogany, buckthorn, shrub oak, prickly pear and hedgehog cacti, and grasses.

Richard A. Anduze and James M. Potter

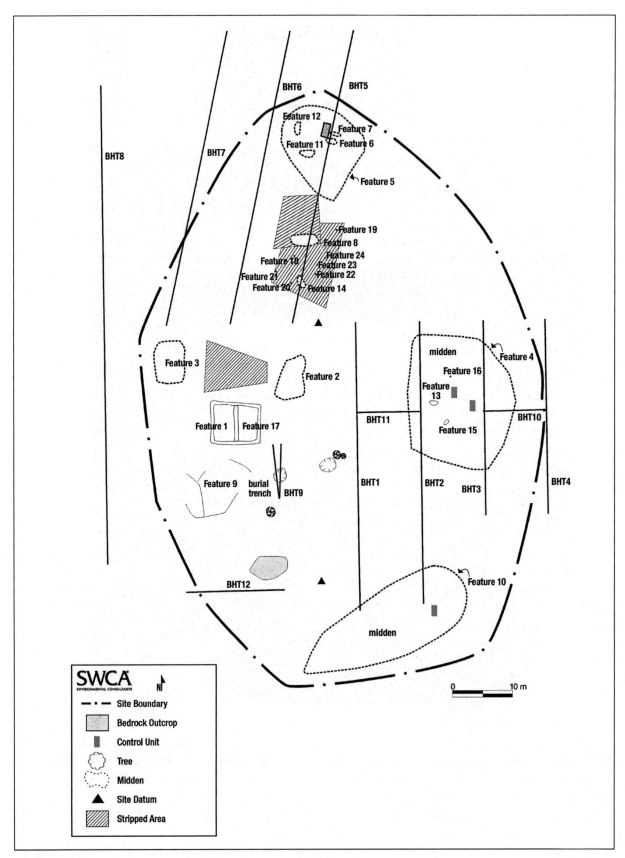

Figure 2.10. AZ N:7:155 (ASM) site map with backhoe trenches.

Table 2.1. Features, AZ N:7:155 (ASM)

Feature	Feature Type	Mitigation
1	masonry room	fully excavated
2	pit house	fully excavated
3	pit house	fully excavated
4	midden	tested, control units
5	midden	tested, control units
6	burial in F5	excavated, reinterred
7	burial in F5	excavated, reinterred
8	pit in F18	excavated
9	rock alignments	not excavated
10	midden	tested, control units
11	burial in F5	excavated, reinterred
12	burial in F5	excavated. reinterred
13	burial in F4	excavated, reinterred
14	pit in F18	not excavated
15	burial in F4	excavated, reinterred
16	burial in F4	excavated, reinterred
17	masonry room	fully excavated
18	extramural surface	mechanically stripped
19	post hole in F18	not excavated
20	ash/charcoal stain in F18	not excavated
21	ash/charcoal stain in F18	not excavated
22	ash/charcoal stain in F18	not excavated
23	ash/charcoal stain in F18	not excavated
24	ash/charcoal stain in F18	not excavated

The site was about 150 m southwest of the old Hassayampa Country Club clubhouse and pool. The area had been disturbed by vehicles, and part of the site may have been bladed during construction of the original nine-hole golf course.

Excavations

Because of the quantity of artifacts on the site surface, field crews point provenienced and mapped only those associated with features. Investigation of the site consisted of backhoe trenching and excavation of control units in the middens and complete excavation of the structures, pits, and burial features. The crews photographed all features, drew individual plan views of the structures, the burials, and the rock alignment feature, and added the middens to the general site plan. After thoroughly recording and analyzing the remains, SWCA

reinterred the burials in accordance with the Memorandum of Agreement between the Arizona State Museum and the Yavapai-Prescott Indian Tribe.

Twelve backhoe trenches were excavated to define the site boundaries and uncover any features (including burials) not apparent on the site surface. Three areas north of the architectural features were mechanically stripped to expose buried features.

AZ N:7:155 (ASM) produced the largest and most diverse prehistoric artifact assemblage of the project sites, accounting for 72 percent of all project ceramic artifacts (excluding the figurines), 70 percent of flaked stone, and 77 percent of ground stone. Seventy-five percent of the nearly 8,500 artifacts were ceramics, 22 percent were flaked stone, and 3 percent were ground stone. Another 39 artifacts were ceramic figurines and figurine fragments, one from a structure and the rest found in middens. Over 325 faunal bone and shell specimens and nearly 100 mineral specimens and pieces of raw material (Chapters 3–7) were collected as well. Burial features yielded small numbers of ceramic, flaked stone, and ground stone artifacts and one worked bone tool.

Features 1 and 17 made up a two-room masonry structure. They were contiguous rectangular semi-subterranean rooms with floors 60 cm below the present ground surface. Both rooms had been heavily disturbed by tree roots, and the field crew left part of each unexcavated because of the presence of large ponderosa pines. There were no indications of doorways, suggesting entry through the roof. Apparently the builders added the interior wall of the structure (west wall of Feature 17/east wall of Feature 1) as a divider after the exterior walls were built, as a different mortar was used in the interior wall.

Feature 1, the western room, had interior dimensions of 5.25 m north-south by 3.20 m east-west (Figure 2.11). The excavators found no floor features and could not determine the function of the room. The floor assemblage included sherds, a tabular ground stone tool, and other lithic artifacts. The presence of a large ponderosa prevented excavation of the northwest corner of Feature 1. The room sat on top of a granite outcrop that sloped southward; the builders apparently had excavated the

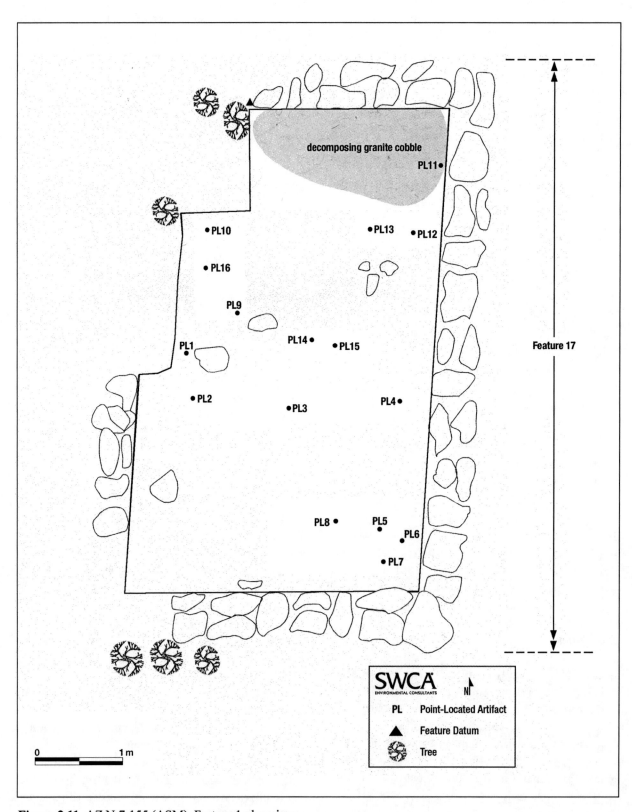

Figure 2.11. AZ N:7:155 (ASM), Feature 1 plan view.

south end of the room to bedrock, then added fill to match the level of the bedrock at the north end of the room. The south wall stood on 35 cm of this leveling fill. The floor of the room was difficult to define but seemed to incorporate a 1-degree slope to the southwest.

The fill above the floor was a homogeneous gray-tan clayey sediment with decomposed-granite sand and charcoal fragments throughout. The fill became more compact (and difficult to excavate) nearer the walls of the structure and extremely hard at the wall edges. Wall fall was present throughout the fill. Artifact density was high in this feature, which yielded 7 percent of the sherds, 7 percent of the flaked stone (including 18 tools), and 8 percent of the ground stone (including seven tabular tools) from this site.

The exterior walls of Feature 1 were one to two stones wide and semi-regularly coursed. The corners appeared to be composites of bonded and abutted types. A substantial amount of mortar remained in the corners, however, masking the contact between the stones and making the joinery difficult to define. The stones used in the walls were granite and ranged in size from 30 by 20 by 15 cm to 50 by 30 by 20 cm, with smaller cobbles used as fillers. The stones varied in shape from rounded to blocky to angular to tabular, but most were rounded to blocky. An abundance of mud had been used in the vertical and horizontal joints. The mortar, which was generally flush with the wall surfaces, varied from a coarse sandy clay loam to a coarse loamy sand and from light brownish gray to yellowish brown.

Feature 17 measured 5.25 m north-south by 3.55 m east-west (Figure 2.12); trees in the southeast corner prevented excavation of that portion of the room. Feature 17 exhibited the same construction methods and elements as Feature 1. The floor was exposed bedrock at the north end of the room, and fill had been added to the southern two-thirds of the room to level the surface. Wall stone size varied more in this room, with smaller cobbles more common and more stones exposed in the walls.

The fill of Feature 17 consisted of a hard clayey sediment with sand of decomposed granite. Pockets of oxidized orange clay may have represented roof fall.

Again, no floor features were evident. Unlike Feature 1, however, this feature contained few artifacts, most of them from the north half of the room. Among them were six flaked stone tools, a grooved axe-head fragment, two tabular tools, a turquoise pendant, and pieces of azurite.

Feature 2 was an irregular pit structure northeast of Features 1 and 17 (Figure 2.13). The interior dimensions of the structure were 7 m north-south by 3.5 m east-west. Preservation was poor, but the walls appeared to have been relatively straight with rounded corners. Construction was probably dry-laid stone, with dirt added for stability; no mortar or plaster was evident. The walls may originally have been two or three courses high. This feature yielded moderate numbers of sherds, flaked stone, and ground stone.

The upper 8 to 10 cm of structure fill was a humic clay loam overlying a hard, compact, brownish-gray clayey sediment. The excavators defined two floors in this structure, one at 38 cm below the ground surface and one 4 to 6 cm higher. Each floor contained a hearth.

The earlier floor of Feature 2 was an unprepared, use-packed surface just above the undulating bedrock, which protruded above the floor in the northeast corner of the structure. Artifacts found in association with this floor included a chert core, fragments of hematite and ocher, a polishing stone, and a mano fragment. A circular, clay-lined hearth, Subfeature 2.01, was also associated with this lower surface. This feature apparently was constructed on the granite bedrock, as burning was evident there. The hearth measured 23 cm across and 10 cm deep and was filled with a hard, compact, dark brown gravelly clay loam. A single black-on-white sherd was embedded in the north wall of the hearth.

Possible economic taxa identified in botanical samples were corn, prickly pear, smartweed, and oak. Subfeature 2.01 was on the west side of the structure and may have been associated with an entry on the west side. However, no evidence of such an entry remained in the poorly preserved walls.

Subfeature 2.02 was an unlined, unprepared circular hearth, 22 cm across and 11 cm deep. The top of this feature was 6 cm above the lower floor, indicating the

Richard A. Anduze and James M. Potter

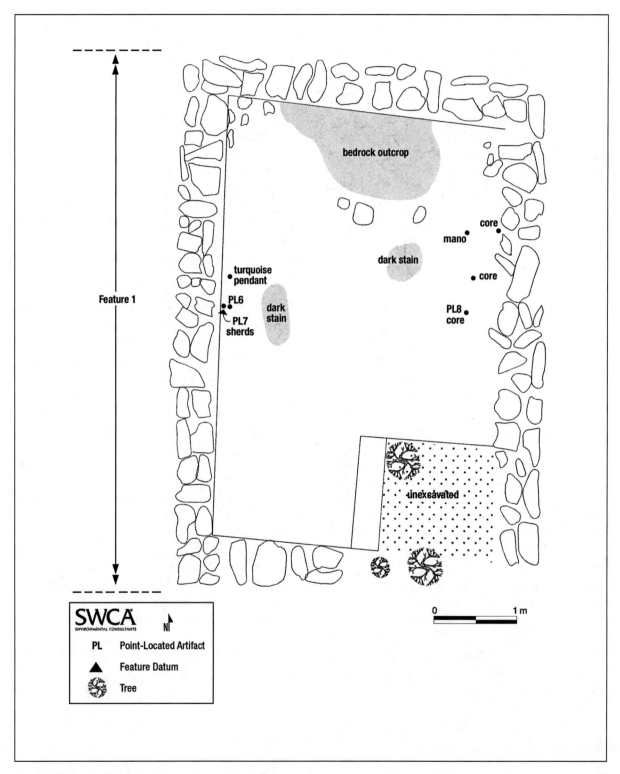

Figure 2.12. AZ N:155 (ASM), Feature 17 plan view.

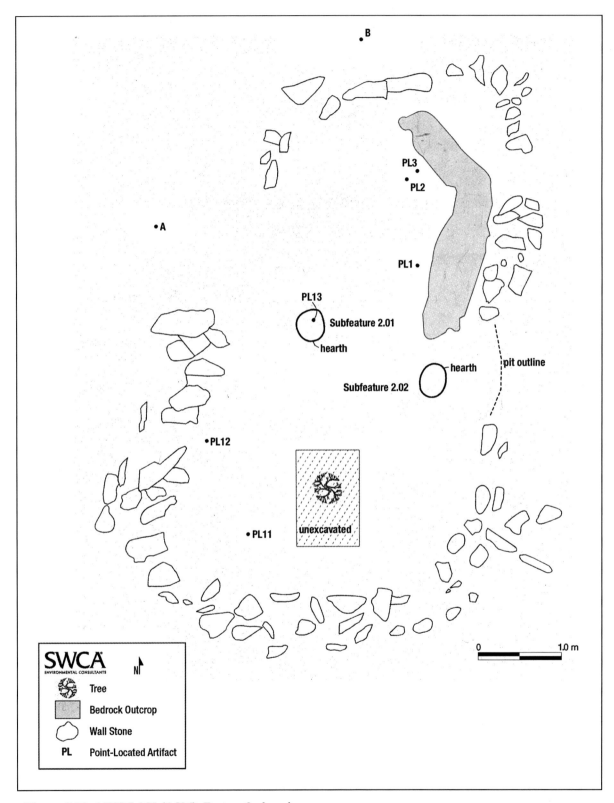

Figure 2.13. AZ N:7:155 (ASM), Feature 2 plan view.

presence of a second, later floor. The hearth extended downward to bedrock. The hearth fill was a compact clayey sediment with pockets of ash. No other evidence of the second floor was found. The placement of Subfeature 2.02 in the eastern portion of Feature 2, along with the lack of rocks in the eastern wall of the structure, suggests that the inhabitants shifted the entryway from the west side of the structure to the east side when constructing the second floor and hearth. In this case as well, the poor preservation of the walls precluded direct identification of an entry if one was present. No artifacts were associated with Subfeature 2.02 or the projected floor. A flotation sample contained walnut shell fragments.

Feature 3 was a rectangular pit structure northwest of Features 1 and 17 (Figure 2.14). The interior dimensions of this feature were 6.6 m north-south by 3.5 m east-west, with a well-defined floor 20 cm below the present ground surface. The walls of the structure were quite straight, and the corners were fairly sharp. The builders had partly backfilled the pit for this structure to create a level floor, which was burned and contained several post features. The feature fill was generally a moderately compacted gray-tan silty sand with pockets of dark gray, humic soil and root disturbance throughout. The fill just above and on the floor was a hard-packed clayey material. The interior of this structure yielded 4 percent of the sherds, 5 percent of the flaked stone, and 4 percent of the ground stone from this site.

The walls of Feature 3 were fairly intact, although they showed signs of severe slumping, and consisted of large granite rocks with smaller rocks used as chinking. In the southwest corner of the structure the extant walls were as much as three courses high, and given the amount of wall fall found in the feature fill were probably at least four courses high originally. The walls exhibited no evidence of mortar or plaster.

The floor of Feature 3 was a clayey surface that had been leveled with cultural fill at the south end. The floor varied in thickness and probably was compacted by use rather than by formal preparation. Many areas of the floor showed signs of burning. Artifacts found in association with the floor included several pieces of ground stone (one of them a metate) and a mineral specimen. A pollen wash from the metate did not yield enough pollen for analysis. However, a flotation sample from the floor around the metate contained corn remains and charcoal from pine, mountain mahogany, cliffrose, and oak.

All eight of the floor features encountered in Feature 3 were holes from posts that apparently were added to the structure well after its initial construction. None were formal post holes; it appeared that the inhabitants simply stuck wooden posts into the floor to support the western wall, which had slumped inward prior to abandonment. A small burned portion of a clay rim north and east of the doorway was the only evidence of a possible hearth. On the east side of the structure was a formally prepared ramp entryway with walls of tiered cobbles.

Features 4, 5, and 10 were middens, east, north, and southeast of the architectural features. The field crews examined each one with hand-excavated control units and backhoe trenches. Features 4 and 5 produced the greatest quantities of artifacts on the site, including all but one of the faunal specimens recovered.

Feature 4 was roughly rectangular in plan, measuring 20 by 15 m across and 80 cm deep. The surveyors described this feature as a "trash mound" because it was slightly higher than the adjacent ground surface. The fill was a moderately compact, dark gray to black sandy silt from the ground surface to the bottom of the feature, which lay on bedrock. The artifact assemblage recovered from this feature was the largest at this site. Two 2 by 1 m control units excavated in the center of the feature yielded nearly half of the sherds from the site, over half of the flaked stone artifacts, and 30 percent of the ground stone. Other cultural materials recovered were six objects made from faunal bone and five shell artifacts, as well as numerous faunal remains, mineral specimens, and pieces of raw material. Pollen and flotation samples from a control unit near the center of the midden yielded remains of corn, walnuts, and manzanita seeds from all four levels. Other possible economic taxa identified were squash/pumpkin, goosefoot and other Cheno-ams, cholla and prickly pear, members of the rose family, grapes, cattail, juniper, oak, pine, and cherry/plum. Feature 4 contained three inhumations, Features 13, 15, and 16 (see below).

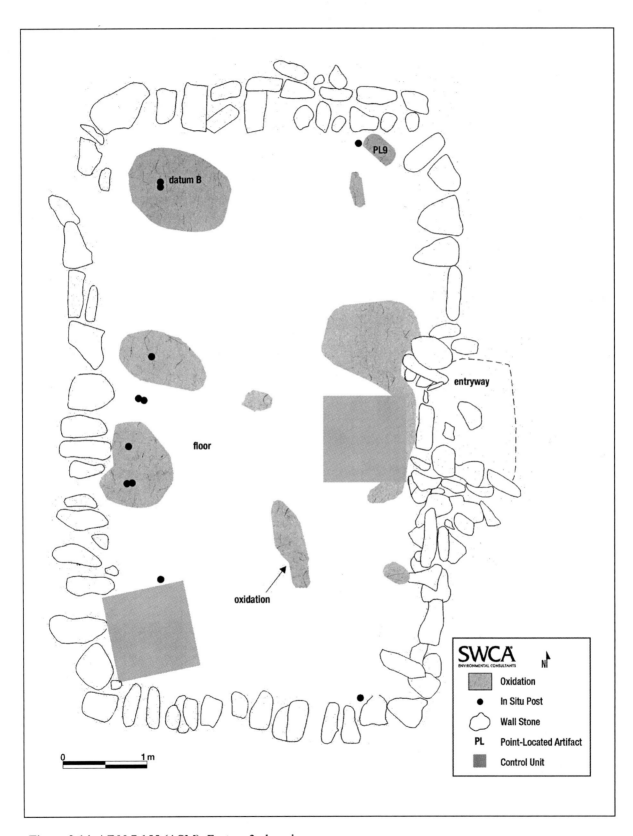

Figure 2.14. AZ N:7:155 (ASM), Feature 3 plan view.

Feature 5 was roughly oval, measuring 15 by 12 m in plan, and 60 cm deep. The fill in this feature was also a moderately compact, dark gray to black sandy silt, with charcoal flecking throughout. The substrate was decomposing granite bedrock. Artifact density was high in this midden as well. A single 2 by 1 m control unit yielded 30 percent of the site ceramic assemblage, 19 percent of the flaked stone artifacts, 13 percent of the ground stone, a quantity of faunal remains, and three shell artifacts. Corn, walnut, and cholla remains occurred regularly in the botanical samples from this feature. Other possible economic taxa present were purslane, squash/pumpkin, cultivated beans, cattail, manzanita, Chenoams, pine, and oak. Feature 5 contained four inhumations, Features 6, 7, 11, and 12 (see below).

Feature 10 was an elongated midden, 25 m long by 10 m wide and 40 cm deep. The fill was a moderately compact, very dark gray ashy sandy silt. The fill contained only a few sherds but yielded 6 percent of the flaked stone and 12 percent of the ground stone from the site. A single 2 by 1 m control unit near the northeast end of the feature exposed the underlying bedrock. Botanical samples indicated possible use of corn, grasses, goosefoot and other Cheno-ams, cholla, walnuts, grapes, juniper, oak, and pine.

Feature 18 was an extramural occupation surface north of the architectural features. Two rather amorphous pits, one poorly defined post hole, and five amorphous ash and charcoal stains exposed during mechanical stripping defined this feature. Backhoe trenching exposed Features 8 and 14, the two pits, in profile. Feature 14 was not examined further. Feature 8, an informal pit feature, measured 1.66 m north-south by 1.45 m east-west and was 40 cm deep (Figure 2.15). The fill was a dark gray-brown sandy silt with extensive charcoal staining, particularly in the deep central portion of the pit. The fill contained very few artifacts: small pieces of burned human bone, a few heavily oxidized sherds, six lithic artifacts, and a clay effigy. Since there was no evidence that the soil had been burned or that a fire had been built in this location, the pit probably served as an ash dump or the repository for a cremation. Heavy mottling of the bottom and sides made determining the exact limits of the pit difficult.

Feature 9 was a series of fairly straight rock alignments (Figure 2.16) on the surface of the site just south of the architectural features, within the portion of the site that was preserved. They were not excavated, and their function is not known. A depression within the alignments may mark the location of a subsurface pit structure, but bedrock is exposed 10 m to the south, so any pit feature at this location is unlikely to have much depth.

Burials

The burials recorded as Features 13, 15, and 16 were within Feature 4. Feature 13 was a primary inhumation found 2 m west of the control units. The burial rested on bedrock at a depth of 70 cm. The body was extended and supine, with the legs together and the head to the east. Much of the upper body was absent, including the arms (except for one humerus fragment) and the cranium (except for a mandible fragment and a small cranial fragment). However, most of the innominate and the legs were in situ. Grave goods associated with this burial included a spindle whorl fragment and a ceramic cylinder found in the screen, as well as four shell beads or pendants beneath the left hip.

Feature 15 was a possible secondary inhumation found south of the control units. The bones were badly disturbed, either through prehistoric activity (i.e., secondary deposition) or from construction of the original golf course. This burial was higher in the midden fill than the other two inhumations found at Feature 4, suggesting that it was more susceptible to disturbance. No burial goods were present, but a few artifacts, including a tabular tool and a shell bracelet fragment, were nearby.

Feature 16 was the remains of a primary inhumation, consisting of the left leg bones. This burial was just north of the control units excavated in Feature 4 and was 2 cm above bedrock, 70 cm below the ground surface. The orientation of the complete individual could not be determined, and no grave goods were present.

The burials recorded as Features 6, 7, 11, and 12 were also from a midden, Feature 5. Feature 6, a primary inhumation, was southeast of the excavation control unit. This extended burial was oriented southeast to

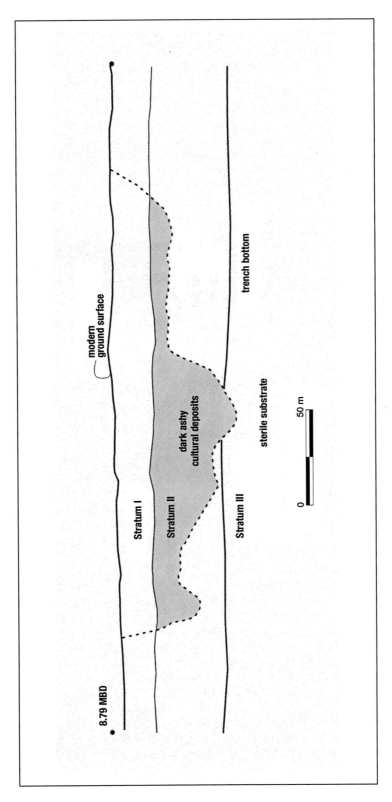

Figure 2.15. AZ N:7:155 (ASM), Feature 8 profile.

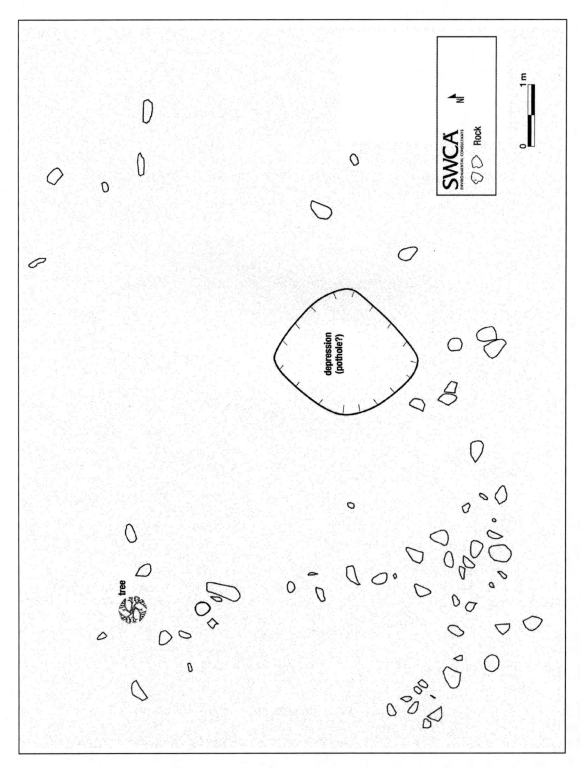

Figure 2.16. AZ N:7:155 (ASM), Feature 9 plan view.

northwest; the remains rested on bedrock, 50 cm below the ground surface. Most of the skeleton was preserved, except for a portion destroyed by the backhoe trench. A bone awl was underneath the left forearm, near the elbow, and a large sherd was near the left side of the head.

Feature 7 was a primary inhumation just east of the control unit excavated in Feature 5; this burial was also extended and oriented southeast to northwest. This individual had been interred in a pit-like crevice in the bedrock, and the remains were thus well preserved. No grave goods were present, but two shell fragments were nearby.

Feature 11, a double primary inhumation found south of the control unit, contained the remains of an adult woman (identified in the field) and a child (identified in the laboratory). The adult individual was on her back in an extended position, with arms and legs parallel to the torso. Orientation of the body was southeast to northwest. This was the only burial in the midden found in a discernible pit. The pit was 80 cm wide at the head, 45 cm wide at the feet, and 2 m long, and extended to within 20 cm of bedrock. This burial was unique in the large number of associated grave goods. Two whole ceramic vessels and two reconstructible vessels were near the head, and a broken ceramic vessel and a large uniface were near the hip.

Feature 12 was a badly disturbed, poorly preserved primary inhumation west of the control unit in Feature 5. Surviving evidence indicated that the burial was in a pit-like crevice in the bedrock, in an extended position, oriented north-south. The only articulated part of the skeleton was the left leg. No artifacts were in this feature; a single piece of ground stone was nearby.

Discussion

The artifacts recovered from AZ N:7:155 (ASM) were numerous and diverse. The amount and variety of flaked stone and ground stone indicate long-term occupation and year-round activities (Chapter 5). Of particular note is the abundance of minerals, such as azurite, hematite, and malachite, suggesting ritual activity, and the large number of tabular tools, suggesting harvesting of wild

plants, particularly agave. The botanical remains in pollen and flotation samples indicated use of corn, squash/pumpkin, and beans and a wide variety of wild plant foods from local and riparian environments. Recovered charcoal came from at least seven woody plants. The faunal remains, which included a high relative frequency of large game such as deer, elk, and antelope, indicate exploitation of multiple environmental zones (Chapter 6). The proportion of large game also suggests that the site was strategically situated to target multiple species. In short, this site yielded evidence of a wide variety of activities, both economic and non-economic, characteristic of long-term, year-round habitation.

The ceramic data suggest that AZ N:7:155 (ASM) was occupied between A.D. 1100 and 1200 (Chapter 3). The high frequency of Prescott Gray sherds indicates that this pottery was probably locally produced, perhaps at this site. Two radiocarbon samples recovered from the site, one from the floor of Feature 3 and one from the floor of Feature 2, dated from A.D. 1025 to 1260 (calibrated results, two sigma) and from A.D. 1275 to 1410 (calibrated two sigma). The sample from Feature 3 correlates with the ceramic date for the feature. Note that the two-sigma ranges (95 percent confidence intervals) do not overlap, suggesting that the structures were not contemporaneous and that Feature 3 was earlier. Unfortunately, two radiocarbon samples do not constitute sufficient data for solid chronological conclusions.

AZ N:7:156 (ASM)

Site Type: temporary habitation, ceremonial
Size: 24,000 m²
Elevation: 5,550 feet (1,692 m)

AZ N:7:156 (ASM) measured about 200 m north-south by 120 m east-west (Figure 2.17). It consisted of an irregular occupation surface with a hearth (Feature 1), a rock alignment (Feature 3), and a possible check dam (Feature 4), and a possibly Archaic bedrock grinding slick (Feature 9) with four associated petroglyph panels (Features 5–8). The site components were scattered along small drainages on a slope, 100 m north of Aspen Creek. The area has an overstory of ponderosa pine, piñon, alligator juniper, and oak; the understory includes manzanita, mountain mahogany, buckthorn,

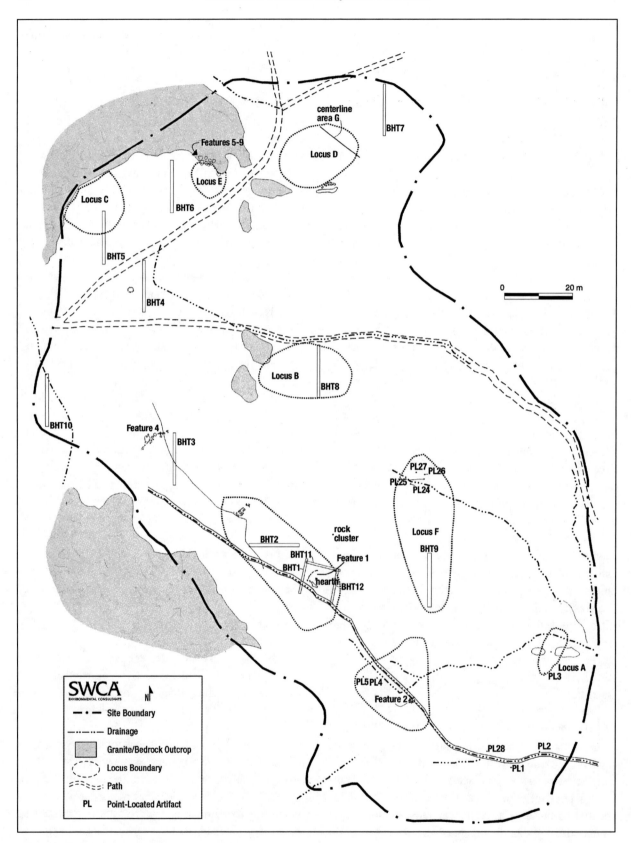

Figure 2.17. AZ N:7:156 (ASM) site map.

shrub oak, prickly pear, hedgehog cactus, and grasses. Several granitic rock outcrops on the site undoubtedly supplied raw material for the structure walls and other stone features.

Excavations

Field crews photographed all features, drew individual plan views of the structure and rock features, and point provenienced diagnostic artifacts on features and on the site surface within defined loci. Twelve backhoe trenches placed across the site in an attempt to uncover features not apparent on the surface exposed no additional cultural remains. Feature investigations consisted of complete excavation of the occupation surface and associated hearth and placement of a 2 by 1 m control unit over Feature 3.

AZ N:7:156 (ASM) produced a substantial number of artifacts, primarily from surface collections. The assemblage contained approximately 15 percent of the ceramic artifacts, 12 percent of the flaked stone, and 10 percent of the ground stone collected during this project. Sherds accounted for 76 percent of the site assemblage, flaked stone for 21 percent, and ground stone for 3 percent.

Feature 1 was an activity area consisting of an occupation surface and a hearth in the southwest portion of the site, next to a small drainage (Figure 2.18). A substantial amount of rubble and an artifact concentration were on the ground surface. The overlying sediment graded from duff at the modern ground surface to a hard-packed tan clay loam just above the prehistoric surface, at a depth of 25 cm. The prehistoric surface, a hard-packed decomposed granite, measured 4.9 m north-south by 4.1 m east-west. It was heavily disturbed by roots and by water erosion along the drainage. The associated hearth, Subfeature 1.01, was a circular pit dug into the prehistoric surface. The pit was 28 cm in diameter and 16 cm deep and was partly lined with clay, which extended over the edge of the pit to form a collar. The fill was a highly compact dark brown sediment.

Artifacts associated with this feature, surface and subsurface, included approximately 20 percent of the sherds (primarily Prescott Gray Ware) and flaked stone items

from this site, and 88 percent of the ground stone. Fifteen flaked stone artifacts and 20 ground stone items were tools; all of them but one metate were found during excavation of the feature. The large number of grinding tools indicates fairly intensive plant processing at this feature. Most of the metates and manos were medium to coarse grained, suggesting that maize was probably the primary plant resource being processed.

Feature 2 was a loose pile of granitic cobbles and boulders two to three courses high and 2 m in diameter. This feature was in the middle of a small drainage or trail at the southeast end of the site and appeared to be on the modern ground surface. The lack of lichen buildup and post-construction animal burrowing suggested that this feature was a recent rock pile used to mark the trail or that it consisted of rocks cleared from the trail. However, a concentration of prehistoric sherds, flaked stone, manos, and grinding slabs surrounded the feature.

Feature 3 was a semicircular rock alignment next to a small drainage, 30 m northwest of Feature 1. The alignment was 2.3 m long east-west by 1.9 m wide north-south. One of the rocks was a slab metate. A 2 by 1 m control unit excavated next to the alignment did not expose any subsurface remains. The surrounding fill was 30 cm of a loose, sandy clay loam overlying a hard, compacted clay loam, possibly an ancient ground surface. No cultural material was associated with this earlier surface, and rocks visible on the modern ground surface were 3 to 7 cm above the clayey layer and thus not directly associated with it. The lack of subsurface material suggests that this alignment probably was the foundation or other support for a temporary structure. The only artifacts associated with Feature 3 were a few flaked stone items recovered from the surface in and around the feature and from the subsurface testing unit.

Feature 4 was a linear concentration of granitic rocks one course high. The rocks ranged from less than 10 cm across to 2.6 m across. The alignment extended across a small south-flowing drainage and continued east for 6 m. Sediment was trapped behind the feature, and it had most likely served as a check dam. The sediment around the feature was a compact decomposed granitic alluvium. A few artifacts were on the surface of the site near the rocks.

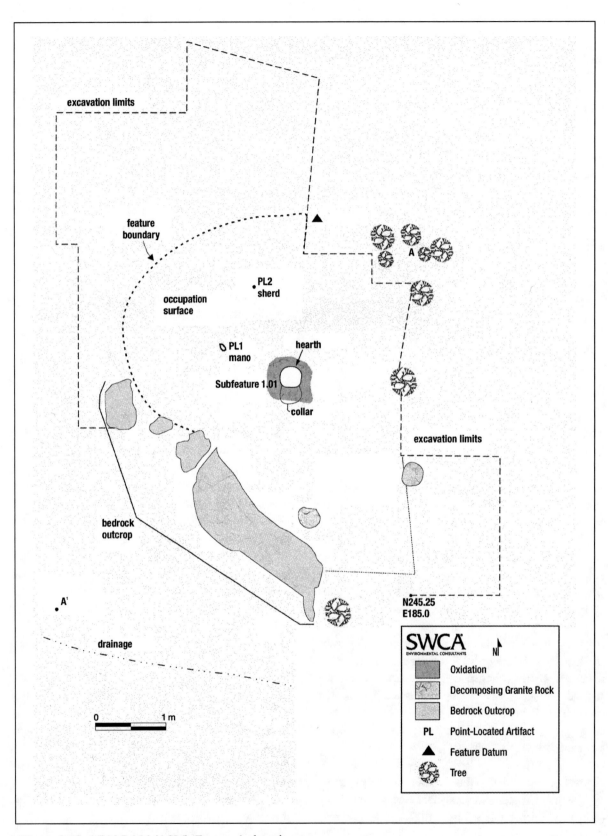

Figure 2.18. AZ N:7:156 (ASM), Feature 1 plan view.

Features 5 through 8 were petroglyphs on boulders at the north end of the site (Figure 2.19). Feature 9 was a bedrock grinding slick near the petroglyphs. These features may predate the rest of the site and possibly are Archaic, but no firm evidence supports that hypothesis. An artifact concentration associated with these features (Locus E) consisted of numerous sherds and flakes, a flake uniface, a core, and a slab metate.

Five other surface artifact concentrations (Loci A–D, F) were identified and collected, and Loci B, C, and F were tested with backhoe trenches. The backhoe trenches exposed no subsurface features.

Locus A was at the southeastern end of the site, next to two granitic outcrops. It measured 15 by 7.5 m and yielded four sherds, three pieces of debitage, and one flaked stone artifact, which was point provenienced.

Locus B, in the center of the site next to two large granitic outcrops, measured 27 by 15 m and consisted of six sherds and one piece of debitage. Seven additional sherds and a flake biface came from the backhoe trench excavated in this locus.

Locus C was adjacent to the large granitic outcrop defining the northern boundary of the site, west of the petroglyphs, and measured 15 by 15 m. Locus C produced sherds and one piece of lithic debitage, and the backhoe trench yielded additional sherds.

Locus D, the northernmost locus on the site, measured 22 by 18 m. Only one piece of debitage and two sherds were in this locus.

Locus F was a long, narrow concentration in the southeast portion of the site containing sherds, pieces of debitage, and four point-provenienced artifacts: a core/hammerstone, a hammerstone, a mano, and a handstone. Trenching yielded more than 60 sherds.

Discussion

AZ N:7:156 (ASM) was a prehistoric Prescott Culture site with a possible Archaic component. The site consisted of an occupation surface with an associated hearth, three rock features, four petroglyph panels, a bedrock grinding slick, and a large quantity and variety of artifacts. The site probably supported long-term use on a year-round or regular seasonal basis and may have been a farmstead related to maize agriculture. The dense concentration of manos and metates at the occupation surface indicates intensive plant processing, probably corn grinding, at this feature. The presence of rock art suggests a possible earlier use of the site, probably for ceremonial purposes.

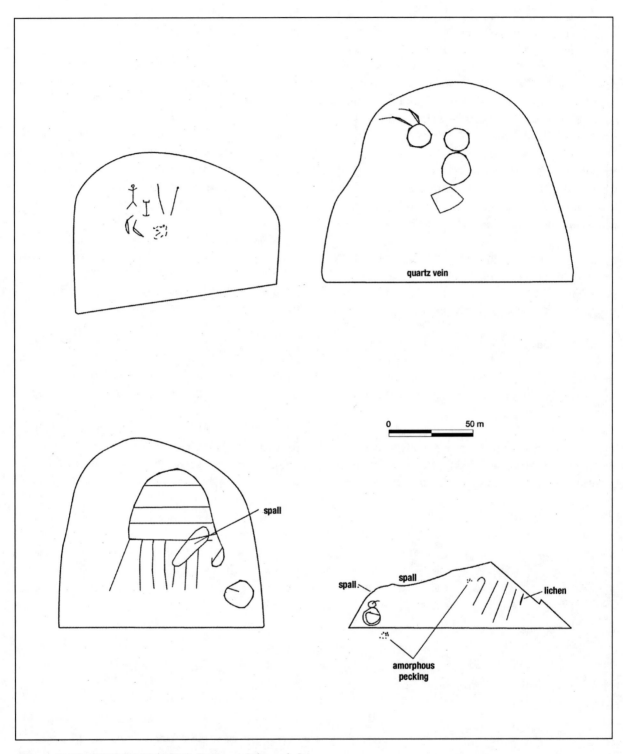

Figure 2.19. AZ N:7:156 (ASM), Features 5 through 8.

CHAPTER 3

Ceramic Artifact Analysis: An Examination of Technological Variation in Prescott Gray Ware

Mary-Ellen Walsh and Andrew L. Christenson

In this chapter we present the results of the ceramics analysis for six of the Hassayampa Country Club sites: AZ N:6:9, AZ N:6:13, AZ N:6:19, AZ N:6:20, AZ N:7:155, and AZ N:7:156 (ASM). Of the 5,979 sherds analyzed (Table 3.1), we have focused on the assemblage from AZ N:7:155 (ASM), which constituted 84 percent of the total. The local pottery, traditionally defined as Prescott Gray Ware (Caywood and Spicer 1935; Colton and Hargrave 1937), includes a number of types based on the presence or absence of paint on reduced or oxidized surfaces. For this study, we examined correlations between specific technological attributes, such as temper type and surface finish, to define the variation within Prescott area pottery and to distinguish Prescott Gray Ware and Alameda Brown Ware (which are often confused with each other). We also conducted a petrographic analysis (Appendix A) and an oxidation study (Appendix B) in an attempt to define mineralogical composition of tempering material and characterize variation in ceramic clays.

The analysis was completed in several phases. Walsh analyzed the bulk of the assemblage, conducted the oxidation study (Appendix B), and compiled the chapter. Christenson wrote the historical overview, analyzed all rim sherds, and did the petrographic research (Appendix A). Although the analysts did not work directly with one another during the course of this research, they jointly developed and designed the analysis and worked together to record attributes from a sample of sherds to ensure some level of consistency. The similar results of the separate rim sherd and body sherd analyses, which were later compiled into a single discussion, confirmed the success of these efforts. The results of these analyses have helped to determine the range of variation in Prescott Gray Ware and define a few key attributes that may

help to describe the group of pottery identified as "intergrades," which may have temporal importance.

The ceramics data suggest that AZ N:7:155 (ASM), a habitation site of four or five rooms, was occupied between A.D. 1100 and 1200. The high frequency of Prescott Gray sherds indicates that this pottery was locally produced. Low frequencies of sherds at the other sites, except perhaps AZ N:6:20 (ASM) and AZ N:7:156 (ASM), indicate less intensive use, perhaps on a seasonal basis. Contemporaneous or overlapping occupations are a possibility, however. The ratios of Wingfield Plain, Prescott Gray, and Prescott Black-on-gray pottery may offer additional chronological information, as discussed later in this chapter.

To put our research into proper perspective, we begin with an overview of ceramics studies for the local area. The Prescott ceramics typology, which has presented researchers with confusing type descriptions over the years, has led to three separate conferences, two of them discussed briefly below. Proceedings of the most recent conference, held in November 1996, are on file at the Museum of Northern Arizona. This report incorporates some of the decisions made by the 1996 conference participants, particularly the revised Prescott Gray Ware typology.

Overview of Ceramic Studies in the Prescott Area

This review of approximately 70 years of research on Prescott area pottery concentrates on the major studies and the most commonly found types. As defined here, the Prescott area is the region where Prescott Gray Ware pottery is common: a circle with a radius of 50 miles,

Mary-Ellen Walsh and Andrew L. Christenson

Table 3.1. Ceramic Ware and Type Frequencies, Analyzed Assemblage

Ceramic Ware/Type	Site (AZ N:_[ASM])						Total
	6:9	6:13	6:19	6:20	7:155	7:156	
Prescott Gray Ware	*65*	*139*	*4*	*300*	*4,458*	*341*	*5,307*
Prescott Gray	65	136	4	262	3,946	341	4,754
Prescott Black-on-gray				38	473		511
Prescott Red-on-gray					16		16
Prescott Red		3			23		26
Wingfield Brown Ware	*5*	*5*		*22*	*484*	*39*	*555*
Wingfield Plain	5	5		22	481	39	552
Wingfield Red					3		3
Alameda Brown Ware					*5*		*5*
Tuzigoot Brown					4		4
Verde Red					1		1
Hohokam Buff Ware					*13*	*2*	*15*
Sacaton Red-on-buff					4	1	5
Sacaton/Casa Grande Red-on-buff					1		1
Casa Grande Red-on-buff					2		2
Untyped					6	1	7
Little Colorado and Tusayan White Ware				*1*	*9*	*1*	*11*
Sosi Black-on-white					1		1
Holbrook A Black-on-white				1			1
Holbrook B Black-on-white					4		4
Untyped Little Colorado White Ware					1		1
Flagstaff Black-on-white					3		3
Untyped Tusayan White Ware						1	1
San Francisco Mountain Gray Ware					*34*		*34*
Kirkland Gray					12		12
Deadmans Gray					4		4
Deadmans Black-on-gray					18		18
San Juan Red Ware					*1*		*1*
Deadmans Black-on-red					1		1
Tsegi Red-on-orange					*1*		*1*
Untyped Brownware				*6*	*31*	*6*	*43*
Other Buffware					*5*	*1*	*6*
Other Orangeware					*1*		*1*
Total	**70**	**144**	**4**	**329**	**5,042**	**390**	**5,979**

centered on Prescott. Conveniently, this area coincides with most of Yavapai County (although Simonis [2000] has recently claimed an extension of the ware all the way to the Colorado River).

The first part of the review focuses on the abundant sand-tempered gray or brown pottery that is commonly assumed to have been made in the area, including Prescott Gray (and its associated decorated types or varieties) and Verde Brown, as well as Tizon Brown Ware. The second part briefly considers the phyllite-tempered or mica-schist-tempered brownware usually called Wingfield Plain. The review concludes with a short summary of technical studies of Prescott area pottery.

Sand-tempered Grayware and Brownware

As was frequently the case in other parts of the Southwest, J. W. Fewkes was the first professional archaeologist to visit the Prescott area (Fewkes 1912), but it was not until 1930 that descriptions of the local pottery were published. Beginning in 1926, Winifred Gladwin and Harold S. Gladwin conducted surveys east and west of the Prescott area proper. In their first report, on the western area (Gladwin and Gladwin 1930b), they named, described, and illustrated the local ceramic types, including Verde Black-on-white:

> Verde Black-on-white; a variety which is, more accurately, a dull Black-on-grey; the ware is thick and crude, of a coarse sandy paste. Designs are simple, chiefly linear, wide and sloppy, drops and splashes often included. Vessel shapes are ollas and deep bowls, decorated in many repetitions of one motif.

> A second type is found in association with Verde Black-on-white ... this variety is coarse and heavy, usually grey in color, and contains a high percentage of fine gravel and mica [Gladwin and Gladwin 1930b:140].

The Gladwins may have chosen the term *Verde* because they found these types in their Verde Valley survey. They quickly realized that calling the type black-on-white was an error, and they changed the name to Verde Black-on-gray (Gladwin and Gladwin

1930a:176). At about the same time that the Gladwins were examining the peripheries of the region, an amateur archaeologist, J. W. Simmons, was working in its heart (Christenson ca. 2004). Based on his work at Fitzmaurice Ruin and elsewhere, he published an article on what he called the Black on Grey Culture (Simmons 1931a).

Simmons contacted Byron Cummings at the University of Arizona, and this contact led to the university's brief involvement in the area, excavating at two sites where Simmons had already worked (Simmons 1931a, 1931b). Simmons began work on burials at King's Ruin on Big Chino Wash in late 1931 and the following summer was joined by Cummings and his students, who excavated the associated pueblo (Spicer 1933, 1936). Excavations continued at Fitzmaurice Ruin on Lynx Creek in the following year (Caywood 1936). Spicer described the pottery from King's Ruin in his Master's thesis and suggested the name Prescott Black-on-gray in preference to the Gladwins' Verde Black-on-gray (Spicer 1933:2).

In 1933 and 1934 Caywood and Spicer excavated at Tuzigoot in the Verde Valley (Caywood and Spicer 1935). Here the most abundant type was what they called Verde Brown Ware, and they published the first comparison of Prescott and Verde plainwares (Caywood and Spicer 1935:42) (Table 3.2). They contrasted the two types in seven different categories, including temper size, abundance, type, and shape; surface characteristics; and paste color and porosity. Prescott Gray "Ware" generally had a gray paste with more than 50 percent granitic temper, angular and nonuniform in size; both surfaces always showed mica. Verde Brown "Ware" had a porous, dark brown paste, with a smaller amount (30–50 percent) of a feldspar temper that was frequently rounded and that did not show on the surface. Mica was uncommon in this pottery.

In the first comprehensive guide to Southwest ceramic types, Hawley (1936) followed Caywood and Spicer, except that she left the ware designation off the type names and placed both in a category called "Plain Ware." The following year Colton and Hargrave (1937) published their *Handbook*, which solidified the ware and type names and definitions for the next 25 years.

Table 3.2. Original Type Descriptions, Prescott Gray and Verde Brown

Characteristic	Prescott Gray	Verde Brown
Temper Size	large, non-uniform, coarse	fine to extremely fine
Temper Abundance	>50%	30–50%
Temper Type	quartz, feldspar, mica (generally muscovite) – granite origin	feldspar
Temper Shape	angular	generally rounded
Surface	temper, especially mica, always visible	temper not visible
Paste Color	gray, often reddish-brown in spots	dark brown
Porosity	very porous	very porous

From Caywood and Spicer 1935:42

Using the criterion of priority that they had established (Colton and Hargrave 1935), Colton and Hargrave kept the Gladwins' name, Verde Black-on-gray, for the decorated Prescott pottery but gave no name for the undecorated type. They did not distinguish the brown sherds as a separate type; their Verde Black-on-brown (Colton and Hargrave 1937:186–187) is not the same as Caywood and Spicer's Prescott Black-on-brown. Colton and Hargrave introduced Prescott Gray Ware as a ware name. Their description of the ware and type generally followed Caywood and Spicer, except they classified the ware as fired in an oxidizing atmosphere, partly reduced (Colton and Hargrave 1937:184), and described the temper for the type as "opaque angular fragments, gray, [whitish] or tan, with smaller quantities of water-worn sand" (Colton and Hargrave 1937:185).

Colton and Hargrave (1937:167) copied the Verde Brown definition unchanged from Caywood and Spicer (1935:42) and identified this type as an Alameda Brown Ware, thus separating it even farther from the Prescott material. In his 1958 update of ceramics definitions, Colton made no changes, but he introduced an error in quoting Caywood and Spicer on the temper description for this type.

In a survey of northwestern Arizona, Colton (1939b) added three new types to Prescott Gray Ware: Aquarius Orange, Aquarius Black-on-orange, and Aquarius Black-on-gray. This modification separated out some differences in temper and surface color that Colton

thought were important, but it increased the difficulty of applying the system in a consistent way. He also placed Prescott Gray Ware in the Prescott Branch of the Patayan Root, a cultural unit thought to represent prehistoric Yuman groups (Colton 1939b:25). Colton (1939a:8–25) also created a new ware, Tizon Brown Ware, for a subculture called the Cerbat Branch of the Patayan Root. Types in this ware were differentiated from Verde Brown by the presence of a rough, scummy surface and less mica and from Prescott Gray Ware by a finer temper and less mica (Colton 1939b:10–11, 17). Colton (1939a:31) supported placing Tizon Brown Ware and Prescott Gray Ware in the same root by arguing the existence of a typological and chronological series from Cerbat Brown to Aquarius Black-on-brown to Verde Black-on-gray, with a less-perfect series joining Verde Black-on-gray with Tonto Red, a common type of the Mogollon Root to the east.

The 1940s and 1950s were a fairly quiet period for Prescott area archaeology, but in the 1960s things picked up again. To the east, in the Verde Valley, Schroeder and Breternitz conducted work that suggested a different placement for Verde Brown. Schroeder (1960) felt that this type should be in the Beaver Creek Series of Hohokam Plain Ware, while Breternitz (1960:11) went even further and suggested that it was merely the Verde Valley variety of Gila Plain. He also argued that Tonto Brown, Wingfield Plain, Adamana Brown, Rio de Flag Brown, Winona Brown, and perhaps some Tizon Brown and Prescott Gray types were actually series within a single, basic, paddle-and-anvil brownware tradition in central and western Arizona (Breternitz 1960:27).

Euler and Dobyns (1962) excavated a site west of Prescott with pottery that was predominantly a Prescott Gray Ware–Tizon Brown Ware intergrade (on the basis of temper); they stated that "it is sometimes difficult to place these sherds objectively in either one type or the other" (Euler and Dobyns 1962:79). Euler and Dobyns also noted that the Prescott Gray Ware in their area had less mica and less controlled firing and that there was a west-to-east gradient in these two characteristics. They concluded that because Prescott Gray Ware was fired in an uncontrolled atmosphere, surface color should not be used to define types within the ware (Euler and Dobyns 1962:76–77). Thus, they rejected Colton's (1939b) additional Prescott types and suggested that there is only one Prescott type, or two if decorated and undecorated are distinguished. Later, in a study of sherds from excavations in the Bagdad area, Linford (1979:192) created a transitional category between Prescott Gray Ware and Tizon Brown Ware.

Between 1966 and 1976, the avocational archaeologist Franklin Barnett excavated 10 sites in the Prescott area, including extensive work at Fitzmaurice Ruin. As all but one of these excavations were published (Barnett 1970, 1973a, 1974, 1975, 1978), his work has been important in increasing understanding of Prescott area pottery. Barnett had a close relationship with the Museum of Northern Arizona (MNA), and all of his major ceramics studies were undertaken by MNA ceramics analysts. Although these studies involved no type or ware changes, they did add important information on variation in firing atmosphere and temper (James 1973, 1974).

Using materials from the Matli Ranch sites, Mueller and Schecter (1970) distinguished micaceous and sandy varieties of Prescott Gray Ware based on the quantity of mica present: the Aquarius variety had finer temper and less mica than Prescott Gray. They differentiated oxidized and reduced varieties on the basis of surface color. The micaceous or sandy distinction has carried over into later analyses, but the oxidized or reduced distinction has not been found to be particularly useful (James 1973:19; but see Frampton 1981:85). The Aquarius

variety has not been used since, in part because Mueller and Schecter's type sherds apparently do not show the characteristics that they claimed (James 1973:19).

James (1974) was the first ceramics analyst in 40 years to look closely at Verde Gray and Verde Brown from the same site (Fitzmaurice Ruin). She felt that the two categories intergraded but decided on second examination to define the intergrade category as Verde Gray, Sandy variety (James 1974:112–113). She characterized Prescott Gray Ware as having clear quartz temper, sometimes crushed, and mostly silver mica; Verde Brown, in contrast, was porous and had abundant subangular quartz and occasional gold mica. James did not mention feldspar for either type.

Because of archaeological projects southeast of the Prescott area, a two-session Agua Fria–Verde River Brownware Conference was held at MNA in 1973 and at Prescott College in 1974 (Bradford 1974) to discuss issues relevant to the pottery of the area. One of the most interesting observations made at the conference was that

> [t]he Type and Ware concepts do not tend to hold up well in Central Arizona; rather, plainwares of this region all seem to follow a continuum. The basis for differences is primarily temper, the choice of which is assumed to be geographically determined, but may be culturally determined as well. At the extremes of the continuum, the ceramic differences are obvious, but a great deal of intermediary blending occurs [Gratz and Fiero 1974:2].

With regard to Verde Brown, the conference participants felt that the definition should allow more temper variation. In the expanded definition, "temper is composed mainly of quartz granules with smaller amounts of hornblende and/or white angular fragments, and/or red fragments, and sometimes small quantities of schist. The paste nearly always contains variable amounts of gold colored flakes of mica" (Gratz and Fiero 1974:7). This was a major change from Caywood and Spicer's temper description.

The conferees also noted a temper and surface finish intergrade between Verde Brown and Verde Gray, with the intergrade form usually oxidized. The only sugges-tion about Prescott Gray Ware was that the sandy and micaceous varieties might reflect functional differences, the sandy variety representing utility vessels and the micaceous variety non-utilitarian and trade vessels (Gratz and Fiero 1974:9).

Examination of the ceramic assemblage from the Cop-per Basin Project led the analysts to suggest that a major reorganization of ceramic typology in central Arizona might be useful (Westfall and Jeter 1977:379). Although they continued using the terms Prescott Gray Ware and Verde Gray, Westfall and Jeter (1977:381–383) sug-gested that it might be more appropriate to use the terms Prescott Ware (also recently suggested by Horton [1994a:44]) and Prescott Plain. Thus, they reacted nega-tively to both the geographic term and the color term, although their suggested changes have problems as well.

Westfall and Jeter (1977:379) found an intergrade between Verde Brown and Verde Gray, as have others more recently (Frampton 1978:62; Fryman 1988:32; Higgins 1997); however, they decided on second exami-nation to use paste color as the sole typological criterion to force all the sherds into named categories. Thus, they contravened the suggestions of the 1973–1974 Brown-ware Conference (of which the authors may not have been aware) that single attributes not be used to catego-rize central Arizona brownwares and that intergrade cat-egories be used to handle transitional pottery (Gratz and Fiero 1974:2). Westfall and Jeter also briefly discussed a study by Lerner (1976) of variation in Verde Brown between the Copper Basin sites and sites to the east, not-ing minor differences in surface color, surface treatment, texture, and paste color and the presence of gold mica and suggesting that these characteristics related to local clay and temper variations (Westfall and Jeter 1977:379). Keller (1993:67) has recently suggested that Verde Brown may simply be a regional or early tempo-ral variety of Prescott Gray Ware.

Problems with sorting the brownwares did not disappear with increasing research; the response was the West-Central Arizona Ceramic Conference in 1980. Unfortunately, the results were never published or dis-tributed, and information from the meeting has been transmitted primarily by word of mouth. The conference

participants agreed, with few dissenters, to change the Prescott Gray Ware type names, from Verde Gray to Prescott Gray, Verde Black-on-gray to Prescott Black-on-gray, and so forth. They also maintained the Aquar-ius types in the ware, in spite of considerable unhappi-ness with these ceramic categories (e.g., Euler and Dobyns 1962; Mueller and Schecter 1970; Westfall and Jeter 1977). Wood (1987:51) provided the only pub-lished information on the decisions of the conference; he did not use the traditional ware names in his over-view, placing the Prescott types in the "Prescott Series" and using the term Tonto Plain, Verde variety, for Verde Brown, which he placed in the "Verde Series" (Wood 1987:48).

Wood (1987:52) also added a new variety to Prescott Plain, unfortunately called "micaceous"; this pottery, which was also reported by Fryman (1988:31), is tem-pered with crushed mica schist. Note that this definition of the micaceous variety differs from that used by most ceramics analysts in the Prescott area, where mica is derived mostly from granitic rocks, not from schist.

A comparison by Dosh (1987:12–13) of Prescott Gray Ware and Verde Brown from the Iron Springs area found a possible correlation with mica type, silver mica occur-ring in the Prescott types and gold in Verde Brown. Dosh (1987:13–14) also found that Verde Brown sur-faces were smoother, had less color variation, and had no visible temper. However, Dosh complicated her oth-erwise simple typological scheme by noting that some sherds show gold mica in the oxidized areas and silver mica in the reduced areas, opening the possibility that mica color may be partly a function of firing atmosphere (Christenson 1997a). She also saw a similarity between Verde Brown and Tizon Brown Ware, with a greater angularity of temper and a slight variation in color in the Verde Brown.

Two recent additions to Prescott Gray Ware by Horton (1994b) represent temper variations of unknown signifi-cance. One is a Black Mineral variety, defined as having "one or more heavy minerals, such as hornblende or augite, and what appears to be biotite or a biotite schist" (Horton 1994a:44–45). The second is Granite Basin Plain, a type with temper of an unknown "distinct white platy" material (Horton 1994b:22).

As archaeological studies in the Prescott area increased in the 1990s, and with the results of the 1980 conference so poorly known, ceramics analysts in the area were uncertain how to proceed. In 1996 a new conference was called to resolve some of the issues and to provide a stronger foundation for future research. One of the first steps of the conference was to accept the type-name changes from Verde to Prescott recommended by the 1980 conference, thus finally implementing the suggestion made by Spicer over 60 years earlier. The conference retained most of the standard type names but did make a major addition, Prescott Red-on-buff (white-slipped, mineral painted jars from A.D. 1200s Prescott sites). The type had been reported earlier in small quantities at Fitzmaurice Ruin and possibly other sites but was found in abundance at the Neural site in Prescott (Higgins 1997, 2000).

Wingfield Plain

A type present on most Prescott area sites, and occasionally predominant, is a phyllite-tempered brownware consistently called Wingfield Plain. Because it is a common plainware and because it has implications for the interpretation of ceramic production and interaction in the area, we provide a brief history (for more detailed discussions see Doyel and Elson 1985 and Spoerl et al. 1984).

The first mention of what is probably Wingfield Plain appears in Caywood's (1936:103) discussion of the Fitzmaurice Ruin ceramics assemblage, where he described but did not name a brownware tempered with mica schist, possibly meaning phyllite. It is this type that Colton and Hargrave (1937:186–187) apparently termed Prescott Black-on-brown, although Caywood did not describe the type as decorated. This is one of the rare occasions when Colton and Hargrave incorrectly described a type with which they were not personally familiar. Caywood and Spicer (1935:42) used Prescott Black-on-brown for a type of Prescott Gray "Ware" found at King's Ruin (Spicer 1936:29), differing from the black-on-gray only in the color of the background.

Colton (1941:46) defined Wingfield Plain using specimens from the Verde Valley. He recognized the type as being included in Gladwin's definition of Gila Plain, but

differing from Gila Plain in having "very, very coarse ... crushed mica schist." (Mica schist and phyllite are different stages in the metamorphism of sedimentary rocks. If individual flakes of mica can be seen, then the rock is mica schist; if the flakes are visible only under high magnification, then the rock is likely phyllite. This distinction has not been adhered to by archaeologists, and so the term *schist* or *mica schist* has been commonly used for rock that is actually phyllite.) Colton made no mention of Prescott Black-on-brown, which seems to have disappeared from the literature. Colton placed Wingfield Plain within Hohokam Plain Ware, which he named at the same time.

Since its original definition, Wingfield Plain has been moved from ware to ware. Colton (1955) seems to have later changed his mind about the ware designation, placing Wingfield Plain in Alameda Brown Ware. In the second edition of his southwestern pottery type checklist (Colton 1965), Wingfield Plain is absent. Breternitz (1960:27) felt that Wingfield Plain was merely a variety of Gila Plain. Hudgens (1975:40) put it into Pimeria Brown Ware, while Wood (1987:18) called it a central Arizona plainware. More recently, Horton (1994a:46, 1994b:23) has suggested incorporating Wingfield Plain within a new ware, Phyllite Plain Ware, that includes additional types in an attempt to encompass the range of phyllite colors.

The prior discussions of Wingfield Plain have taken the presence of mica schist or phyllite temper as the defining characteristic of the type, with no discussion of intergrades with other types. The participants in the Agua Fria–Verde Valley Brownware Conference were an exception. They decided to define Wingfield Plain as containing at least 50 percent schist temper (including phyllite), regardless of the other particles, and to classify sherds with less than 50 percent schist on the basis of the other materials present (Gratz and Fiero 1974:10–11). This system recognized intergrades with wares such as Prescott Gray Ware, where occasional mica schist or phyllite temper had been noted, but violated a basic conclusion of the conference: that single attributes should not be used to make type identifications (Gratz and Fiero 1974:2).

The record of the conference also reports the results of porosity and strength tests on schist-tempered and sand-tempered pottery, which suggested that schist-tempered pottery fires harder at lower temperatures, is stronger, and has greater cooling and heating capacity than sand-tempered types. Finally, the conference raised the question of whether Wingfield Plain was a Hohokam type or a ceramics tradition shared by several groups (Gratz and Fiero 1974:12). The 1996 ceramic conference decided that the Wingfield types appeared to have been manufactured over a large area of Arizona by several archaeological "cultures," including that of the Prescott area, and that they should be placed in a separate ware: Wingfield Brown Ware (Hays-Gilpin and Walsh-Anduze 1997).

Technical Studies of Prescott Pottery

While the Prescott area has never been a hot spot for technical research, there have been a few studies of note. In what must be one of the earliest uses of spectroscopy (presumably optical emission) to study prehistoric pottery, Byron Cummings commissioned an analysis of a number of sherds and clays from the Verde Valley, including five specimens of Prescott Black-on-gray and some "Verde Common Ware" (possibly Verde Brown; Fowler 1934, 1935). No specific interpretation of these sherds was offered, although similarities and differences were evident. The only other physical study of Prescott pottery was a pilot electron microprobe analysis of a Prescott sherd from the Neural site (NA 20788), conducted to look at the chemical composition of galena grains (Lundin 1995).

A number of tests have been conducted on Prescott pottery to determine whether the paints used were organic (carbon) or mineral (iron), including analysis of a single Prescott Black-on-gray sherd from Tuzigoot (Fowler 1935:111). Spicer (1936:34) found the black paint on King's Ruin pottery to be carbon, as did Colton for Verde Black-on-gray (Colton and Hargrave 1937:185) and Hawley (1938:14) for Prescott Black-on-gray. At Las Vegas Ruin East, 62 of the 63 Verde Black-on-gray sherds were decorated with carbon paint (Frampton 1978:55). James's (1973:18) refiring experiments found that the paint on Prescott pottery burned off at between 800°C and 850°C. Noting a tendency for the paint to burn off before the paste was oxidized, she concluded that Prescott potters were trying for incomplete oxidation or reduction and that the fully oxidized sherds were misfires (James 1973:19; see also Frampton 1981:85).

Petrographic examination of Prescott pottery has begun only in the last decade. Field (1992) analyzed a single Prescott Gray Ware sherd from a site near Cameron. In an examination and comparison of 26 Prescott Gray Ware sherds and 12 Tizon Brown Ware sherds from sites near Seligman, Zedeño et al. (1993:194) found both wares to have mineralogically similar tempers, although the Prescott Gray Ware had more crushed rock. Closer to Prescott, Christenson has analyzed 72 sherds from 19 sites, including the six in this report. Of most importance, analysis of sherds from the Neural site found no significant mineralogical difference between Prescott Gray Ware and Alameda Brown Ware sherds (i.e., Verde Brown and Verde Red), suggesting that these types may have been made locally (Christenson 1995, 2000). Accumulation of sufficient samples of both Prescott Gray and Prescott Black-on-gray has led to the realization that the latter type is tempered with a high quartz, high mica rock that has not been reported locally, while a portion of the samples of the undecorated type is often near or at least closer to the mineral composition of local granitic bedrock (Appendix A; Christenson 2001).

Although no chemical sourcing has yet been done on Prescott area clays, a few refiring studies provide some information on iron content. Bubemyre and Mills (1993:270–272) refired sherds of Tizon Brown Ware and Prescott Gray Ware from an area near Seligman. Both wares had clays that refired most commonly to a yellowish red, although the Tizon sherds had a greater frequency of red (Bubemyre and Mills 1993:271). Christenson (1995:8) refired a few sherds from the Neural site and obtained a consistent yellowish-red color for all but one. In a refiring study of sherds from two sites near Pioneer Park, Walsh (Walsh-Anduze1996:17) found the clays of most Prescott Gray Ware and Wingfield Plain pottery to be of similar composition, with most refiring red.

Discussion

This brief synopsis of Prescott area ceramics studies, emphasizing classifications, leads to a few observations on future directions for research. The early workers on central Arizona graywares or brownwares (Caywood and Spicer, Colton and Hargrave, the Gladwins) were applying a new system, the ware-type system, to an area whose characteristics were poorly known. Although these pioneers occasionally recognized that the differences between types could be subtle, they were satisfied to place all sherds in a fairly narrow range of discrete types. When the range of variation became too great, they created new types or wares (e.g., Colton in 1941).

When ceramics research increased in the area from the late 1950s into the 1970s, gradations between types or wares became more of an issue, but the almost universal approach was to force all sherds into the old types rather than create new ones. No significant new types have been added until quite recently. In fact, in this period there was actually a reduction in the number of types, as several of the types created by Colton (e.g., Aquarius Orange) were absorbed into the standard types.

Rather than create transitional categories or new types, since the 1970s some ceramics analysts have employed varieties, such as sandy and micaceous, in an attempt to account for variation within the few existing types. Although the Agua Fria–Verde River Brownware Conference took a positive stand on the acceptability of transitional categories and advocated an attribute approach to ceramics variation (Gratz and Fiero 1974:2), neither of these ideas had taken hold until recently. Mueller and Schecter (1970:81) came the closest to an attribute approach for Prescott area pottery, recording simple dichotomous variables at five Matli Ranch sites. The work discussed in this report initiated a program of attribute recording that is currently being carried out by Christenson and the Yavapai Chapter of the Arizona Archaeological Society. Untimately, such studies will allow us to examine spatial and temporal variation in characteristics that are claimed to have cultural significance.

The presence of gradations between types not only raises the issue of the validity and usefulness of the type system as it now stands, but throws into doubt the ware system currently in use as well. The presence of transitional categories, and not just in the early stages of development, among Prescott Gray, Verde Brown, Aquarius Brown, and Wingfield Plain should make us question whether the four wares that subsume these types (Table 3.3) have any validity. It is interesting that although Wingfield Plain and Verde Brown have been placed in the same ware by Colton (Alameda Brown) and by Breternitz (Hohokam Plain), no one has ever placed Verde Brown and Prescott Gray in the same ware—no one, that is, until Schroeder (1991). In his last statement on the Hakataya concept, Schroeder decided that all of the central Arizona brownwares should be classified as Alameda Brown Ware. A similar idea had been put forward by Breternitz (1960) many years earlier. Wood's concept of a Central Arizona Ceramic Tradition (Wood 1987) is perhaps a better way of indicating that a group of types has been made with a similar technology, with local differences in temper indicated by series of types.

The use of such characteristics as type and quantity of temper as major definers of wares is misleading and inappropriate unless such definers are demonstrated to be of cultural, not geological, origin (see Rice 1976). Pottery studies in the Prescott area have been notable for their almost total lack of ancillary geological studies to support inferences. Observations by Euler and Dobyns (1962) that mica increases in Prescott Gray Ware from west to east and by Westfall and Jeter (1977) that variation in Verde Brown may be related to local geological differences were not then and have not yet been backed up by geological data. Only now are the first steps being taken in this important area of research, and only after geological variation is somewhat under control are we likely to determine what portion, if any, of the temper variation is cultural.

Table 3.3. Ware and Type Designations, Prescott Area Sand-tempered Grayware and Brownware and Phyllite-tempered Brownware

Source	Sand-tempered Gray		Sand-tempered Brown		Phyllite-tempered Brown	
	Ware	*Type*	*Ware*	*Type*	*Ware*	*Type*
Gladwin and Gladwin 1930a		Verde Black-on-white*				
Gladwin and Gladwin 1930b		Verde Black-on-grey*				
Spicer 1933		Prescott Black-on-grey				
Caywood and Spicer 1935			Verde Brown			
Caywood 1936		Prescott Grey				unnamed
Hawley 1936	Plain		Plain			
Colton and Hargrave 1937	Prescott Gray	Verde Black-on-grey*	Alameda Brown		Prescott Gray	Prescott Black-on-brown
Colton 1941					Hohokam Plain	Wingfield Plain
Colton 1955					Alameda Brown	
Schroeder 1960			Hohokam Plain			
Breternitz 1960					Gila Plain	Gila Plain
Hudgens 1975					Pimeria Brown	
Westfall and Jeter 1977	Prescott	Prescott Plain				
WCACC** 1980	Prescott Plain	Prescott Plain				
Wood 1987	Prescott Series		Verde Series	Tonto Plain	Central Arizona Plain	
Schroeder 1991	Alameda Brown		Alameda Brown		Alameda Brown	
Horton 1994	Prescott	Prescott Gray			Phyllite Plain	

*no name given for undecorated type
**West-Central Arizona Ceramic Conference

The Hassayampa Ceramic Assemblage

Analysis Methods

Selection of sherds for analysis was based on sherd size, archaeological context, or both.

- Regardless of context, sherds 2 cm on a side or smaller were not analyzed because of the limited information they would yield. They were saved for future research but not included in the artifact counts.

- Ware, type, temper type, and presence/absence of mica were recorded for sherds 3 cm on a side (size 3) from all contexts. This information was also recorded for sherds size 3 or larger from contexts of questionable integrity, such as site surfaces, overburden, and backhoe piles.

- Detailed analysis included sherds larger than size 3 from all features except the trash middens (Features 4, 5, and 10) from AZ N:7:155 (ASM).

- Most of the body sherds from Features 4, 5, and 10 were grouped by differences in temper type observed with a 10X hand lens. Detailed recording was reserved for decorated sherds, rim sherds size 4 and larger, and other sherds size 4 or larger that had qualities (usually surface treatment) that set them apart from the rest.

The variables examined in the detailed analysis included vessel form, temper type, texture and abundance of temper, presence/abundance of mica by color, paste color, interior and exterior surface color, and interior and exterior surface treatment. For rim sherds, five additional variables were examined: rim diameter, rim length, neck height (jar sherds only), rim curvature, and lip shape.

For body sherds, attributes of surface finish (smoothed or rough) determined definition of vessel form. Sidewall curvature was a more reliable determinant for rim sherds. For all sherds, we identified temper type with the aid of stereoscopic microscopes, making no distinction between natural inclusions and deliberately added material. Because the presence of mica (principally silver) was originally a defining characteristic of Prescott Gray Ware (Colton and Hargrave 1937:184; Gladwin and Gladwin 1930a:140; Spicer 1936:29), mica color (silver, gold/copper, mixed) and abundance were recorded separately from the basic temper type. Mica was coded as absent if no or very few flakes were visible on the surface, and as minimal if flakes were clearly visible but were not abundant enough to be a dominant characteristic of the surface. Temper texture was an ordinal measure of temper size from fine to coarse. Fine texture was what sedimentologists would call medium to coarse sand, while coarse texture ranged into what would be called very coarse sand to gravel (Pettijohn et al. 1972:71).

Because of inconsistencies in type descriptions for Prescott Gray and Verde Brown pottery through the years, the authors decided in advance that the presence, texture, and abundance of specific tempering materials would be equated with specific ceramic types and that these attributes would be given more weight than others, such as the abundance and type of mica and surface treatment and color. We would then carry out a statistical analysis using all of the attributes as an independent evaluation of the success of our imposed typology. We further decided that Prescott Gray Ware sherds should have an abundance of (crushed) arkosic sand temper (decomposed granite consisting predominantly of quartz and feldspar) ranging in size from medium to coarse and either light or dark in color. We originally thought that an abundance of silver mica (muscovite) would aid in the type identification, but modified our opinion when

many of the sherds we examined had little or no mica but otherwise had the "correct" temper type for Prescott Gray Ware.

Based on conversations with Peter Pilles, Jr., Coconino National Forest Archaeologist, the analysts also decided a priori to distinguish Verde Brown, an Alameda Brown Ware type, from Prescott Gray on the basis of temper and surface characteristics. Thus, sherds identified as Verde Brown were tempered with a small to moderate amount of round or subangular arkosic sand, often with gold mica, and had a smoother surface than sherds classified as Prescott Gray.

Descriptions of Site Assemblages

AZ N:6:9 (ASM)

Only 70 of the 235 sherds collected from this site were large enough for analysis. Sixty-two were body sherds and eight were rim sherds; 65 were Prescott Gray and five were Wingfield Plain. All of the Prescott Gray sherds were tempered with a moderate to abundant amount of light arkosic sand, while the Wingfield Plain sherds had phyllite temper. Three of the rim sherds were from Prescott Gray bowls, and two were from Prescott Gray jars; the other three were from Wingfield Plain bowls. No other information was recorded, because all of the sherds were collected from the site's surface and the rim sherds were smaller than the analysis parameters.

AZ N:6:13 (ASM)

The analyzed sample from this site consisted of 136 Prescott Gray sherds, three Prescott Red sherds, and five Wingfield Plain sherds, 23 percent of the 628 sherds collected. All sherds were from surface collections. Vessel form could be determined for 27 sherds. All seven rim sherds were Prescott Gray; five were from bowls, one was from a jar, and one was of indeterminate form. Attributes were not recorded for these sherds because of their small size. Among body sherds, 19 were Prescott Gray (3 bowls, 16 jars) and one was from a Wingfield Plain bowl. The Prescott Gray bowl sherds tended to have smoothed but unpolished interior surfaces and rougher exterior surfaces. In contrast, 11 of the 16 Prescott Gray jar exteriors had smoothed surfaces and four had rough surfaces (one sherd was eroded). Interior surfaces of jars were rough or unmodified, as expected. The Wingfield Plain bowl sherd had smoothed, unpolished surfaces.

Light arkosic sand dominated the temper in the Prescott Red and Prescott Gray pottery. Two Prescott Gray sherds had quartz temper; all of the Wingfield Plain sherds were tempered with phyllite. All of the Prescott Gray sherds had a moderate to abundant amount of medium-coarse particles. Silver mica was visible in 28 sherds; the rest of the Prescott Gray sherds (including the two with quartz temper) had no obvious mica inclusions. As most of the sherds were from jars, the analysts could not examine the correlation between vessel form and the presence or absence of mica.

AZ N:6:19 (ASM)

Of the 26 sherds collected from this site, only four Prescott Gray sherds were large enough to be analyzed. Attributes of these sherds were not recorded in detail because they were from surface collections. One sherd not included in the assemblage count (Table 3.1) because of its small size was identified as a Tizon Brown Ware (Tizon Wiped), based on the presence of deep striations across the surface from wiping with a fibrous material.

AZ N:6:20 (ASM)

The analyzed assemblage from this site consisted of 329 sherds: 262 (79.6 percent) Prescott Gray, 38 (11.6 percent) Prescott Black-on-gray, and 22 (6.7 percent) Wingfield Plain. One intrusive sherd was identified as Little Colorado White Ware (Holbrook A Black-on-white). Six sherds were untyped brownware. The assemblage included rim sherds, but no measurements were recorded because the sherds were size 3 or smaller or were irregular in shape.

Vessel form was identified for 154 sherds: 108 (70.1 percent) from jars, 45 (29.2 percent) from bowls, and one (0.6 percent) (a rim sherd) from a seed jar. Table 3.4 shows the distribution of sherd forms by ceramic type. More Prescott Gray and Wingfield Plain sherds were

from jars than from bowls, but more Prescott Black-on-gray sherds were from bowls.

Table 3.4. Vessel Form Frequencies by Ceramic Type, AZ N:6:20 (ASM)

Ceramic Type	Vessel Form			Total
	Bowl	Jar	Seed Jar	
Prescott Gray	23	92	1	116
	*19.8	79.3	0.9	**75.3
	**51.1	85.2	100.0	
Prescott Black-on-gray	18	7		25
	72.0	28.0		16.2
	40.0	6.5		
Wingfield Plain	3	9		12
	25.0	75.0		7.8
	6.7	8.3		
Holbrook A Black-on-white	1			1
	100.0			0.6
	2.2			
Total	45	108	1	154
	*29.2	70.1	0.6	100.0

*Row %
**Column %

Most Prescott Gray and Black-on-gray sherds were tempered with a moderate or abundant amount of light, medium-coarse arkosic sand (Table 3.5). Silver mica was present in very small amounts in 12 percent of these sherds, was abundant in 17 percent, and was not visible in almost 58 percent. Nine percent contained minimal amounts of gold mica. Quartz temper was present in 18 percent of Prescott Gray sherds but in only 5 percent of the Prescott Black-on-gray sherds. As in most of the pottery tempered with arkosic sand, mica inclusions were relatively uncommon. Dark arkosic sand was rare, occurring in only two Prescott Gray sherds. Temper in Wingfield Plain pottery was phyllite.

Analysis of Prescott Gray and Prescott Black-on-gray sherds from this site included examination of the relationship of ceramic type to surface color and paste color. Prescott Gray pottery was fired under more variable conditions than was Prescott Black-on-gray pottery, and surface and paste colors of Prescott Black-on-gray sherds were more often reduced than oxidized.

Table 3.5. Texture and Abundance of Temper, Arkosic-Sand-Tempered Prescott Gray and Prescott Black-on-gray Pottery, AZ N:6:20 (ASM)

Type/Texture	Abundance			Total
	Mod-erate	Mod-Abun	Abun-dant	
Prescott Gray				
Medium	5		6	11
Medium-coarse	8	2	186	196
Coarse		3	1	4
Total	*13*	*5*	*193*	*211*
Prescott Black-on-gray				
Medium	1	1		2
Medium-coarse		34		34
Coarse				
Total	*1*	*35*		*36*
Total	14	40	193	247

The sherds from AZ N:6:20 (ASM) were distributed among five features (Table 3.6): two structures (Features 1 and 9) and three middens (Features 2, 3, and 5.)

Half of the assemblage (51.1 percent) was associated with Feature 1. Wingfield Plain sherds were most common only at Feature 3. A single Holbrook A Black-on-white sherd came from Feature 1. Breternitz (1966:77) suggests a date of A.D. 1075–1130 for this type.

AZ N:7:155 (ASM)

The Assemblage

Twenty percent of the sherds recovered from AZ N:7:155 (ASM), a habitation site, were too small to include in the analysis. Nevertheless, 84 percent of the analyzed Hassayampa project assemblage was from this site. In the analyzed site assemblage of 5,042 sherds (Table 3.1), 88 percent were Prescott Gray Ware and just under 10 percent were Wingfield Brown Ware, the second most abundant pottery group. If frequencies are any indication, either one or both of these wares may have been produced locally. Intrusive pottery represented the Alameda Brown Ware, Hohokam Buff Ware, Little Colorado White Ware, Tusayan White Ware, San Francisco Mountain Gray Ware, and San Juan Red Ware traditions.

Table 3.6. Distribution of Analyzed Ceramic Types, AZ N:6:20 (ASM)

Ceramic Type	Feature					Total
	1	2	3	5	9	
Prescott Gray	148	69	18	26	1	262
	*56.5	26.3	6.9	9.9	0.4	**79.6
	**88.1	84.1	40.9	76.5	100.0	
Prescott Black-on-gray	15	12	7	4		38
	39.5	31.6	18.4	10.5		11.6
	8.9	14.6	15.9	11.8		
Wingfield Plain	4	1	13	4		22
	18.2	4.5	59.1	18.2		6.7
	2.4	1.2	29.5	11.8		
Holbrook A Black-on-white	1					1
	100.0					0.3
	0.6					
Untyped			6			6
			100.0			1.8
			13.6			
Total	168	82	44	34	1	329
	*51.1	24.9	13.4	10.3	0.3	100.0

*Row %
**Column %

To reduce the size of the sample, the temper analysis for AZ N:7:155 (ASM) excluded most of the sherds collected from the trash features (4, 5, and 10); these sherds were examined by a rough sort. Of the 1,461 Prescott Gray Ware sherds in the temper analysis, 97 percent were tempered with light arkosic sand, including 915 of 953 sherds identified as Prescott Gray and 460 of 472 sherds identified as Prescott Black-on-gray. Twelve of the 13 red-on-gray sherds and 21 of the 23 Prescott Red sherds also had light arkosic sand temper. Thirty-three sherds (23 Prescott Gray, 7 Prescott Black-on-gray, 1 Prescott Red-on-gray, 2 Prescott Red), or 2 percent of the Prescott sherds, had quartz temper. Temper in the remaining Prescott Gray sherds included dark arkosic sand (6), sand and minor quantities of phyllite (3), a minor quantity of schist (1), unknown rock (1), and multilithic sand (1); three of the sherds tempered with dark arkosic sand were decorated with black paint.

Results of the petrographic analysis (Appendix A) indicated that most of the sand-sized inclusions in the paste were crushed rock. Most often, the light arkosic sand used in tempering Prescott Gray Ware was medium to medium-coarse in size and was moderate to abundant in quantity. It is difficult to estimate the proportion of temper on a broken sherd edge, but "abundant" might indicate a temper component of around half of the paste and "low" a temper content of around one-third. Although Spicer (1936:39) defined Prescott Gray Ware as consisting of at least 50 percent temper, the proportion of temper point-counted in thin-sections from several sites has never reached 50 percent (Christenson 1995; Appendix A). In other words, temper abundance appears to have been consistently overestimated.

Table 3.7 shows temper type and abundance for Prescott Gray and Prescott Black-on-gray pottery from this site. The rest of the Prescott sherds were excluded from the table because they constituted only 2.5 percent of the assemblage. Only slight differences in temper size and abundance were noted between the two types, such as the higher proportion of decorated sherds in the medium-coarse and moderate-abundant categories. A stronger correlation was evident between ceramic types

and the presence and type of mica (Table 3.8). Silver mica was much more common in Prescott Black-on-gray than in Prescott Gray sherds; the latter split fairly evenly between no mica and silver mica, while biotite or gold mica occurred rarely in both decorated and plain pottery. These patterns held regardless of vessel form.

Wingfield Plain, the second most abundant type at AZ N:7:155 (ASM), was easily identified by the presence of phyllite temper; quartz sand occurred in varying amounts but was never dominant. Mica-schist-tempered sherds were classified as untyped brownware and may, in fact, have been Gila Plain. The phyllite in Wingfield Plain sherds was usually silver or steel gray, although purple and reddish-brown were also noted. Horton (1994a:46) has used phyllite color to name some new types of Wingfield, but as phyllite outcrops vary significantly in internal color, this may not be a valid procedure, and the 1996 conference did not recognize any of her types. However, Horton's study suggests the need for additional work to determine the range of variation among specific phyllite sources.

No Verde Brown pottery was in the assemblage from AZ N:7:155 (ASM). However, one sherd was identified as Verde Red, which is Verde Brown with a red slip (Colton and Hargrave 1937).

Kirkland Gray, a type of San Francisco Mountain Gray Ware generally considered to have been manufactured by the Cohonina, may intergrade with Prescott pottery in western Arizona (D. Simonis, personal communication 1996). Twelve sherds of this type, identified by the presence of translucent quartz temper and a smoothed, lightly polished, uniform light gray surface color, were recorded in the assemblage from AZ N:7:155 (ASM). Four sherds of Deadmans Gray and 18 of Deadmans Black-on-gray, from the same ceramics tradition as Kirkland Gray, were also present. It is possible that some of the Kirkland Gray sherds were misidentified and should have been typed as Deadmans Gray, since there seems to be a gradation between the two types.

Table 3.7. Texture and Abundance of Temper, Arkosic-Sand-Tempered Prescott Gray and Prescott Black-on-gray Pottery, AZ N:7:155 (ASM)

Type/Abundance	Texture					Total
	Fine	Fine-Medium	Medium	Medium-Coarse	Coarse	
Prescott Gray						
Low	2 *50.0 **50.0		2 50.0 0.6			4 **0.4
Low-Moderate	1 4.2 25.0	14 58.3 38.9	8 33.3 2.5	1 4.2 0.2		24 2.6
Moderate	1 0.5 25.0	13 6.0 36.1	146 67.0 44.8	56 25.9 10.9	2 0.9 5.7	218 23.8
Moderate-Abundant		5 1.4 13.9	64 18.1 19.6	284 80.4 55.2		353 38.6
Abundant		4 1.3 11.1	106 33.5 32.5	173 54.7 33.7	33 10.4 94.3	316 34.5
Total	*4* **0.4*	*36* *3.9*	*326* *35.6*	*514* *56.2*	*35* *3.8*	*915* *100.0*
Prescott Black-on-gray						
Low					1 100.0 10.0	1 **0.2
Low-Moderate		1 *100.0 **12.5				1 0.2
Moderate		2 4.8 25.0	28 66.7 26.7	12 28.6 3.6		42 9.1
Moderate-Abundant		2 0.7 25.0	41 13.8 39.0	254 85.5 75.4		297 64.6
Abundant		3 2.5 37.5	36 30.2 34.3	71 59.7 21.1	9 7.6 90.0	119 25.9
Total		*8* **1.7*	*105* *22.8*	*337* *73.3*	*10* *2.2*	*460* *100.0*
Total	4 *0.3	44 3.2	431 31.3	851 61.9	45 3.3	1,375 100.0

*Row %
**Column %

Table 3.8. Relationship between Presence and Type of Mica and Prescott Gray Ware Ceramic Types, AZ N:7:155 (ASM)

Mica Presence/ Type	Ceramic Type		Total
	Prescott Gray	Prescott Black-on-gray	
Not present	384	39	**423**
	*90.8	9.2	**30.8
	**42.1	8.4	
Silver	415	385	**800**
	51.9	48.1	**58.2**
	45.4	83.3	
Other	114	38	**152**
	75.0	25.0	**11.0**
	12.5	8.2	
Total	**913**	**462**	**1375**
	*66.4	33.6	100.0

*Row %
**Column %

Analysis of Form, Surface Finish, and Color

The vessel-form analysis included 338 rim sherds (Table 3.9), 184 (54 percent) from bowls and 144 (43 percent) from jars. Two rim sherds were from plates, two were from seed jars, and six were from vessels of undetermined form. Because these numbers matched fairly well with body-sherd data, we may assume that they are representative. Of 511 body sherds (including two partly reconstructible vessels), 58 percent were from bowls and 41 percent were from jars. One sherd from a Prescott Black-on-gray scoop was analyzed with the body sherds because use wear had completely modified the rim.

Rim-sherd attributes such as shape and side-wall curvature provide a means of identifying vessel form more specifically than is possible from body sherds. In the AZ N:7:155 (ASM) assemblage, 79 bowl rim sherds were outcurved, 73 were hemispheric (slightly outcurved), 10 were slightly incurved, 5 were vertical, and 11 were recurved (slightly flaring at the rim). One association between ceramic type and bowl form emerged from the data: in the Wingfield Plain pottery, sherds from hemispheric bowls were twice as numerous as sherds from outcurved bowls, whereas outcurved bowl forms were slightly more prevalent in Prescott Gray.

In shape, 72 bowl rim sherds were rounded, 57 were flat, 37 were beveled (flat, at an angle to the rim), 5 were tapered (flat and beveled on both sides), and 10 were coded as irregular because the rim shape varied. Distribution varied by ceramic type. Thirty-nine plain Prescott Gray sherds had round rims and 16 had flat rims; 27 Prescott Black-on-gray bowl sherds had round rims, only 8 had flat rims, and 11 had beveled rims; and 11 Wingfield Plain bowl sherds were flat, 6 were round, and 5 were beveled.

A lip (a protuberance but not necessarily an extra fillet) was present on 12 examples. Lips were usually exterior and were found most often on Wingfield Plain bowl sherds (7). These differences may be associated with ceramic type, production area, function, or a combination of factors.

Rim diameters on bowl sherds ranged from 4 cm to 38 cm. The mean for all types was in the range of 25 to 29 cm.

Prescott Gray jars from AZ N:7:155 (ASM) most commonly had recurved rims, with 62 examples. Twenty-one, about one-fourth, had slightly incurved rims, and eight had vertical rims. Incurved and vertical rims were rare in the decorated pottery (two of each); 36 had recurved rims. Six Wingfield Plain jar sherds had vertical rims, and two had vertical or recurved rims. Prescott Gray and Prescott Black-on-gray jars were not significantly different in rim form. About one-third of all Wingfield Plain jars had lips. Jar rim forms showed a similar range among types, but decorated and undecorated Prescott types differed significantly in frequency of flat rims. In the bowls this association was present but not strong enough to be significant.

Jar orifice diameters in decorated and undecorated pottery were very similar, with a mean diameter of 32 cm for all types. Because jars were most frequently broken at or above the shoulder, it was almost impossible to measure neck height on recurved jars. The mean neck height for Prescott Gray jars (3.3 cm) was slightly higher than that for the other types. Prescott Black-on-gray and Wingfield Plain jars had mean neck heights of 2.8 cm and 2.7 cm.

Table 3.9. Vessel Form by Ceramic Type, Rim Sherds, AZ N:7:155 (ASM)

Ceramic Type	Vessel Form					Total
	Bowl	Jar	Plate	Seed Jar	Undeter-mined	
Prescott Gray	101	94	2	2	3	202
	*50.0	46.5	1.0	1.0	1.5	**59.8
	**54.9	65.3	100.0	100.0	50.0	
Prescott Black-on-gray	50	40				90
	55.6	44.4				26.6
	27.2	27.8				
Prescott Red-on-gray	2					2
	100.0					0.6
	1.1					
Prescott Red	4				1	5
	80.0				20.0	1.5
	2.2				16.7	
Wingfield Plain	23	9			2	34
	67.6	26.5			5.9	10.1
	12.5	6.3			33.3	
Wingfield Red	1	1				2
	50.0	50.0				0.6
	0.5	0.7				
Verde Red	1					1
	100.0					0.3
	0.5					
Sosi Black-on-white	1					1
	100.0					0.3
	0.5					
Holbrook B Black-on-white	1					1
	100.0					0.3
	0.5					
Total	184	144	2	2	6	338
	*54.4	42.6	0.6	0.6	1.8	100.0

*Row %
**Column %

Two Prescott Gray rim sherds were from plates and two were from seed jars. One sherd of each form was fairly large, a plate fragment 22 cm in diameter and a seed jar fragment with an orifice diameter of 18 cm.

Since bowl and jar body sherds could be distinguished by the relative smoothness of their interior surfaces, and the AZ N:7:155 (ASM) assemblage was so large, the analyst conducted separate statistical studies for the sherds representing the two forms. Surface treatments recorded included polishing (both random and allover), smudging, and slipping; most vessels were either untreated or just smoothed. Frequencies of surface fin-ish attributes for bowls and jars are shown in Tables 3.10 and 3.11. Only one significant association between vessel form and surface finish within or between ceramic types emerged from the data, although some weaker patterns were evident.

The strong association was the presence of wiping on Wingfield Plain bowls, with 81.8 percent of the exterior surfaces exhibiting some degree of this treatment. Only three other examples of wiped surfaces were recorded: one interior surface of a Wingfield Plain bowl, one interior surface of a Prescott Gray bowl, and one exterior surface of a Prescott Gray jar.

Table 3.10. Distribution of Surface Finish Attributes by Ceramic Type, Bowl Rims, AZ N:7:155 (ASM)

Surface Finish	Ceramic Type													
	Prescott Gray		Prescott Black-on-gray		Prescott Red-on-gray		Prescott Red		Wingfield Plain		Wingfield Red		Verde Red	
	Int	*Ext*	*Int*	*Ext*	*Int*	*Ext*	*Int*	*Ext*	*Int*	*Ext*	*Int*	*Ext*	*Int*	*Ext*
None/unmodified	23	27	9	11	1	1	1		4	1				
Wiped	1								1	18				
Smooth (not polished)	45	58	37	38	1	1			12					
Random Polish	1	4												
All-over Polish	5	8	3	1					3	3				
Smudge	10		1						1					
Smudge and Polish	10								1				1	
Slip							6	4			2	2		1
Slip and Polish							1	2						
Indeterminate	2							2						
Total	97	97	50	50	2	2	8	8	22	22	2	2	1	1

Int=interior surface
Ext=exterior surface

Table 3.11. Distribution of Surface Finish Attributes by Ceramic Type, Jar Rims, AZ N:7:155 (ASM)

Surface Finish	Ceramic Type							
	Prescott Gray		Prescott Black-on-gray		Wingfield Plain		Wingfield Red	
	Int	*Ext*	*Int*	*Ext*	*Int*	*Ext*	*Int*	*Ext*
None/unmodified	29	44	17	24		1		
Wiped		1						
Smooth (not polished)	46	35	22	16	6	7		
Random Polish	1	6						
All-over Polish	7	4			2			
Smudge	5							
Smudge and Polish	5		1					
Slip							1	1
Slip and Polish								
Indeterminate	1	4			1	1		
Total	94	94	40	40	9	9	1	1

Int=interior surface
Ext=exterior surface

One weaker pattern was a trend for Prescott Black-on-gray pottery to have more bowls and jars with smooth interiors and exteriors than was found in the undecorated vessels. Also, polishing, which was uncommon in the assemblage as a whole, was not present on any Prescott Black-on-gray jars sherds but appeared on decorated bowl sherds and undecorated (i.e., Prescott Gray) bowl and jar sherds. The two Prescott Red-on-gray bowl sherds were smoothed but not polished on both interior and exterior surfaces, and three of the four Prescott Red bowl sherds were slipped (and smoothed) on both surfaces; one sherd had a rough interior. In contrast, the Verde Red sherd had a smudged and polished interior and a slipped exterior.

Three ceramic types not represented by rim sherds were present as body sherds: Deadmans Black-on-gray, Kirkland Gray, and Tuzigoot Brown. Seven Deadmans Black-on-gray bowl sherd interiors were smoothed, eight were polished, and one had an unmodified interior. Ten bowl sherd exteriors were smoothed, five were polished, and one was unmodified. On Kirkland Gray bowls, four interiors were smoothed, two were smudged, and one was polished; five exterior surfaces were smoothed and two were polished. The single Tuzigoot Brown bowl sherd had a smudged and polished interior and polished exterior. All three Kirkland Gray jar sherds had smoothed exteriors; the interior surfaces of two sherds were unmodified, and one sherd was smoothed. The three Tuzigoot Brown jar sherds had polished exterior surfaces and unmodified interiors.

The smudged and polished Prescott Gray Ware sherds do not fit any of the published type descriptions. Such examples are sometimes perceived as intergrades with other types, such as Verde Brown or Kirkland Gray (Gratz and Fiero 1974; P. Pilles, personal communication 1996), although they are classified as different ceramic wares. In all cases, the smudged and polished plainware sherds identified on the basis of temper as Prescott Gray in the assemblage from AZ N:7:155 (ASM) were noted as intergrades. As discussed below, this classification appears to be statistically valid.

Surface and paste colors in the assemblage ranged from black and gray to brown, orange, and even yellow. For purposes of discussion, surface colors were categorized as reduced (black and gray), oxidized (orange, orange-brown, red, yellow), and neutral (brown); the variation suggests incomplete reduction or oxidation on one or both surfaces. Most Prescott Black-on-gray bowls and jars were fired in a reducing atmosphere, whereas firing of Prescott Gray bowls and jars appeared to vary more (Table 3.12). Paste color was recorded as the dominant color in the vessel core, using the same system as for surface color (Table 3.13). When two colors were equally dominant, color was coded as indeterminate. Like surface color, paste color was reduced more often in Prescott Black-on-gray bowls and jars than in the undecorated pottery.

Table 3.12. Surface Color, Prescott Gray and Prescott Black-on-gray Pottery, AZ N:7:155 (ASM)

Firing Atmosphere	Ceramic Type			
	Prescott Gray		Prescott Black-on-gray	
	Bowl	Jar	Bowl	Jar
Variable	110	165	179	53
Reducing	49	35	147	18
Oxidizing	10	20		
Neutral	31	52	20	11
Total	200	272	346	82

Table 3.13. Paste Color, Prescott Gray and Prescott Black-on-gray Pottery, AZ N:7:155 (ASM)

Firing Atmosphere	Ceramic Type			
	Prescott Gray		Prescott Black-on-gray	
	Bowl	Jar	Bowl	Jar
Reduced	141	142	250	62
Oxidizing	22	68	8	2
Neutral	47	69	64	9
Indeterminate	4	3	26	9
Total	214	282	348	82

Taken together, the data presented in Tables 3.12 and 3.13 indicate that Prescott Black-on-gray pottery was generally fired in a *controlled* reducing atmosphere. The scarcity of oxidized surfaces was probably related to the use of black carbon paint, which would burn off under more oxidizing (hotter) conditions (Joanne Cline, personal communication 1996; James 1974). In contrast, Prescott Gray pottery was often fired under more variable, *uncontrolled* conditions, although reduction was most likely the intent.

Discussion

Examination of pottery frequencies and intrasite distribution at AZ N:7:155 (ASM) provided general information about site chronology (Table 3.14). According to Colton (1939b), Prescott Gray Ware has a broad manufacturing date, from about A.D. 900 to 1200; Breternitz (1966) places the date between A.D. 1025 and 1200 for Prescott Gray and A.D. 1023 and 1185 for Prescott Black-on-gray. Gumerman et al. (1973) revised Colton's dates to A.D. 850–1025 for the Prescott focus and A.D. 1025–1310 for the Chino phase, thus eliminating the 25-year hiatus (A.D. 1000–1025) between the foci as defined by Colton. More recent dating of Prescott area sites clearly indicates that Prescott Gray Ware was made through most of the thirteenth century and perhaps into the fourteenth century. The principal occupations at the Las Vegas East and West ruins, Fitzmaurice Ruin, and the Neural site have been dated by mean ceramic dating of trade sherds to A.D. 1232–1254 (Christenson 1997b). The Neural site radiocarbon dates range from A.D. 1040 to 1550, but most are in the A.D. 1150–1300 range.

Table 3.14. Distribution of Analyzed Ceramic Types, AZ N:7:155 (ASM)

Ceramic Type	Provenience										Total
	NF	F1	F2	F3	F4	F5	F8	F10	F17	F18	
Prescott Gray	7	327	73	180	1,817	1,130	4	375	32	1	**3,946**
Prescott Black-on-gray	4	4	7	13	253	129		61	1	1	**473**
Prescott Red-on-gray					11	4		1			**16**
Prescott Red		4			9	4	5	1			**23**
Wingfield Plain	1	28	5	17	193	202		34	1		**481**
Wingfield Red				1		2					**3**
Tuzigoot Brown						4					**4**
Verde Red					1						**1**
Sacaton Red-on-buff		1			2			1			**4**
Sacaton/Casa Grande Red-on-buff					1						**1**
Casa Grande Red-on-buff						2					**2**
Sosi Black-on-white					1						**1**
Holbrook B Black-on-white				1	2	1					**4**
Flagstaff Black-on-white					3						**3**
Kirkland Gray					6	6					**12**
Deadmans Gray			1			2	1				**4**
Deadmans Black-on-gray					6	5		7			**18**
Deadmans Black-on-red					1						**1**
Tsegi Red-on-orange				1							**1**
Unknown Ware/Type		12	2	4	17	7		2			**44**
Total	**12**	**376**	**88**	**217**	**2,323**	**1,498**	**10**	**482**	**34**	**2**	**5,042**

NF=nonfeature; F=feature

Dates for intrusive pottery (using Breternitz's [1966] best trade dates) suggest that AZ N:7:155 (ASM) was occupied no later than A.D. 1200, but assigning the initial occupation date is more difficult. Deadmans Gray and Deadmans Black-on-red have the earliest trade dates, at A.D. 850–1100 and A.D. 775–1066. Deadmans Black-on-gray, Sosi Black-on-white, Flagstaff Black-on-white, Holbrook B Black-on-white, and Sacaton Red-on-buff have overlapping dates ranging from A.D. 1000 to 1200. Tsegi Red-on-orange (which may have been locally manufactured; P. Pilles, personal communication 1996) and Casa Grande Red-on-buff have slightly later dates: A.D. 1150–1285.

Examination of selected sherds from control units within the trash features (4, 5, and 10) aided in reconstructing the chronology for AZ N:7:155 (ASM). This discussion excludes most of the Prescott Gray and Wingfield Plain sherds, which were examined in a rough sort only. The largest sample—300 sherds—was associated with Feature 4. Prescott Black-on-gray sherds were collected from each level, increasing in frequency from 47 sherds in Level 1 to 65 in Level 2, then decreasing to nine in the lowest sample context, Level 4. Intrusive pottery occurred in all four excavation levels in Feature 4. Level 1 yielded four intrusive sherds (1 Deadmans Black-on-gray, 2 Flagstaff Black-on-white, 1 Kirkland Gray); Level 2 contained 10 intrusive sherds (1 Holbrook B Black-on-white, 1 Deadmans Black-on-red, 4 Deadmans Black-on-gray, 3 Kirkland Gray, 1 Deadmans Gray); and Level 3 contained four intrusive sherds (one each of Flagstaff Black-on-white, Kirkland Gray, Sacaton Red-on-buff, Sacaton/Casa Grande Red-on-buff). Level 4, which should reflect the earliest types, yielded three intrusive sherds: one Sacaton Red-on-buff and two Deadmans Black-on-gray. The data from Feature 4 indicate disturbance of the first two levels (which is very likely, as a golf course was built around the feature in the 1960s). Less mixing was evident in deposits from Levels 3 and 4, and the relatively minor presence of Prescott Black-on-gray in these levels suggests that production of this type was minimal during the earlier occupation or use of the site.

The control sample from Feature 5 included 40 Prescott Black-on-gray sherds, which were fairly evenly distributed among the three levels of the control unit. Level 1 yielded one sherd each of Deadmans Black-on-gray, Deadmans Gray, and Sacaton/Casa Grande Red-on-buff. Three Deadmans Black-on-gray sherds were collected from Level 2, along with one sherd each of Deadmans Gray and Kirkland Gray. One Kirkland Gray sherd was associated with Level 3. These data suggest a relatively narrow period of time, ca. A.D. 1000–1075 (based on Downum 1988 and Fairley and Geib 1989; see also Ahlstrom 1985 and Samples and Wilcox 1991:71) for the creation of the trash midden.

Twenty-three sherds were recovered from the control unit in Feature 10, all but six from Level 1; the count included 15 Prescott Black-on-gray sherds and one sherd each of Deadmans Gray and Deadmans Black-on-gray. One Deadmans Black-on-gray sherd was also recovered from Level 2. Although the data are limited, they suggest that this feature was contemporaneous with Feature 5.

AZ N:7:156 (ASM)

Of the 1,235 sherds recovered from AZ N:7:156 (ASM), 845 were size 2 or smaller and therefore excluded from the attribute analysis. Of the 390 sherds that were analyzed, 87.4 percent were Prescott Gray Ware (none painted or slipped). One sherd was classified as an unknown buffware, possibly of local manufacture. Thirty-nine Wingfield Plain sherds and six sherds that were not assigned to a type accounted for the remaining plainwares. Intrusive sherds included one untyped Tusayan White Ware and two Hohokam Buff Wares. One of the buffwares was identified as Sacaton Red-on-buff by its design; the other was unpainted and therefore not typed.

Initial examination of 247 sherds for temper type revealed that most were tempered with a moderate to abundant amount of medium to coarse particles. All Wingfield Plain sherds from this site contained phyllite temper, occasionally with small amounts of quartz sand. Temper in Prescott Gray pottery included light arkosic sand (209 sherds), quartz (4 sherds), dark arkosic sand (2 sherds), and unidentified rock (2 sherds). Four of the untyped brownware sherds were also tempered with unidentified rock; quartz and quartz with micaceous schist were present in two sherds. Mica was present in

135 of 242 Prescott Gray sherds (55.8 percent); in 115 (85.2 percent) of these sherds the mica was silver.

Seventy-nine (82.3 percent) of the 96 sherds that were large enough for vessel form to be identified were from jars; 71 were Prescott Gray, seven were Wingfield Plain, and one was an untyped brownware. Fifteen Prescott Gray sherds and two Wingfield Plain sherds were from bowls. Orifice diameters recorded on 10 Prescott Gray bowl rims varied, to a maximum of 34 cm. Rims from Prescott Gray bowl sherds suggested two common forms: outcurved (two specimens) and hemispheric (six examples). Specific form was not identifiable for two bowl rim sherds. One Wingfield Plain bowl was hemispheric. Nine Prescott Gray jar rims had a mean orifice diameter of 4.67 cm; the maximum diameter was 42.0 cm. All other rim sherds were either too small or too irregular for diameter to be measured. Seven of nine Prescott Gray jar rims were recurved; curvature was not visible on two sherds. One Wingfield Plain jar rim was incurved, one was vertical, and one was recurved.

Surface and paste colors, which ranged from dark gray to orange-brown, indicated firing conditions for Prescott Gray bowls and jars. (The frequency of Wingfield Plain sherds was too low to allow meaningful analysis.) Of 66 sherds examined, 10 had reduced surfaces (both interior and exterior) and 24 were considered neutral (either light or dark brown in color). The remaining 32 sherds indicated variable firing conditions, with one surface reduced and the other oxidized. Paste colors, in comparison, indicated that 37 sherds were fired in reducing atmospheres and 18 sherds were fired under oxidizing conditions. In 21 sherds the paste was brown, the neutral color.

Of the 390 analyzed sherds from AZ N:7:156 (ASM), 221 (56.7 percent) were from Feature 1, a habitation. One sherd was from Feature 3, a rock alignment, and the remaining 113 sherds came from nonfeature areas across the site.

Intersite and Regional Comparison

According to Anduze and Potter (Chapter 2), Sites AZ N:6:9, AZ N:6:13, and AZ N:6:19 (ASM), and possibly AZ N:6:20 (ASM) and AZ N:7:156 (ASM), were

resource-procurement sites. AZ N:7:155 (ASM) was a substantial habitation site, with four or five rooms, three trash middens, several pits, an occupation surface, and seven burials. AZ N:7:156 (ASM) and AZ N:6:20 (ASM), especially the latter, reflect possible year-round occupation as well. In addition to architectural remains, these two sites had larger material culture assemblages than AZ N:6:9, AZ N:6:13, and AZ N:6:19 (ASM), and their ceramics assemblages included higher proportions of Wingfield Plain and some intrusive pottery. One important difference between Sites AZ N:7:156 (ASM) and AZ N:6:20 (ASM) is that 14.5 percent of the Prescott Gray Ware sherds from AZ N:6:20 (ASM) were Prescott Black-on-gray, but no sherds of this type were in the assemblage from AZ N:7:156 (ASM). This dichotomy may indicate differences in function between the two sites, along with differences in their relationship with AZ N:7:155 (ASM)—especially in the case of AZ N:6:20 (ASM). Overall, however, the distribution of ceramic types was relatively uniform (see Table 3.1), which tends to support the hypothesis that the sites were in some way related. It is also likely that most of the Prescott Gray Ware collected from the Hassayampa sites was made elsewhere. The presence of this pottery at these sites may reflect seasonal population movement for resource procurement, as was suggested earlier.

The lack of variation in surface finish attributes in the Prescott Gray sherds is additional evidence for close relationships among the sites. In the Phoenix Basin, Abbott (1994) has identified potentially close relationships between Pueblo Grande and other Hohokam sites within Canal System 2 on the basis of similar proportions of specific technological attributes, such as presence and type of polishing. In the Hassayampa assemblage, not only were polished or smudged surfaces rare on Prescott Gray sherds, but most of the examples were from AZ N:7:155 (ASM). This one group of pottery, which appeared to be better made than the rest of the plain graywares, may indicate a social or functional difference (or both) among sites. However, temporal variation should not be ruled out.

On a regional scale, and based on proportions of ceramic types, the assemblages from the Hassayampa sites were found to be similar to ones from King's Ruin (Spicer 1936) and the Neural, Sundown, and Sandretto sites (Elizabeth Higgins, personal communication 1996). Sherds from all of these sites were dominated by Prescott Gray Ware. In contrast, assemblages from other sites, such as Fitzmaurice Ruin (James 1974), Lonesome Valley Ruin (James 1973), and many sites of the Copper Basin project area (Westfall and Jeter 1977) had more Verde Brown.

Spicer (1936:28–49) described the pottery from King's Ruin, which was about 55 km miles northwest of Prescott on Chino Creek. Ceramic frequencies for Rooms 1 and 5 of the pueblo showed that the assemblage was dominated by plain gray (i.e., Prescott Gray) sherds and that decorated sherds accounted for only 5 percent of the analyzed assemblage of 2,150 (with black-on-gray pottery most common). The undecorated sherds were smoothed but not polished (Spicer 1936:32–33). Although Spicer did not explicitly draw this conclusion, the site inhabitants may have preferred the black-on-gray pottery over other decorated and undecorated types for burials (see Spicer 1936:33–34, 74).

In 1933 Spicer and Caywood partially excavated Fitzmaurice Ruin to compare this site with King's Ruin. They chose the site because of its proximity to Prescott, its size, and its location at what was thought to be the periphery of the black-on-gray region; it was also in a different drainage basin than King's Ruin (Caywood 1936:87). The sherds were similar to those recorded at King's Ruin, with the addition of two plainware types: undecorated grayware (Prescott Gray) and a "mica-schist"-tempered brownware. (Recent work on earlier sites nearby indicates that what Caywood saw was a local gabbro-tempered brownware, now called the Fitzmaurice Series [Christenson 2002]). Caywood reported that the Fitzmaurice Ruin pottery was better made. A statement about influences from the southeast (Caywood 1936:101–102) suggests that some of the pottery was smudged, polished, or both.

James (1973) typed 42 percent of the 2,600 sherds from Lonesome Valley Ruin as Prescott Gray Ware and nearly 41 percent as Alameda Brown Ware, primarily Verde Brown. In discussing the Prescott Gray Ware, James (1973:17–19) suggested that the potters attempted to reduce their ceramic wares and that they generally did not paint vessels that were to be oxidized.

James (1973:20–21) also suggested that the inhabitants of Lonesome Valley Ruin had contact with Hohokam, Cohonina, and Sinagua groups, based on the presence of intrusive pottery and the use of certain forms, such as shouldered vessels.

Westfall and Jeter's analysis of pottery from the Copper Basin project found the assemblage split between Prescott Gray (43 percent) and Verde Brown (46 percent) (Westfall and Jeter 1977:Table G-2). Westfall and Jeter (1977:379) identified an "intergrade" category between the two types during the preliminary sort, as had James (1974:112–113) with the Fitzmaurice collection, but they later discarded it in favor of sorting the sherds by paste color. In their summary, Westfall and Jeter (1977:383–84) noted that the high proportion of Verde Brown might have chronological implications.

The large percentage of Verde Brown pottery in the assemblages from Fitzmaurice Ruin, Lonesome Valley Ruin, and the Copper Basin sites needs further examination. We need to determine whether the identifications are valid based on current standards—and, if the types are valid, whether they represent production by one or more groups of people. A third issue is the temporal relationship between the two types. If we are to understand the mechanisms of ceramics production more fully in this region, we also need to undertake attribute analyses to address the so-called intergrade category. Results of such analyses can be used to document variations in production technology over both time and space, and thus to draw inferences about cultural affinity and social and economic interaction.

Discussion and Interpretation: Technological Variation and the Traditional Prescott Typology

The ceramics assemblages from the Hassayampa Country Club sites were similar, with Prescott Gray Ware constituting most of each. Prescott Gray Ware, in the revised description of the 1996 Prescott Ceramic Conference, was constructed by coiling and thinned using a paddle and anvil, with light wiping and scraping marks often visible on the interior surfaces (especially on jars), surface finishes ranging from rough (usually jar interiors) to smooth, light polishing sometimes present on bowl interiors, and rare smudging. Firing atmosphere varied, with more of an attempt to control reducing atmospheres for decorated pottery and less for plain gray. (Orange types appear to have been deliberately oxidized.) Temper generally includes an abundance of poorly sorted, angular, granitic sand dominated by translucent quartz or arkosic sand, in particle sizes ranging from fine to coarse, with medium to coarse grains predominating. Mica inclusions, usually silver, are common, especially in decorated vessels, but may be rare in plain vessels. This description accords well with the results of the Hassayampa project analysis and typology.

Results of the oxidation study undertaken to characterize the clays (Appendix B) suggested little variation in the clays used to manufacture Prescott Gray Ware. However, at least two differences recorded between Prescott Gray and Prescott Black-on-gray pottery may be behaviorally significant. First, plain Prescott Gray vessels were most often fired in uncontrolled (i.e., partly oxidizing and partly reducing) atmospheres, whereas Prescott Black-on-gray pottery was nearly always reduced. Refiring studies have demonstrated that the black carbon paint used to decorate the black-on-gray pottery disappears when the temperature reaches 850°C (1560°F) (J. Cline, personal communication 1996; James 1974), indicating that the gray surfaces consistently recorded for the decorated pottery are deliberate. Second, the more common presence and greater abundance of silver mica in Prescott Black-on-gray, in contrast to the undecorated Prescott Gray pottery, was statistically significant (see Table 3.8). The presence/absence of mica in undecorated Prescott Gray pottery can also be the basis for identifying two varieties that have previously been called "Sandy" and "Micaceous" (James 1973; Mueller and Schecter 1970; Westfall and Jeter 1977), but the contrast is not as strong as that between plain and decorated pottery.

Aside from the use of paint, the deliberate addition of high-mica granite and intentional firing in a controlled reducing atmosphere suggest that production cost was higher for Prescott Black-on-gray pottery than for the plain counterparts. Other researchers (Feinman et al. 1981) have used the number of steps in pottery manufacture, which is equated with production cost, to infer differences in the social or economic value of the pottery. Among the Classic period Hohokam, one example

of selective use of higher-value pottery is that redwares are more common than plainwares in mortuary assemblages (Abbott 1994; Walsh-Anduze 1994). Moreover, redwares from a specific production zone were preferred for this purpose over other redwares. It is possible that the inhabitants of the Hassayampa project sites valued Prescott Black-on-gray vessels more highly than plain pottery, especially for trade and other forms of exchange, although this possibility has yet to be documented systematically.

Surface finish was also consistent in Prescott Gray Ware pottery. Few sherds in the Hassayampa project collection exhibited polishing or any type of surface modification (excluding painted design) other than smoothing. The sherds that were well polished or smudged were more similar to Verde Brown, Kirkland Gray, or Deadmans Gray than to other Prescott sherds; this group of pottery seems to represent the extreme range of variation within Prescott Gray Ware and is consistent with what others have referred to as "intergrades," despite the designation as Prescott Gray Ware (see Gratz and Fiero 1974; E. Higgins, personal communication 1996). Further analysis is needed to determine whether polished and smudged surfaces on Prescott Gray Ware vessels had social or cultural significance.

Earlier we noted that we typed each analyzed sherd and that we based differences between types—especially Prescott Gray and Verde Brown—primarily on a single attribute: temper. As a result, no Verde Brown pottery was recognized in the Hassayampa assemblage. To test the validity of the imposed classification, we examined the data statistically using a clustering procedure (Ward's method) in the SPSS-PC+ (version 5.0) software package. The statistical study included all analyzed body sherds tempered with arkosic sand from AZ N:7:155 (ASM); other temper types were excluded because the sample sizes were too small for statistical manipulation. Overall, the results showed a lack of significant clustering, with numerous small clusters separated only by short and fairly equal distances. Differences among the clusters reflected the addition of individual attributes, one at a time. Clusters at one end of the series were dominated by a moderate to abundant amount of medium to coarse arkosic sand and smooth surfaces. Sherds with polished and smudged surfaces occurred at the other end of the series. The statistical difference between these two clusters of sherds (Student's t-test) was not significant. We can thus infer that smudged and polished surfaces fall within the range of variation that can be expected for Prescott Gray Ware.

The full context of this pottery should be considered further so that we can understand why these differences occur—do they represent variation over time or space? As indicated above, some sherds seemed to be more like Verde Brown, while others were more like Deadmans Gray or Kirkland Gray. Does the presence of smudging or polishing reflect interaction between cultural groups, in the form of direct contact via trade or population movement?

The suggested similarities between Prescott Gray, Verde Brown, Kirkland Gray, and Deadmans Gray pottery may, in fact, reflect a widespread ceramics tradition throughout central Arizona from about A.D. 700 to 1300 (Walsh-Anduze 1996; Wood 1987, personal communication 1996). The idea is not new. Schroeder (1957) recognized the widespread distribution of the paddle-and-anvil method of ceramics manufacture in his "Hakataya Concept." A few years later, Breternitz (1960) suggested that Prescott Gray, Tonto Brown, Verde Brown, Wingfield Plain, and Tizon Brown were all local variants of Hohokam Gila Plain. Euler (1982) suggested that the Prescott ceramics tradition developed out of the Hohokam Gila Plain and Estrella Gray ceramics complex in the northern Agua Fria River drainage. In one of the few statistical studies published to date, Stone (1982:109–111) found that a discriminant analysis procedure reclassified Prescott Gray Ware sherds from the Granite Reef Aqueduct Project as Hohokam plainwares. Stone (1982:111) suggested that the types might better reflect the range of variation within a single ware rather than differences between two wares. Wood (1987) has characterized the Central Arizona Ceramic Tradition as a series of related pottery types, produced by local Hohokam, Salado, Sinagua, Verde Valley, Payson, Anchan, and Prescott groups (J. S. Wood, personal communication 1996) who shared a common ancestral cultural development. Additional research, including advanced analysis, is necessary before this theory can be tested.

Summary and Conclusions

The analyzed assemblage from the Hassayampa Country Club project consisted of 5,979 sherds from six sites, at least four of them probably occupied by the same group of people. Three were established for resource procurement; the largest, AZ N:7:155 (ASM), was established for long-term habitation. Sites AZ N:7:156 (ASM) and AZ N:6:20 (ASM) may also have been habitation sites, but they were probably not occupied as intensively as AZ N:7:155 (ASM). This conclusion is based not only on ceramics counts but on the numbers of types encountered in the assemblages. Sites AZ N:6:9, AZ N:6:13, and AZ N:6:19 (ASM) yielded only Prescott Gray Ware and Wingfield Plain pottery (and one Tizon Brown Ware sherd, from AZ N:6:19 [ASM], possibly transported from the large habitation site). Few intrusive sherds were in the assemblages from AZ N:6:20 (ASM) and AZ N:7:156 (ASM), but those that were present indicate that the sites may have been contemporaneous with AZ N:7:155 (ASM). Differences in the intrusive types may suggest that the sites were involved in different (perhaps overlapping) interaction spheres with their neighbors to the north and south. San Francisco Mountain Gray Ware sherds were recorded only at AZ N:7:155 (ASM), which suggests interaction to the north. Based on the dates for intrusive types, the best estimate for the occupation of the sites is between about A.D. 1100 and 1200.

Due to constraints imposed by sherd size and context (most were from surface collections), we analyzed few of the sherds from Sites AZ N:6:9, AZ N:6:13, and AZ N:6:19 (ASM) in detail. The larger assemblages from the other three sites, especially AZ N:7:155 (ASM), provided most of the ceramics data generated in this report. Attribute analyses suggest that Prescott tradition ceramic technology was fairly basic but not necessarily uncontrolled or careless, as a glance at the pottery might suggest. As a general conclusion, undecorated vessels (Prescott Gray) do not exhibit characteristics considered diagnostic of Prescott Gray Ware: abundant silver mica and reduced firing atmosphere. It is the decorated vessels (Prescott Black-on-gray) that have these characteristics. In the Matli Ranch site assemblage, analyzed using a limited attribute approach, both decorated and undecorated Prescott Gray Ware pottery was micaceous and fired in an oxidized atmosphere (Mueller and Schecter 1970:82). More attribute analyses are needed to determine whether these differences between the sites have temporal or other implications.

Because of the brown residual clays of the Prescott area (see Appendix A), potters had to consciously control firing conditions to attain a gray or reduced color. The observed attempts at reduced firing conditions suggest that Prescott area potters were influenced by their neighbors to the north and northeast, who produced grayware pottery. The statistical analysis confirmed the qualitative observations in part: Prescott Black-on-gray sherds were reduced significantly more often than they were oxidized or mottled. Other researchers using experimental data (e.g., James 1974; J. Cline, personal communication 1996) have demonstrated that reducing conditions were necessary for paint to adhere to a vessel surface during firing. Also, design styles in the assemblage (not discussed in this report) tended to resemble ones from the north and northeast more often than Hohokam models from the south (Higgins 1996). With additional research we may find that painted designs changed through time and that the pattern can be correlated with a specific history of interaction.

Another important finding of the Hassayampa ceramics study was the abundance of Prescott Black-on-gray sherds with silver mica inclusions, relative to their plain counterparts. Recent research has suggested that the black-on-gray pottery is tempered with a high-quartz, high-mica granite, the origin of which is not yet identified (Christenson 2001). The difference between the types suggests that the use of mica increased the social value of the decorated pottery. The idea that Prescott Black-on-gray vessels had a higher social value than the plain types can be evaluated by examining burial and nonburial assemblages (following Abbott 1994). At King's Ruin, Prescott Black-on-gray vessels were, in fact, favored for mortuary offerings over other types (Spicer 1936:33–34, 74).

The detailed attribute analysis has also allowed us to be more specific about the variation in Prescott Gray Ware pottery. Vessels with polished and smudged surfaces, while infrequent, nevertheless point to a change in ceramic technology that may have temporal or other behavioral implications. Re-analysis of previous collections may be necessary to determine whether such finishing techniques were more common than has been reported to date. With a larger database, we can then look for patterns that may correlate with increased or decreased mobility and interaction.

The results of the petrographic analysis and the oxidation study (Appendixes A and B) have also added to our knowledge of Prescott ceramic technology and production. Although both studies are preliminary, they suggest that the pottery recovered from the Hassayampa project sites was produced with locally available materials. The oxidation study further suggests that the clay used to manufacture Wingfield Plain was similar to the clays used for Prescott Gray Ware. Phyllite sources in the area have yet to be tested systematically, however, and such studies would allow us to refine our understanding of the relationship between Wingfield Plain and Prescott Gray Ware.

CHAPTER 4

Ceramic Figurines

Thomas N. Motsinger

The Prescott region has yielded intriguing hand-molded human and animal figurines that are surprisingly abundant at some sites. Probably the first person to note and study the ceramic figurine complex in the Prescott area was a self-trained archaeologist, J. W. Simmons, who began excavating at Fitzmaurice Ruin and in the Groom Creek area (about 10 km south of Prescott) about 1930. The figurines continue to arouse the curiosity of residents of the area and are periodically featured in local media (e.g., Lin 1995; O'Connor 1981) but have attracted little professional study.

SWCA's field crews collected one intact figurine and 38 fragmentary specimens at the Hassayampa Ruin (AZ N:7:155 [ASM]) and two more fragments from the Stoney Ridge site (AZ N:6:20 [ASM]). This chapter provides a brief review of what is known about the ceramic figurine phenomenon, followed by descriptions of the figurines from the project area.

Range of the Figurine Phenomenon

In his field notes and in correspondence with A. V. Kidder and others in the 1930s, Simmons (n.d.) noted that the distribution of ceramic figurines did not coincide with the distribution of black-on-gray pottery or of other traits attributed to the Prescott Culture. In fact, Simmons was agitated by what he felt were Caywood's (Spicer and Caywood 1936:110–111) uninformed assertions that such figurines were common throughout the Prescott region and that they were generic in form. In a 1939 letter to Mr. W. E. Davis of Prescott, Simmons wrote:

> That Caywood had not studied his subject is borne out by the fact that the figurines are NOT COMMON in the PRESCOTT REGION, and, furthermore, that the majority of the animal fetishes found on the Groom Creek divide exhibit a wealth of detail—to that I feel you will agree [Simmons n.d.:86; emphasis in original].

The abundance of ceramic figurines in the Groom Creek area was so great that Simmons referred to the prehistoric inhabitants of the area variously as the "Groom Creek Effigy Culture" or, simply, the "Groom Creek Culture," considering it different (although not wholly distinct) from the Prescott Culture. In all, Simmons recovered over 400 animal and human figurines from the Groom Creek area. This collection, which Stuart Scott (1960) later analyzed, is now housed at the Arizona State Museum in Tucson. Apparently echoing what Simmons had found, Haury (1937a:239–240) noted that the forested area south of Prescott was one of only a handful of locales in the Southwest where ceramic figurines were produced in relative abundance.

The Copper Basin Project, about 4 miles southwest of the Hassayampa property, turned up only one animal figurine and two human forms (Westfall and Jeter 1977:381), indicating that those sites lay outside the core distribution of the figurine phenomenon. Recent surveys south of Groom Creek along the upper Hassayampa River have revealed a plethora of sites, some containing figurines (Horton and Logan 1992, 1993, 1994, 1995, 1996). Although it is difficult to assess the abundance of such artifacts from surface assemblages that have been subjected to unauthorized collecting (the Hassayampa Ruin, for instance, had no figurines on its surface as excavations began), the phenomenon appears to extend as far south as the upper Hassayampa drainage. Prescott Culture site densities and figurine occurrences drop off markedly south of this area (Horton and Logan 1995; Macnider et al. 1989).

Simmons (n.d.:86) placed the boundary between the Prescott Culture to the north and the Groom Creek Culture to the south at the southern boundary of Township 14 North, which coincides with East Gurley Street in the center of Prescott. The Hassayampa Ruin, although some 6 km northwest of Groom Creek proper, lies less than 1 km south of this line, placing it in Simmons's Groom Creek Culture area. The abundance of figurines at the Hassayampa Ruin places this site squarely in Simmons's alternative culture area as well. In his informal summary of sites in west Prescott, Ogg (1973b) also noted an abundance of "clay figurines," representing humans, bears, foxes, deer, and mountain sheep. Euler (1956) described a particularly large (27 cm long) specimen of a human female and an associated quadruped from another site on the south side of Prescott. These finds serve as further evidence that sites in the vicinity of the Hassayampa property are associated with this remarkable, albeit localized, phenomenon.

Speaking in rough terms, then, the core range of figurine use appears to be bounded by the southern boundary of Township 12½ North, the eastern and western boundaries of Range 2 West, and the northern boundary of Township 13 North. This area, south of present-day Prescott, covers only about 13 square kilometers. Further survey and excavation near the margins of this region will better define the geographic limits of this figurine "cult."

Hassayampa Forms

The figurine forms from the two Hassayampa sites (Table 4.1) resemble those described in detail by Scott (1960), who examined 403 specimens recovered by Simmons, mostly from the Groom Creek area. The Hassayampa figurines were about evenly split between human (17) and animal (19) forms; five pieces were too fragmentary to assign to either of these broad categories.

As with the Groom Creek assemblage, various animal forms were represented, including a possible bear, possible artiodactyls (deer or antelope), and a bird-in-flight

(Figure 4.1). Most of the animal figurines could be assigned only to the broad category of quadrupedal mammals, partly because of their fragmentary condition but mostly because of lack of detail. Two quadrupeds had molded perforations that extended entirely through the long axis of their bodies, from chest through hind end, indicating that they were molded around a small twig and may have been suspended from a string. The hindquarter fragment from another quadruped had a molded perforation that would also allow for suspension. Only two animal-form specimens had facial features, in each case a small slit representing the mouth.

Human forms exhibited a fair range of variation (Figure 4.1). Typically, they were made from a cylinder of clay with one end flattened into a head and the other terminating in either a blunt point or an expanded base that might or might not allow the figure to stand on its own. A pinch of clay added to the center of the head represented the nose, and linear grass or twig impressions represented the eyes. Two examples had a vertical hole pressed in below the nose to represent a mouth. When present, limbs ranged from stubby suggestions to cylinders of clay roughly proportional to the body length. Only two torsos exhibited breasts, and no indication of genitalia was present on any of the specimens.

Condition

Only one specimen (FN 116) (Figure 4.1) in the assemblage was recovered intact. This breakage rate is far greater than chance would allow and is consistent with the deliberate mutilation of figurines that occurs throughout the region. Animal figurines were recovered with any number of appendages broken off (including legs, tails, ears, noses, and entire heads); some unfortunate figurines were not discarded until all appendages had been removed. Still others were broken in half across the midsection. Although at first blush the dismembered condition of these animal figurines seems related to either real or hoped-for hunting results, it should be emphasized that human figurines generally suffered the same fate. Heads were commonly snapped off at the neck, noses were broken off of heads, limbs were removed from torsos, and torsos were broken into two or more pieces. Simmons (n.d.) notes some patterns to the disfigurement of Groom Creek human figurines:

Table 4.1. Ceramic Figurines and Fragments from the Hassayampa Property

Type	FN	Subtype	Condition	Notes
Hassayampa Ruin				
Human	115		Torso only	No apparent features
	118	Female	Missing head, 1 arm	Flared base, suggestion of 1 arm, breasts
	119		Head and neck only	Slit eyes, pinch nose
	122		Head only, missing nose	Flat head, slit eyes
	136		Base and torso only	Straight base, no apparent features
	141		Torso and legs	No arms, short legs
	172		Missing head, 1 arm	Straight base, appended arm
	173	Female	Missing head	Breasts, flared base, no arms
	202		Torso only	Appended arms
	258		Head only	Slit eyes, pinch nose
	323		Top of head only	Slit eyes, pinch nose
	350		Portion of base (?)	
	410		Head and neck only	Slit eyes, pinch nose, punctate mouth
	551		Base and torso only	Flat base, no appendages
	553		Torso only	Possibly one arm, no other features
Animal	116	Quadruped	Intact	Made from very coarse paste
	117	Bird	Missing feet	Extended wings, thumbnail impressions suggesting feathers
	120	Quadruped	Missing ears	Slit mouth and upturned tail
	137	Quadruped (?)	Leg	
	142	Quadruped	Hind end only, legs and tail broken	Upturned tail
	166	Quadruped	Missing head, 2 legs	
	171	Quadruped	Missing legs, tail, head	Molded perforation through long axis
	344	Quadruped	Head only	Slit mouth
	379	Quadruped	Hind end only, 1 leg broken	Molded perforation through tail
	380	Quadruped	Head, 2 legs missing	Molded perforation through long axis
	381	Quadruped (?)	Leg	
	385	Quadruped	Missing legs, head	Flat body
	396	Quadruped	Missing hind end, 3 legs, ear, nose	
	409	Quadruped	Hindquarter fragment	
	409	Quadruped (?)	Leg	
	423	Quadruped	Missing legs, head	Arched back suggests bear
	457	Quadruped	Missing legs, ears	Upturned tail suggests artiodactyl
	550	Quadruped (?)	Leg	
	553	Quadruped (?)	Missing all appendages	Very crude
Indet.	167		Broken at each end	Cylindrical and curved, may be handle
	395		Broken at each end	May be animal leg or human torso
	549		Broken on three sides	Animal or human torso fragment
	552		Leg fragment (?)	Curved, may be handle fragment
	554		Leg or torso fragment	
Stoney Ridge Site				
Human	37		Head fragment only, nose broken	Large, flat head
	119		Head only, nose missing	Coffee-bean eyes, punctate mouth

FN=field number

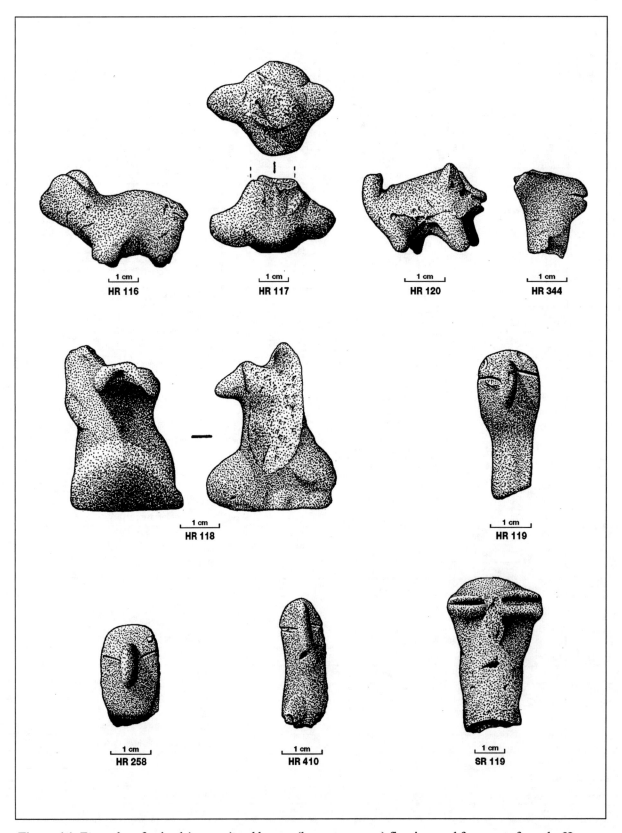

Figure 4.1. Examples of animal (top row) and human (lower two rows) figurines and fragments from the Hassayampa property. HR=Hassayampa Ruin; SR=Stoney Ridge.

An identical disfigurement noted on a number of human figurines seemed to smack of superstitious practices— probably the killing or injury of an enemy by remote control. The injury or mortal wound (?) was identical on each. The injury, or kill, was made by slicing off the right half of the face leaving the well defined nose and left side of the face normal—not damaged. Too, a peculiar feature was the fact that only heads were recovered— never a trace of the bust [Simmons n.d.:9].

The right half of the face was not missing from any of the Hassayampa figurines, and there was no lack of torsos among the fragments, but patterns such as the one Simmons points out may offer clues to what role dismemberment had in the use of the figurines.

Context

Simmons (n.d.) notes that figurines in the Groom Creek area were recovered from three types of contexts: funerary, as isolates in middens, and within "shrines" among middens:

> Quite a number of figurines were recovered by screening middens. Others were recovered from what appeared to be crude shrines. These shrines occurred in middens and consisted of four or five stones or small boulders formed in sort of a housing over and around the fetish. The recovering of figurines at random in the middens may have been due to the fact that a few hearths were found in them and that in digging these, the shrines were disturbed. Whenever a cluster of rocks were uncovered it was almost a safe bet that they hid a figurine [Simmons n.d.:134].

In a 1931 letter to A. V. Kidder, Simmons (n.d.:44–45) also noted that he sometimes found figurines in association with extramural fireplaces, although his later comments suggest that this may have been due to the fact that he often found fireplaces near or beneath middens.

At the Hassayampa sites we found no evidence of the types of "shrines" that Simmons describes, and none of the nine inhumations contained figurines as offerings. Five figurines recovered during excavation of inhumations appeared to be associated with the overlying midden fill rather than the interred individuals. One human-figurine head at the Hassayampa Ruin and one at the Stoney Ridge Site were recovered from structure fill, and one head at Stoney Ridge was on the surface. All other figurines on the Hassayampa property were from middens. Regarding the shrine-like features Simmons reports, most of the Hassayampa figurines were recovered from machine-excavated backdirt from trenching or stripping, so association of some of these items with shrines may not have been recognized.

Conclusions

The ceramic figurines from the project area represent a fascinating cultural phenomenon peculiar to about 130 square kilometers of ponderosa forest south of Prescott. They were apparently used for ritual purposes, and analysis of their breakage patterns and depositional contexts may eventually offer clues to what these purposes may have been. Thousands of figurines are scattered among private collections in the Prescott area, and most site surfaces have been scoured clean of them. For this reason, future archaeological investigations within the known distribution range of the figurines should include careful documentation and analysis of those figurines and the contexts in which they were found.

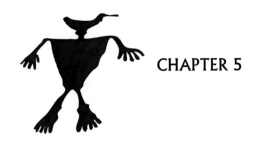

CHAPTER 5

Flaked Stone and Ground Stone Analysis

Dawn M. Greenwald

The goal of the analysis of the flaked stone and ground stone assemblages from the Hassayampa Country Club project sites was to examine and evaluate tool function and technology by site and, if possible, through time (Motsinger 1995:17). The variables chosen have proven, in previous analyses, to be reliable identifiers and aids in tracking technological and functional patterns both temporally and spatially. The analytical systems used (one for flaked stone and one for ground stone and miscellaneous stone) were the same for artifacts from all sites to ensure comparability of data and are similar to those used for regions to the north, east, and south of the project area (Ancestral Puebloan, Sinagua, and Hohokam regions) to facilitate interregional comparisons.

Methods

Flaked stone in this analysis comprised debitage, cores, and tools. The ground stone and miscellaneous stone category included ground and pecked stone, worked and unworked minerals, and nonlocal raw materials that had been carried to the site.

Flaked Stone Analysis

The analytic variables for flaked stone were morphological type, material type, grain size, cortex, size (debitage and used flakes only), facial and margin evaluation (tools only), tool completeness, use wear, and weight (tools and cores). Other characteristics, such as material color, heat alteration, and core platform symmetry, were noted. The morphological type variable provided information on form as well as function:

- Debitage
  - angular debris (shatter)
  - flake fragment (no platform or partial platform)
  - platform-bearing flake (broken flake with intact platform)
  - whole flake (intact maximum dimensions and intact platform)
- Core
  - core (no use wear)
  - core tool (use wear other than hammering/battering)
  - core/hammerstone (hammering/battering wear)
- Hammerstone (unflaked cobble with hammering/battering wear)
- Drill
- Projectile point
- Other tool
  - uniface (cobble or flake)
  - biface (cobble or flake)
- Used flake (use wear but no retouch)

Material type, determined from both macroscopic and microscopic (18–110X) observation, included three general geologic groups (igneous, sedimentary, and metamorphic NFS [not further specified]) for specimens of indeterminate type or that were poor examples of local material. The grain-size variable was a relative measure of material grain size, structure, and flaking qualities and included micro- and cryptocrystalline, fine, medium, and coarse. Micro- and cryptocrystalline materials showed no visible grains and had very good flaking characteristics, including conchoidal fracture.

Fine-grained materials had grains that were visible but small enough to provide good flaking characteristics so that fracturing did not appear to have been impeded by granular structure. Medium-grained materials had a rough surface, and their flake morphology was less obvious. Coarse-grained materials contained large crystals or vesicles, their flake morphology was difficult to identify, and their flaking qualities were very poor.

Measures of cortical retention differed for (1) debitage and used flakes and (2) other tools and cores. Reduction stage (primary, secondary, and tertiary) was the criterion for debitage and used flakes. Primary flakes were those with 90 to 100 percent cortex on their dorsal faces, secondary flakes retained 1 to 89 percent cortex, and tertiary flakes had no dorsal cortex. For cores and retouched tools, the criterion was the amount of cortex on the entire specimen (no cortex, 1 to 25 percent, 25 to 50 percent, and so forth).

Sizing followed a technique proposed by Patterson (1982). For all sites except AZ N:6:20 (ASM), a size chart consisting of a series of squares at 1-cm intervals provided an ordinal measure of dimensions for debitage and used flakes. For example, a flake with maximum dimensions between 2 cm and 3 cm fit into the third size interval. All items with a maximum dimension greater than 8 cm were given a value of 9. Length, width, and thickness of complete tools were measured with a tape to the nearest tenth of a centimeter. All tools and cores were weighed on either an electronic digital scale (0–300.0 g) or a triple-beam balance scale (> 300.0 g), to the nearest tenth of a gram. The tool-completeness variable provided a measure of the portion of a tool that was present.

Face and margin evaluations of retouched tools assessed technological stage of production and the amount of energy invested in tool production. Face evaluation is a reduction-stage variable, adopted from Phagan (1976), that allows a consistent description of artifact form through "a ranked evaluation of energy investment into facial regularization or flattening" (Phagan 1976). Phagan described eight levels of facial regularization, ranging from an unworked form with cortex to a highly stylized form. Margin evaluation was a relative measure of the degree to which a tool's margin had been retouched (e.g., < 1/4, < 1/2).

Microscopic examination of artifacts with possible edge damage (18–110X) identified any evidence of use wear that could provide information on tool function. Striations, polish, flake scars, attrition, and surface rounding, and the continuous patterning of these attributes, indicated use wear type, as described by Neusius (1988).

Ground Stone Analysis

The ground stone analysis system incorporated eight variables: morphological type, material type, grinding-surface texture, condition, weight, production investment and technique, and, for manos and handstones, profile. Other significant attributes, such as heat alteration, multiple wear patterns, and artifact reshaping or recycling, were noted. Morphological categories were traditional Southwestern types such as trough metate, 3/4-grooved axe, and mortar, descriptors that often combine form and function. As with the flaked stone analysis, macroscopic and, when necessary, microscopic (18–110X) identification of materials provided as precise an identification as possible. Each artifact was weighed to the nearest 0.1 gram on a triple-beam balance scale (< 3000.0 g) or a bathroom scale (≥ 3000.0 g). The evaluation also included measurements of complete maximum dimensions and degree of completeness.

Assessment of grinding-surface texture (fine, medium, or coarse) on milling stones and other grinding tools included material grain size as well as any surface pecking. Prehistoric tool users artificially roughened grinding surfaces to achieve a desired texture. Latitudinal profiles of manos and handstones (biplanar, plano-convex, etc.) provided a basis for comparison of grinding patterns among tool types and through time.

The production investment and manufacturing technique variables applied to all ground stone artifacts. The amount of shaping each artifact had undergone defined level of production investment. For example, a metate pecked only on the grinding surface was categorized as "minimally altered," a metate flaked and/or pecked on less than one-half of its entire form, including edges, ends, and faces, was "shaped," a metate flaked and/or pecked on half or more of its form was "well shaped," and one with evidence of production over all or nearly all of its form was "completely shaped." These categories indicated the amount of energy invested in the manufacturing process and whether the investment correlated with artifact type, functional groupings, or other factors. Production techniques, such as flaking, pecking, and grinding, reveal varying degrees of energy investment in the application of different horizontal and vertical forces.

Site Assemblage Descriptions

The following discussion groups the flaked stone and ground stone assemblages by site. The primary foci are artifact category characteristics and variation, with an emphasis on specialized and diagnostic items.

AZ N:6:9 (ASM)

Two ground stone tools and 159 flaked stone items recovered from this site indicated that core reduction and activities involving grinding and hammering/battering were the primary functions associated with stone tools at this site. Evidence of plant-resource processing was also present.

The flaked stone assemblage consisted of debitage, five used flakes, six cores, 11 cores/hammerstones, and nine hammerstones (Table 5.1), with little variation from site to site in artifact type or material type (Table 5.2). Most raw materials were local igneous types such as basalt and diorite; two chert flakes were the only examples of nonlocal material. Most locally derived materials were fine- or medium-grained (Table 5.3), obviously sufficient for on-site activities. Flaked stone artifacts of these materials exhibited primarily hammering/battering wear. The relatively high frequency of hammerstones and core/hammerstones, the absence of unifacial or bifacial tools, and the almost exclusive use of local materials suggest that site inhabitants were processing resources that did not require tools with sharp edges or tips for extensive scraping, slicing, drilling, or piercing. Used flakes exhibited cutting/sawing wear (three speci-

mens), scraping wear (one specimen), and piercing wear (one specimen). Although some of the hammering/battering wear found on the core/hammerstones and hammerstones probably reflected core reduction, other activities responsible for similar wear patterns may have included processing of plant materials and ground stone tool production (e.g., pecking the surfaces of manos and metates; Dodd 1979). As neither of the ground stone artifacts from Site AZ N:6:9 (ASM) was pecked, it is reasonable to infer that processing of plant resources was the dominant site activity.

Fifty-seven percent of the debitage was whole flakes (Table 5.4), and flake size was large compared with other project assemblages (Table 5.5). These attributes indicate minimal flake breakage due to trampling and suggest that site occupation was short term. Sixty-four percent of the whole flakes were tertiary (Table 5.6). The absence of thinning flakes and facially reduced flakes, combined with debitage characteristics, argues for a generalized core reduction strategy, a trait associated with Ceramic period flaked stone technology (Parry and Kelly 1987). One hammerstone (FS 5) and one core/hammerstone (FS 66) found on the modern ground surface were recycled hand grinders.

The ground stone at Site AZ N:6:9 (ASM) consisted of a complete grinding slab and a complete slab metate (Table 5.7), both with fine-textured surfaces. Grinding slabs, also known as "lapstones," are smaller than slab metates and probably served as more generalized grinders (Greenwald 1993:327); slab metates are usually associated with food processing, particularly the grinding of small seeds or grain (Greenwald 1990). The grinding slab was an irregular granite cobble measuring 14.5 by 14.3 by 4.6 cm (length, width, thickness), with a flat ground surface and chopping use on one side. The slab metate was a large granite boulder with exfoliation due to weathering. Most of the grinding surface was flat, although the central area was slightly concave, to a depth of approximately 0.6 cm. This metate was also irregular in shape and measured 42 by 35 by 12 cm. As noted above, two ground stone items had been recycled as hammerstones.

Dawn M. Greenwald

Table 5.1. Flaked Stone Artifact Type by Site

Artifact Type	Site (AZ N:_[ASM])						Total
	6:9	6:13	6:19	6:20	7:155	7:156	
Debitage	128	102	24	151	1,650	297	2,352
	*80.5	85.7	70.6	82.5	86.7	88.1	*86.0
Used Flake	5	4		3	58	5	75
	3.1	3.4		1.6	3.0	1.5	2.7
Core	6	4	2	9	67	10	98
	3.8	3.4	5.9	4.9	3.5	3.0	3.6
Core Tool			1		9	2	12
			2.9		0.5	0.6	0.4
Core/Hammerstone	11	6	3	12	54	7	93
	6.9	5.0	8.8	6.6	2.8	2.1	3.4
Hammerstone	9	2		7	27	5	50
	5.7	1.7		3.8	1.4	1.5	1.8
Uniface			1		13	2	16
			2.9		0.7	0.6	0.6
Biface		1	2		13	6	22
		0.8	5.9		0.7	1.8	0.8
Drill			1				1
			2.9				tr
Serrated Flake					3		3
					0.2		0.1
Projectile Point				1	7	1	9
				0.5	0.4	0.3	0.3
Indeterminate Tool					2	2	4
					0.1	0.6	0.1
Total	**159**	**119**	**34**	**183**	**1,903**	**337**	**2,735**
	**5.8	**4.4**	**1.2**	**6.7**	**69.6**	**12.3**	**100.0**

*Column %; **Row %; tr=trace (<.05%)

Table 5.2. Flaked Stone Material Type by Site

Material Type	Site (AZ N:_[ASM])						Total
	6:9	6:13	6:19	6:20	7:155	7:156	
Quartz	7	11	1	42	212	14	287
	*4.4	9.2	2.9	23.0	11.1	4.2	*10.5
Chert	2	1	8	13	232	63	319
	1.3	0.8	23.5	7.1	12.2	18.7	11.7
Jasper		1	1	1	76	1	80
		0.8	2.9	0.5	4.0	0.3	2.9
Obsidian		3	4	1	47	9	64
		2.5	11.8	0.5	2.5	2.7	2.3
Chalcedony		1	4		53	3	61
		0.8	11.8		2.8	0.9	2.2
Basalt	79	18	4	41	715	148	1,005
	49.7	15.1	11.8	22.4	37.6	43.9	36.7
Granite/			2	1	15	3	21
Vesicular Basalt			5.9	0.5	0.8	0.9	0.8
Igneous NFS	62	77	10	69	369	82	669
	39.0	64.7	29.4	37.7	19.4	24.3	24.4
Metamorphic NFS	9	7		14	167	14	211
	5.7	5.9		7.7	8.8	4.2	7.7
Miscellaneous				1	17		18
				0.5	0.9		0.7
Total	**159**	**119**	**34**	**183**	**1,903**	**337**	**2,735**
	**5.8	**4.4**	**1.2**	**6.7**	**69.6**	**12.3**	**100.0**

*Column %; **Row %; NFS=not further specified

Table 5.3. Flaked Stone Material Grain and Texture by Site

Material Grain/ Texture	Site (AZ N:_[ASM])						Total
	6:9	6:13	6:19	6:20	7:155	7:156	
Micro-/Crypto- crystalline	1	6	13	15	386	64	485
	*0.6	5.0	38.2	8.2	20.3	19.0	*17.7
Fine	82	42	9	61	909	166	1,269
	51.6	35.3	26.5	33.3	47.8	49.3	46.4
Medium	66	51	5	85	439	86	732
	41.5	42.9	14.7	46.4	23.1	25.5	26.8
Coarse	10	20	7	22	169	21	249
	6.3	16.8	20.6	12.0	8.9	6.2	9.1
Total	159	119	34	183	1,903	337	2,735
	**5.8	4.4	1.2	6.7	69.6	12.3	100.0

*Column %
**Row %

Table 5.4. Debitage Type by Site

Debitage Type	Sites (AZ N:_[ASM])						Total
	6:9	6:13	6:19	6:20	7:155	7:156	
Angular Debris	12	6	1	36	163	26	244
	*9.4	5.9	4.2	23.8	9.9	8.8	*10.4
Flake Fragment	31	21	9	41	526	115	743
	24.2	20.6	37.5	27.2	31.9	38.7	31.6
Platform-bearing Flake	12	9	1	9	129	34	194
	9.4	8.8	4.2	6.0	7.8	11.4	8.2
Whole Flake	73	66	13	65	832	122	1,171
	57.0	64.7	54.2	43.0	50.4	41.1	49.8
Total	128	102	24	151	1,650	297	2,352
	**5.4	4.3	1.0	6.4	70.2	12.6	100.0

*Column %
**Row %

Dawn M. Greenwald

Table 5.5. Flake Size by Site

Size	Site (AZ N:_[ASM])					Total
	6:9	6:13	6:19	7:155	7:156	
1	1	1	1	75	43	121
	*0.8	0.9	4.2	4.4	14.2	*5.3
2	36	20	8	704	158	926
	27.1	18.9	33.3	41.3	52.3	40.8
3	46	49	6	448	55	604
	34.6	46.2	25.0	26.3	18.2	26.6
4	27	15	7	261	23	333
	20.3	14.2	29.2	15.3	7.6	14.7
5	17	16	1	133	15	182
	12.8	15.1	4.2	7.8	5.0	8.0
6	4	5		57	4	70
	3.0	4.7		3.3	1.3	3.1
7	1			22	3	26
	0.8			1.3	1.0	1.1
8	1		1	5	1	8
	0.8		4.2	0.3	0.3	0.4
9				1		1
				0.1		tr
Total	133	106	24	1,706	302	2,271
	**5.9	4.7	1.0	75.1	13.3	100.0

Note: Includes debitage and used flakes (2 pieces of debitage were not sized). Site AZ N:6:20 (ASM) not included.
*Column %; **Row %
 tr=trace (<.05%)

Table 5.6. Whole Flake Reduction Stage by Site

Reduction Stage	Site (AZ N:_[ASM])						Total
	6:9	6:13	6:19	6:20	7:155	7:156	
Primary	5	5	2	8	32	5	57
	*6.8	7.6	15.4	12.3	3.8	4.1	*4.9
Secondary	21	32	4	16	213	34	320
	28.8	48.5	30.8	24.6	25.6	27.9	27.3
Tertiary	47	29	7	41	587	83	794
	64.4	43.9	53.8	63.1	70.6	68.0	67.8
Total	73	66	13	65	832	122	1,171
	**6.2	5.6	1.1	5.6	71.1	10.4	100.0

*Column %
**Row %

Table 5.7. Ground Stone Artifact Type by Site

Artifact Type	Site (AZ N:__[ASM])						Total
	6:9	6:13	6:19	6:20	7:155	7:156	
Polishing Stone				4 11.8	6 1.6		10 *2.0
Round/Oval Mano			2 11.1		19 5.0	5 9.8	26 5.3
Rectangular Mano				6 17.6	47 12.4	6 11.8	59 12.1
Indeterminate Mano			3 16.7		16 4.2	3 5.9	22 4.5
Handstone		1 16.7			9 2.4	4 7.8	14 2.9
Slab Metate	1 *50.0	1 16.7	2 11.1	1 2.9	7 1.9	14 27.5	26 5.3
Trough Metate					30 7.9	3 5.9	33 6.7
Indeterminate Metate				5 14.7	9 2.4	3 5.9	17 3.5
Grinding Slab	1 50.0		1 5.6	1 2.9	1 0.3	1 2.0	5 1.0
Netherstone NFS			4 22.2		3 0.8	4 7.8	11 2.2
Mortar/Pestle					2 0.5		2 0.4
Axe/Maul					6 1.6		6 1.2
Tabular Tool		3 50.0		1 2.9	58 15.3		62 12.7
Mineral				6 17.6	45 11.9		51 10.4
Worked Stone				2 5.9	6 1.6		8 1.6
Raw Material		1 16.7			47 12.4	1 2.0	49 10.0
Abrader					1 0.3		1 0.2
Stone Bowl					1 0.3		1 0.2
Stone Ball					1 0.3		1 0.2
Pendant					1 0.3		1 0.2
Grooved Grinder					1 0.3		1 0.2
Notched Stone				3 8.8	1 0.3		4 0.8
Figurine					1 0.3		1 0.2
Slag					4 1.1		4 0.8
Other Stone				3 8.8	5 1.3		8 1.6
Ground Stone NFS			6 33.3	2 5.9	51 13.5	7 13.7	66 13.5
Total	**2** **0.4	**6** **1.2	**18** **3.7	**34** **6.9	**378** **77.3	**51** **10.4	**489** **100.0

*Column %; **Row %
NFS=not further specified

Site AZ N:6:13 (ASM)

The stone assemblage from AZ N:6:13 (ASM) consisted of 119 items of flaked stone and six pieces of ground stone from eight artifact concentrations (Loci A–H). Reduction technology characteristics indicated Ceramic period culture, and the artifact types were consistent with resource procurement and processing.

The flaked stone from this site was similar to the assemblage from AZ N:6:9 (ASM), consisting of debitage, used flakes, cores, hammerstones, and a single biface. Material types were primarily local, but a small percentage were nonlocal jasper, chert, and obsidian. Dacite was the most common igneous type. Overall, the material tended to be coarser grained than at other sites.

Whole flakes constituted 65 percent of the debitage, the highest proportion of this type at any of the project sites. Flake size was limited to sizes 1 through 6, with size 3 most frequent. Secondary flakes were more numerous than tertiary flakes, the opposite of the pattern at other sites and for the project assemblage as a whole. These data imply that reduction was not intensive at this site, an inference supported by retention of more than half of the cortex on 60 percent of the cores.

Four flakes (two quartz, one chalcedony, one basalt) showed evidence of use. All four were complete. The chalcedony flake had scraping wear; the other three exhibited cutting/sawing use wear. Although the internal structure and flaking qualities of the quartz flakes were not good, the material was obviously deemed adequate for site tasks, as one flake showed quite extensive use on both lateral margins and the other showed use on most of one lateral margin. Both quartz flakes were recovered from Locus A; the chalcedony flake came from Locus B and the basalt flake from Locus D.

Four cores (two quartz, one basalt, one dacite), six core/hammerstones, and two hammerstones were recovered from Site AZ N:6:13 (ASM). The basalt core was a recycled piece of ground stone. Due to the reduction of their mass, cores, with an average weight of 230.2 g, were smaller and lighter than hammerstones, which averaged 642.9 g. In addition, hammerstones are often of denser, heavier material to be effective for their ham-

mering or battering tasks. Core/hammerstone average weight, as expected, fell between the cores and hammerstones, at 437.4 g. Seven of these 12 implements were found in Locus C. The basalt core was from Locus D, and one quartz core and one core/hammerstone were from Locus H.

The single flake biface, found in Locus D, was made of reddish-brown Perkinsville jasper and measured 3.1 by 2.6 by 1.3 cm. It was only marginally retouched, but on the entire margin. No use wear was visible on its edges.

The six ground stone artifacts recovered from AZ N:6:13 (ASM) were three tabular knives, one slab metate, one handstone/scraper, and one piece of unworked phyllite. One of the tabular tools was quartzite and two were phyllite. The only complete specimen was one of the phyllite tools. It was more or less oval, measured 6.3 by 2.9 by 0.4 cm, and appeared to have been reshaped by flaking. Cutting/sawing use wear was present on both longitudinal edges of this specimen, as well as on the intact edges of the other two tabular tools.

The metate was a natural slab of sandstone with a partly exfoliated surface. Most of the intact surface was ground, and the grinding surface was fine grained. The metate was irregular in shape and measured 36.4 by 33.5 by 8.2 cm.

The handstone/scraper was a recycled artifact (probably a mano) and was multi-functional. Both surfaces had been used for grinding and shaving/planing, and hammering/battering wear was evident on a broken corner. Scraper-plane wear included much polish and rounding near the edges and along the broken longitudinal edges.

Although the ground stone artifacts were dispersed throughout the site (Loci A–E, G), collectively their presence strongly suggests processing of plant materials. Such processing would have included cutting/sawing of plant stalks, leaves, and possibly hearts with tabular knives, scraping and pulping of some plant parts with the scraper plane, possibly on the metate, and grinding of seeds, nuts, or other foods on the metate. In the Southwest, evidence from both ethnography and archaeology links tabular knives with agave processing. Ethnographic data (Castetter et al. 1938; Russell 1975), experimental and use wear analyses of tabular knives (Bernard-Shaw 1983, 1984, 1985; Greenwald 1988:172–187), and the association of tabular knives with features related to agave cultivation (Fish, Fish, and Madsen 1985; Fish et al. 1985) suggest that tabular knives were used in the initial processing of plants or plant parts such as removal or trimming of leaves, especially agave. Agave may not, however, have been the only economic plant reduced with these tools.

Tabular knives are common components of stone assemblages in and around the Prescott area. Barnett illustrated them and described them as saws (Barnett 1978) and as fleshers (Barnett 1973, 1974). They have been found in the Williamson Valley (Barnett 1978), west of Prescott near Bagdad (Dosh and Halbirt 1985), along the middle Verde and Agua Fria Rivers (Bernard-Shaw 1983:Figure II.1.6; Greenwald 1994), at Lonesome Valley Ruin (Barnett 1973a), and at Fitzmaurice Ruin (Barnett 1974). Fitzmaurice Ruin yielded 56 of these tools, making them one of the most numerous of all stone artifacts at that site. Materials included schist, slate, and rhyolite (Barnett 1974:68). Ethnographic data and archaeological experimentation have also shown that scraper planes were used in processing agave or yucca plants (Salls 1985) by placing the plant material on a flat rock or metate and using the scraper to push the pulp from the leaves (Rogers 1939:49–51). The presence of both tabular knives and a scraper plane at AZ N:6:13 (ASM) is convincing evidence for the prehistoric processing of agave or similar plants at this site.

AZ N:6:19 (ASM)

The stone artifact assemblage at the site consisted of 34 flaked stone artifacts and 18 pieces of ground stone. The flaked stone assemblage was diverse for the small number of artifacts found. Use wear evidence indicated cutting/sawing, scraping, hammering/battering, and drilling. All of the ground stone was grinding equipment. Together, the assemblages suggest site occupation for resource processing.

The few flaked stone artifacts yielded only general patterns. Debitage constituted 70.6 percent of the assemblage and included mostly flake fragments and whole flakes. Most of the of flakes (87.5 percent) were sizes 2–

4, and 54 percent had no dorsal cortex—proportions similar to those for debitage from other sites. The wide variety of debitage material types did not include jasper, rhyolite, or quartz diorite, although these materials were identified in other flaked stone categories from this site.

The two cores, both unused, were a small, exhausted core of chert and a large nodule of quartz diorite. One small core tool of jasper had been reduced with a bipolar technique and had cutting/sawing use wear on one of its edges. The three core/hammerstones were basalt, granite, and igneous NFS and weighed 199.0 g, 345.4 g, and 548.4 g.

The rest of the flaked stone assemblage consisted of a cobble uniface, two flake bifaces, and a drill. The uniface was a complete specimen of rhyolite with scraping wear along an edge from which only one flake had been removed. Both bifaces were chert. The complete biface showed bidirectional edge retouch along one lateral margin; the opposite, unworked margin exhibited both cutting/sawing and scraping use wear. The biface fragment also showed no evidence of thinning, but it had been bidirectionally retouched along all intact edges.

The drill recovered from this site was the only one found in the project area. It was made of obsidian and, although completely worked, was slightly irregular (Figure 5.1a). Slight drill wear, in the form of rounding and flake scars, was present on the distal tip.

Among the ground stone artifacts recovered from AZ N:6:19 (ASM) were five manos from the modern ground surface: two complete oval manos and three fragments of indeterminate types. One of the oval manos was a granite cobble that measured 10.6 by 7.9 by 3.3 cm. It was biconvex in cross section and had one fine-grained grinding surface with bidirectional striations and polish. The other oval mano was smaller, measuring 7.5 by 5.5 by 2.2 cm. It was an igneous NFS cobble, plano-convex in cross section, with two medium-grained grinding surfaces that exhibited bidirectional striations (indicating a back-and-forth grinding pattern). None of the manos or mano fragments showed any production modification. One mano fragment was of igneous NFS material and two were granitic; all had fine-grained grinding surfaces.

88   Dawn M. Greenwald

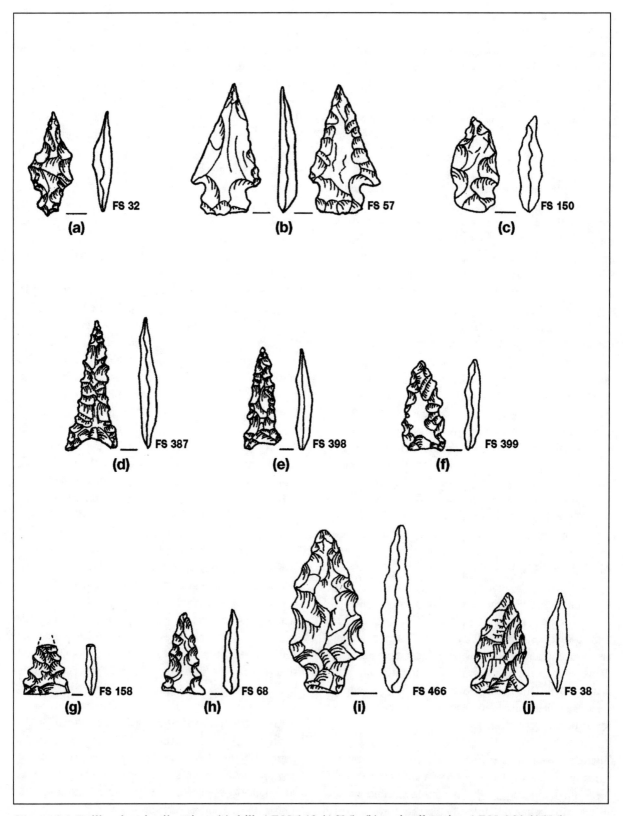

Figure 5.1. Drill and projectile points: (a) drill, AZ N:6:19 (ASM); (b) projectile point, AZ N:6:20 (ASM); (c–h) arrow points, AZ N:7:155 (ASM); (i) dart point, AZ N:7:155 (ASM); (j) projectile point, AZ N:7:156 (ASM).

Stationary grinding stones from the site were two slab metates, one grinding slab, and four netherstones NFS. One of the indeterminate netherstones was of igneous NFS material; the rest of these implements were granite.

One of the slab metates was complete and more or less oval, measuring 44.9 by 38.0 by 12.0 cm. Less than one-half of its perimeter had been shaped, by flaking. Grinding extended over most of its surface, which was medium grained and flat except for a slight (about 0.4 cm) concavity at the center. The slab metate fragment showed no production modification but had also been ground over most of its flat, fine-grained surface.

The grinding slab was an unmodified piece of granite measuring 30.7 by 21.0 by 9.5 cm, with an exfoliated grinding surface. Grinding on the fine-grained surface appeared to be limited to a 12 by 12 cm area, but surface weathering and damage from burning probably had removed the rest.

AZ N:6:19 (ASM) also had two ground stone features. Feature 2 was a bedrock outcrop with two possible mortars and a grinding slick. The possible mortars were 5 cm and 8 cm deep, with eroded interior surfaces. The grinding slick had a partly eroded surface measuring 45 by 30 cm. Feature 3 was a bedrock grinding slick that measured 50 by 19 cm.

AZ N:6:20 (ASM)

The analyzed[1] lithic assemblage from this site consisted of 183 flaked stone artifacts and 34 ground stone items. The tool types were diverse and related to stone tool production, food processing, ceramic manufacture, and habitation. The flaked stone and ground stone assemblages were the third largest in the project area and were from several feature types (Table 5.8).

Angular debris was a larger component of the debitage than at any other site, perhaps indicating that core reduction and tool production were important site activities (Sullivan and Rozen 1985). Given a flaked stone profile with only one retouched tool (a projectile point) and numerous cores and core/hammerstones, the angular debris probably was associated with intensive core reduction. The large number of primary flakes also sug-

gests more initial core reduction at AZ N:6:20 (ASM) than at other project sites.

This site yielded only three used flakes. Two were tertiary basalt flakes, one with cutting/sawing wear and one with scraping wear. The third specimen was a large primary flake of granite, 14.3 cm long and 2.3 cm thick, with cutting/sawing use wear on the distal margin.

Twenty-one artifacts, 11.5 percent of the flaked stone assemblage, were cores and core/hammerstones. These implements were associated with various feature types, including a structure, middens, a rock concentration, and a rock alignment. Twelve cores exhibited hammerstone use. Two-thirds of the cores were reduced from unsymmetrical, multiple platforms. One bipolar core of white chert was found in the fill of Feature 5, a midden.

Nonflaked hammerstones were not as numerous as core/hammerstones. The seven specimens of this tool type were made from heavy, fine-grained igneous and metamorphic rocks.

The single projectile point recovered from this site, from the fill of Feature 3, was a side-notched chert specimen with a triangular blade and slightly convex base (Figure 5.1b). In general form the point resembled the San Pedro side-notched type of the late Archaic period, but the manufacturing details were inconsistent with that style. The notches and base were well made, but one face of the blade was neither thinned nor marginally retouched, resulting in a plano-convex cross section. Most of the other face was thinned, and the unifacial retouch around the margin gave the point a slightly serrated appearance.

The ground stone assemblage from AZ N:6:20 (ASM) was recovered from seven features and nonfeature contexts. The tool types represented, which included polishing stones, grinding implements, and architectural stone, are consistent with use of the site for habitation.

Prehistoric potters used polishing stones to smooth and polish the surfaces of ceramic vessels prior to firing. The stones were usually small cobbles or pebbles with smooth, fine-grained surfaces. All four polishing stones

Dawn M. Greenwald

Table 5.8. Flaked Stone and Ground Stone Artifact Type by Provenience, AZ N:6:20 (ASM)

Artifact Type	Provenience								Total
	NF	F1	F2	F3	F4	F5	F7	F9	
Debitage		51 63.0	55 96.5	42 79.2		3 42.9			151 *69.6
Used Flake		2 2.5	1 1.8						3 1.4
Core		4 4.9		1 1.9	2 100.0	2 28.6			9 4.1
Core/ Hammerstone	7 *53.8	4 4.9					1 14.3		12 5.5
Hammerstone	4 30.8	1 1.2		1 1.9		1 14.3			7 3.2
Projectile Point				1 1.9					1 0.5
Polishing Stone		4 4.9							4 1.8
Rectangular Mano	1 7.7	2 2.5	1 1.8	2 3.8					6 2.8
Slab Metate				1 1.9					1 0.5
Indeterminate Metate		1 1.2		4 7.5					5 2.3
Grinding Slab								1 33.3	1 0.5
Tabular Tool		1 1.2							1 0.5
Mineral	1 7.7	4 4.9				1 14.3			6 2.8
Worked Stone		1 1.2						1 33.3	2 1.0
Unworked Stone		3 3.7							3 1.4
Notched Stone		2 2.5						1 33.3	3 1.4
Ground Stone NFS		1 1.2		1 1.9					2 1.0
Total	13 **6.0	81 37.3	57 26.3	53 24.4	2 0.9	7 3.2	1 0.5	3 1.4	217 100.0

*Column %; **Row %
NF=nonfeature; F=feature
NFS=not further specified

were recovered from Feature 1, three from floor fill and one from feature fill. Two were small granite cobbles and two were igneous NFS cobbles; three exhibited battering wear. All specimens were complete, with mean dimensions of 5.1 by 4.3 by 2.5 cm.

Three of six rectangular manos—two from the floor fill of Feature 1, a pit structure, and one from general site overburden—were complete. Lengths of complete manos ranged from 13.4 cm to 22.5 cm. Four specimens were vesicular basalt, one was granite, and one was igneous NFS material. Four had only coarse-grained surfaces, one had a fine-grained surface, and one specimen had one coarse-grained surface and one fine-grained surface. Four manos had been completely shaped by pecking or a combination of pecking and grinding. Only one specimen exhibited trough wear (a polished and curved end surface caused by contact with the walls of a trough metate).

The complete slab metate came from the fill of Feature 3. Its presence in a midden is baffling, as it appeared to be newly shaped and had a clearly defined and newly pecked grinding area. This metate was large, measuring 59.5 by 35.3 by 11.0 cm, with a use area only slightly smaller pecked into the shape of a trough. The "open" end was pecked completely to the edge; there was no pecking at the "closed" end. This implement showed little use wear and was probably an incipient trough metate. The toolmaker had flaked some of the edges to achieve an approximately subrectangular shape and had roughened the grinding surface to achieve a coarse texture. This metate and the five indeterminate metate fragments found at the site were granite.

A grinding slab, from the floor fill of Feature 9, was a naturally shaped, more or less round cobble of igneous NFS material that had been ground on a small area of one flat surface. This implement measured 21.2 by 20.0 by 8.8 cm and had an oval grinding area measuring 17 by 10 cm.

One tabular tool fragment was found in the floor fill of Feature 1. It was made of phyllite, and although the surfaces exhibited grinding from manufacture, the use edge had been left unworked. Cutting/sawing wear was visible on the edge.

The AZ N:6:20 (ASM) stone assemblage also included one complete notched stone and two notched stone fragments, all made from slabs of naturally tabular schist. The complete specimen came from the floor fill of Feature 9. It was tapered and was 14.0 cm across at its widest point, 35.5 cm long, and 4.0 cm thick. The notch, at the wider end, was bidirectionally flaked to shape and was 8.5 cm wide by 1.5 cm deep. Such stones were structural elements; the notched end held a beam, and the narrow end was set into the floor.

The two fragments fit together but were found in different site contexts. One came from the modern ground surface and the other came from Feature 1 floor fill. Together, they were 23.0 cm long (incomplete), 14.5 cm wide, and 3.4 cm thick. The notch was created by pecking and flaking and measured 9.0 cm wide by 1.7 cm deep. As on the complete specimen, the edges had been partly flaked.

Two other thick slabs of tabular schist, categorized as worked stone, appeared to be fragments of notched stones from the end opposite the notch. Excavators found them as upright slabs set into floor substrate, one in Feature 1 and the other in Feature 9. One fragment was 2.2 cm thick and the other was 2.3 cm thick.

The six mineral specimens found at this site were hematite, azurite, a combination of azurite and malachite, quartz crystal, and an indeterminate mineral. Four of the minerals came from Feature 1; one piece of azurite was in the feature fill, and the indeterminate mineral, the quartz crystal, and the hematite were in the floor fill. The hematite occurred as a smear of pigment on a small slab of unworked granite.

Three small granite slabs found on the floor in the southwest quarter of Feature 1 showed no evidence of production or use. They were all of similar size and thickness, with mean measurements of 14.3 by 12.7 by 2.5 cm. These stones may have been used as trivets.

The two pieces of ground stone NFS were granite fragments. One was flaked and may have been a round/oval mano. The other, a naturally tabular slab 1.1 cm thick, may have been a tabular tool. The edges were worn, possibly from cutting/sawing use.

Possible bedrock grinding slicks (Feature 8) were on a boulder northwest of Feature 1. The slicks were smoothed, possibly ground areas on an exposed portion of bedrock measuring 1.4 by 0.9 m and rising 30 cm above the modern ground surface.

AZ N:7:155 (ASM)

This site had the largest and most diverse stone assemblage by far, with about six times more flaked stone and seven times more ground stone than the next largest assemblage. Assemblage size and diversity were typical for a year-round habitation site (Greenwald 1996:202–211). Flaked stone and ground stone artifacts provided evidence for ceramic production, grinding of corn and wild seeds, plant procurement and processing, wood processing, ornamentation, ceremony, faunal procurement, and core and flake reduction.

Flaked Stone

As at the other project sites, the largest assemblage component was debitage (Table 5.9), about half of it whole flakes. Angular debris was the least common debitage type but was well represented compared to other sites. The large number of broken flakes attests to the longevity of site occupation, and the relatively large quantity of angular debris suggests that flake production was an important on-site activity. Most of the whole flakes and flake fragments were size 2 and had no dorsal cortex. All material types found at the site were represented in the debitage, including the only examples of vesicular basalt (10), hematite (9), phyllite (5), sandstone (5), and agate (1) in the project assemblage. The sandstone, vesicular basalt, and phyllite probably represented ground stone tool production.

The used flake category also included a wide variety of materials, 56.9 percent of it microcrystalline. Most used flakes (67.2 percent) were complete, with wear on less than half of flake edges. Most common was cutting/sawing wear (58.6 percent), with scraping wear (34.5 percent) next in frequency. Three specimens had both cutting/sawing and scraping wear on the same tool, and one example had an indeterminate type of wear. Used flakes were almost equally divided among sizes 3 (16), 4 (15), and 5 (14), with six each in sizes 2 and 6 and one

in size 8. Because site occupants chose larger flakes for use, more used than unused flakes were primary-reduction flakes; 3.8 percent of whole flakes in the debitage category were primary-reduction flakes, whereas 10.3 percent of used flakes retained 90 to 100 percent dorsal cortex. Used flakes were found in a variety of contexts, indicating that they were important tools and probably were used in many different ways.

Sixty-three of the 130 cores recovered exhibited use wear. Fifty-four had been used as hammerstones, four for shaving/planing, two for chopping, one for cutting/ sawing, and one for scraping. One core had been used for both grinding and hammering/battering. On 47.7 percent of the cores, flakes were removed from multiple platforms in no particular pattern, and 16.9 percent had only one platform. Variation in core-reduction patterns was based on the geometry of the core, a production strategy typical of other prehistoric culture groups in the Southwest, and no standard core-reduction model was apparent. Fourteen cores and one whole flake bore evidence of specialized bipolar core reduction, a method often used on small nodules of obsidian and chert when manipulation for freehand percussion was not practical. The toolmaker rested the small nodule on an anvil stone and struck the opposite end with a percussor, removing flakes from both ends (Crabtree 1982:5–6). This technique has been well documented in the Hohokam region. At Site AZ N:7:155(ASM), most evidence of bipolar reduction occurred on cores of obsidian (eight cores and one flake). Other core material types were chert (3), jasper (2), and chalcedony (1). Bipolar cores were most often recovered from midden fill (Features 4, 5, and 10); those found in structures were also in fill contexts (Features 1, 2, and 3).

Unused cores were smaller and of a greater variety of materials than used cores. The mean weight of cores was 222.6 g, with a standard deviation of 421.0; core tools had a mean weight of 264.9 g, with a standard deviation of 313.7. Hammering/battering tools were heavier, with a narrower range of variation: the mean weight of core/hammerstones was 527.6 g, with a standard deviation of 305.6, and the mean weight of the 27 hammerstones was 559.6 g, with a standard deviation of 306.5. These implements were also made from a more

Table 5.9. Flaked Stone Artifact Type by Provenience, AZ N:7:155 (ASM)

Artifact Type	Provenience												Total
	NF	F1	F2	F3	F4	F5	F8	F10	F11	F15	F17	F18	
Debitage	6 *23.1	120 87.0	54 75.0	86 85.1	977 91.3	323 90.7	2 66.7	71 61.7	1 50.0	3 100.0	7 46.7		1,650 *86.7
Used Flake	1 3.8	6 4.3	6 8.3	5 5.0	26 2.4	12 3.4		1 0.9			1 6.7		58 3.0
Core	3 11.5	4 2.9	6 8.3	5 5.0	21 2.0	8 2.2		19 16.5			1 6.7		67 3.5
Core Tool					5 0.5	1 0.3		3 2.6					9 0.5
Core/ Hammerstone	7 26.9	4 2.9	1 1.4	4 4.0	16 1.5	4 1.1		11 9.6			5 33.3	2 100.0	54 2.8
Hammerstone	6 23.1	2 1.4	2 2.8	1 1.0	7 0.7	1 0.3		8 7.0					27 1.4
Uniface	3 11.5				7 0.7	1 0.3			1 50.0		1 6.7		13 0.7
Biface		1 0.7	1 1.4		5 0.5	3 0.8	1 33.3	2 1.7					13 0.7
Serrated Flake		1 0.7			1 0.1	1 0.3							3 0.2
Projectile Point			1 1.4		5 0.5	1 0.3							7 0.4
Indeterminate Tool			1 1.4			1 0.3							2 0.1
Total	26 **1.4	138 7.3	72 3.8	101 5.3	1,070 56.2	356 18.7	3 0.2	115 6.0	2 0.1	3 0.2	15 0.8	2 0.1	1,903 100.0

*Column %; **Row %
NF=nonfeature; F=feature

limited range of material types, most often dense igneous materials such as basalt. Cores and hammerstones were distributed throughout the site. Three core/hammerstones were in a cluster within the entryway of Feature 3, a pit structure.

Thirty-eight flaked stone artifacts were unifacial, bifacial, and indeterminate tools. The unifacial tools were three serrated flakes, four cobble unifaces, and nine flake unifaces. Serrated flakes exhibited cutting/sawing wear along the serrated edge. Two were chert, and one was an igneous NFS material. The chert specimens came from the fill of Features 4 and 5, and the igneous flake was found in Feature 1, a masonry room, in floor fill.

Three cobble unifaces were igneous NFS material, and a fourth was a metamorphic NFS rock. These tools showed retouch only along margins. The two cobble unifaces found in the fill of Feature 4 exhibited use wear (shaving/planing and hammering/battering). One cobble uniface was found on the modern ground surface, and the fourth came from the floor of Feature 17, a masonry room. Lengths of these tools ranged from 6.8 cm to 14.3 cm, widths from 5.2 cm to 11.1 cm, and thicknesses from 1.8 cm to 6.2 cm.

Six of the nine flake unifaces were from midden fill (Features 4 and 5), two were on the modern ground surface, and one was associated with Feature 11, an inhumation. Seven of the nine exhibited use wear: five had scraping wear, one had cutting/sawing wear, and one had both chopping and scraping wear. Flake unifaces had little or no facial thinning, and marginal retouch was usually limited to less than half of the total flake circumference. The seven complete specimens ranged from size 5 to size 8.

Three cobble bifaces, of quartz, basalt, and quartz diorite, came from midden fill in Features 4, 5, and 10. One had cutting/sawing use wear, one exhibited chopping wear, and the third, a recycled piece of ground stone, had been used for both chopping and grinding. Cobble biface production was limited to marginal retouch. These tools had lengths ranging from 5.0 cm to 11.1 cm, widths of 4.4 cm to 8.4 cm, and thicknesses of 2.3 cm to 5.8 cm.

The 10 flake bifaces recovered exhibited a wide range of production investment, from unthinned and only marginally retouched to facially thinned and symmetrical. The six complete flake bifaces were sizes 3 to 7. Material types included chert (2), obsidian (2), basalt (3), and jasper, rhyolite, and igneous NFS (one each). Four specimens had cutting/sawing use wear, two had no wear, two had chopping wear, one exhibited scraping wear, and one exhibited an indeterminate type of wear. Proveniences were structure floor fill (Features 1 and 2), midden fill (Features 4, 5, and 10), and cremation fill (Feature 8).

Six of seven projectile points were arrow points and one was a dart point. Five of the projectile points had serrated blades. The exception was a stemmed arrow point of white chert from the fill of Feature 4 (Figure 5.1c). This point measured 2.2 by 1.2 by 0.5 cm and had considerable damage around the distal tip, part of which had been poorly reworked. Two obsidian arrow points from Feature 4 fill (Figures 5.1d, 5.1e) had expanded concave bases, narrow, serrated blades, and projectile use wear on the tips. One measured 3.15 by 1.3 by 0.5 cm and the other measured 2.4 by 0.9 by 0.4 cm. A triangular obsidian arrow point with a slightly concave base found in Feature 4 fill (Figure 5.1f) had a concave-convex longitudinal cross section that probably represented original flake curvature. This point exhibited projectile use wear and had been reworked near the tip and at the base. It was 2.1 cm long, 1.1 cm wide, and 0.3 cm thick. The fifth arrow point, from the fill of Feature 5, was small and triangular with a straight base; the tip was missing (Figure 5.1g). Extant measurements were 1.2 by 1.1 cm by 0.3 cm. This point had a biplanar longitudinal cross section and was well thinned and symmetrical. The sixth arrow point, from the fill of Feature 2, was a triangular point of chalcedony with the base missing (Figure 5.1h). This fragment was 1.9 cm long (incomplete), 1.1 cm wide, and 0.4 cm thick.

The dart point, from Feature 4 fill, was stemmed and had serrated blades (Figure 5.1i). The sedimentary material was partly discolored by heat. The distal tip of the point had been reused as a punch or drill, and cutting/sawing wear on one edge indicated additional reuse as a knife. This point measured 4.0 by 1.9 by 0.7 cm.

Ground Stone

Table 5.10 shows the distribution of the ground stone artifacts from AZ N:7:155 (ASM) across the site. The amount and variety of ground stone recovered from the site indicates long-term occupation and year-round activities.

Polishing stones, used to smooth and polish the surfaces of ceramic vessels prior to firing, were usually small cobbles or pebbles with smooth, fine-grained surfaces. Six polishing stones were recovered, five from middens (Features 4, 5, and 10) and one from the floor of Feature 2. Two specimens were granite, two were quartzite, and two were an igneous NFS material. The polishing stone from Feature 10 had hematite in the center of its polishing surface.

Manos and handstones are types of hand-held grinding stones. Manos have standard shapes, either round/oval or rectangular/subrectangular. Handstones are irregular in shape. The 82 analyzed manos were divided into three classes: round/oval, rectangular, and indeterminate (too fragmentary for adequate determination of shape). Eighteen manos exhibited trough wear. Sixteen manos (88.9 percent) with trough wear were rectangular types; two (11.1 percent) were round/oval, and one (5.6 percent) was indeterminate.

Nine round/oval manos were granite, five were igneous NFS material, and two were basalt; sandstone, dacite, and metamorphic NFS materials were represented by one mano each. Sizes varied widely. Grinding surfaces on all but one specimen were fine grained; the exception was medium grained. Round/oval manos were usually (78.9 percent) unshaped cobbles that probably had been selected for size, shape, and surface texture. Thirteen of the 19 specimens were complete.

Twenty-seven (57.4 percent) of the 47 rectangular manos from AZ N:7:155 (ASM) were vesicular basalt, 14 were granite, four were quartzite, and two were igneous NFS material. Unlike the round/oval manos, rectangular manos exhibited a variety of grinding-surface textures. Specimens with coarse-grained surfaces outnumbered fine-grained examples 26 to 13; seven had medium-grained grinding surfaces, and one specimen

had one surface that was fine grained and one that was medium grained. Rectangular manos generally differed from round/oval manos in having been pecked to shape, although five were natural rectangular forms. Most (91.5 percent) were fragments, probably due to their thinness and extensive use. Since round/oval manos were usually thicker than rectangular ones (Table 5.11), and their fine-grained surfaces did not require resurfacing by pecking, manos of this type wore down more slowly.

Eight of the nine handstones were of various igneous material types; the exception was quartzite. Six of the nine were either recycled or multiple-function tools, usually with hammerstone use. Two were recycled core/hammerstones, and one was a recycled cobble uniface.

Forty-six of the 50 grinding stones from AZ N:7:155 (ASM) were metates and metate fragments, one was a grinding slab, and three were indeterminate netherstone fragments. Thirty metates were the trough type, seven were slab metates, and nine were indeterminate. The grinding slab, a fragment, was recovered during mechanical stripping of Feature 18, an occupation surface. This specimen was an elongate cobble of diorite with a slightly concave grinding surface exhibiting bidirectional striations. It was 15.5 cm long (incomplete), 9.5 cm wide, and 4.1 cm thick.

The fill of three structures (Features 1, 2, and 17) yielded three complete slab metates and four fragments; five specimens, including one complete metate, were from Feature 1. Six were granite; one was quartzite. Five had a fine-grained surface texture, and two were medium grained. There was little evidence of production.

Two complete trough metates and 28 fragments came from seven features and from nonfeature contexts. Sixteen were granite, 13 were vesicular basalt, and one was granodiorite. Eighteen of the metates had coarse-grained surfaces, seven were medium grained, one was fine grained, and four had an indeterminate texture. Trough depth ranged between 2.7 cm and 11 cm on specimens complete enough to measure. One of the two complete trough metates was vesicular basalt, and the other was

Table 5.10. Ground Stone Artifact Type by Provenience, AZ N:7:155 (ASM)

Artifact Type	NF	F1	F2	F3	F4	F5	F8	F10	F12	F15	F17	F18	Total
						Feature							
Polishing Stone	2 / *33.3	1 / 2.3	1 / 7.1		3 / 1.9	1 / 1.8		1 / 1.9					6 / *1.6
Mano			2 / 14.3	5 / 26.3	32 / 20.4	14 / 25.5	1 / 100.0	19 / 36.5			6 / 28.6		82 / 21.7
Handstone		1 / 2.3				2 / 3.6		6 / 11.5					9 / 2.4
Metate	2 / 33.3	14 / 31.8	2 / 14.3	3 / 15.8	15 / 9.6	3 / 5.5		5 / 9.6			2 / 9.5		46 / 12.2
Grinding Slab												1 / 25.0	1 / 0.3
Netherstone NFS					2 / 1.3			1 / 1.9					3 / 0.8
Mortar/Pestle												2 / 50.0	2 / 0.5
Axe/Maul				1 / 5.3	2 / 1.3	1 / 1.8		1 / 1.9			1 / 4.8		6 / 1.6
Tabular Tool		8 / 18.2	1 / 7.1	3 / 15.8	22 / 14.0	17 / 30.9		7 / 13.5		1 / 25.0	2 / 9.5		58 / 15.3
Mineral		10 / 22.7	5 / 35.7	2 / 10.5	12 / 7.6	4 / 7.3		3 / 5.8			8 / 38.1		45 / 11.9
Worked Stone	1 / 16.7	1 / 2.3			3 / 1.9	1 / 1.8							6 / 1.6
Raw Material		4 / 9.1		2 / 10.5	32 / 20.4	1 / 1.8		5 / 9.6		3 / 75.0			47 / 12.4
Other Stone		1 / 2.3	1 / 7.1								1 / 4.8		5 / 1.3
Miscellaneous[1]				1 / 5.3	3 / 1.9	3 / 5.5		2 / 3.8	1 / 100.0		1 / 4.8	1 / 25.0	11 / 2.9
Ground Stone NFS	1 / 16.7	4 / 9.1	2 / 14.3	2 / 10.5	31 / 19.7	8 / 14.5	1 / 0.3	2 / 3.8					51 / 13.5
Total	6 / **1.6	44 / 11.6	14 / 3.7	19 / 5.0	157 / 41.5	55 / 14.6	1 / 0.3	52 / 13.6	1 / 0.3	4 / 1.1	21 / 5.6	4 / 1.1	378 / 100.0

*Column %; **Row %

NF=nonfeature; F=feature; NFS=not further specified

[1]Includes abrader, grooved handstone, architectural stone, stone bowl, figurine, pendant, slag (4)

Table 5.11. Dimensional Data for Complete Grinding Implements, AZ N:7:155 (ASM)

Artifact Type/FS No.	Complete Dimensions (cm)		
	Length	Width	Thickness
Slab Metate			
FS 72	38.0	23.0	12.0
FS 73	48.0	38.5	14.2
FS 180	45.0	34.0	12.6
Mean	*43.7*	*31.8*	*12.9*
Trough Metate			
FS 174	40.6	40.0	20.4
FS 483	44.3	27.5	15.2
Mean	*42.5*	*33.8*	*17.8*
Round/Oval Mano			
FS 2	7.8	6.8	2.2
FS 44	8.2	7.9	4.8
FS 84	10.4	7.6	6.0
FS 84	15.5	10.5	7.7
FS 84	8.2	7.0	4.9
FS 96	20.1	9.5	7.2
FS 96	15.0	10.5	6.0
FS 96	12.5	11.2	9.1
FS 128	8.4	7.5	6.5
FS 146	9.7	5.9	4.6
FS 211	11.7	9.2	4.5
FS 211	9.1	6.9	4.2
FS 414	9.9	8.6	1.7
Mean	*11.3*	*8.4*	*5.3*
Rectangular Mano			
FS 146	9.0	7.3	3.8
FS 271	24.0	8.9	2.2
FS 285	14.1	8.2	4.1
FS 422	20.8	9.8	2.2
Mean	*17.0*	*8.6*	*3.1*
Handstone			
FS 59	7.0	5.2	4.7
FS 81	9.5	7.5	1.4
FS 96	7.5	6.1	3.2
FS 96	7.0	4.3	3.3
FS 96	6.8	6.2	5.0
FS 96	7.9	5.5	3.7
FS 96	6.0	5.5	2.0
FS 96	10.0	5.6	5.6
FS 200	7.0	6.0	2.5
Mean	*7.6*	*5.8*	*3.5*

granite. The basalt metate had been completely shaped by flaking and pecking to a rough rectangle. Both ends were open, and the trough was deep (11.0 cm), with three distinct mano impressions on the interior of its thin walls. This metate was found on the floor of Feature 3. The granite metate was a large, naturally rounded boulder recovered from the fill of Feature 4. Originally one end was open and the other end was closed, with a shelf; however, the shelf eventually became another open end as the grinding surface extended over it. This metate had a trough depth of 4.9 cm.

Mechanical stripping of fill over Feature 18, an occupation surface, uncovered a double-sided mortar and a pestle. The mortar had been completely shaped by pecking and grinding into a subrectangle measuring 13.5 by 7.6 by 6.1 cm with a shallow, pecked depression centered on either side (Figure 5.2a). One depression measured 4 by 4 cm and was 0.6 cm deep; the other measured 3.5 by 5 cm and was 1.0 cm deep. Both depressions exhibited typical mortar wear. The pestle, 11.1 cm long and 7.7 to 9.5 cm wide, was an unshaped cobble of granite that was naturally wider at one end than the other. Pestle wear was evident on the wide end. The use surfaces of the mortar and the pestle were not the same size, and they probably were not used together.

Hafted tools from the site were one maul, two axes, one indeterminate form, and two indeterminate fragments. The maul, from the fill of Feature 5, was a recycled 3/4-grooved axe of metamorphic material measuring 9.4 by 6.7 by 5.0 cm. The axe appeared to have been worn down and then damaged. Maul/hammerstone wear, exhibited on both ends, was the most recent use.

One of the axes was complete and the other was a fragment. The fragment, from the fill of Feature 4, was the bit end of an axe of indeterminate igneous material. This axe was well made, with production evidence in the form of pecking, grinding, and polishing. Chopping wear was evident on the bit. A complete 3/4-grooved axe of basalt, recovered from the floor of Feature 3, had a bit that had obviously been reshaped after it had been damaged in use. This short axe measured 9.7 by 5.8 by 5.7 cm.

The indeterminate form was a complete hafted tool that had originally been a hand-held grinding tool, as was apparent from grinding use wear and hematite pigment adhesions. The tool had been pecked and ground in preparation for hafting, with a partial groove pecked on one surface. The overall form of the tool suggested that it was an axe blank, but some hammering/battering on the bit end indicated that it may have been used as a maul. It is possible, however, that the battering on the end may have been part of the shaping process. This artifact was made of metamorphic material and was found in the fill of Feature 4.

Both of the hafted tool fragments were 3/4-grooved types. One, probably an axe (Figure 5.2b), was a well-made specimen of greenstone, with a groove and ridges similar to early Ceramic period axes in the Hohokam region (circa A.D. 400–850). This tool was found on the floor of Feature 17. The other fragment, made of igneous material, came from the fill of a midden (Feature 10).

Seven features yielded the 58 tabular tools recovered from AZ N:7:155 (ASM). Thirty-two (55.2 percent) of these tools were made of phyllite; nine were igneous NFS material, eight were quartzite, five were metamorphic NFS rocks, and four were rhyolite. Forty-one (70.7 percent) exhibited evidence of cutting/sawing use on at least one edge, typical of tabular knives that were used for harvesting agave. Two specimens had been reused for different tasks; on one, scraping wear overlapped the cutting/sawing wear, and the other had been reshaped and used as a chopping tool.

Only six tabular tools were complete; most of the rest were small fragments. The complete specimens measured an average of 11.4 by 5.6 by 0.8 cm, with ranges of 5.2 cm to 16.9 cm (length), 4.6 cm to 7.6 cm (width), and 0.4 cm to 2.0 cm (thickness) (Figure 5.3). Two of the complete tabular tools were from Feature 17 (a masonry room), one from floor contact and one from feature fill. The other complete specimens were found in fill contexts in Features 1, 4, 5, and 10.

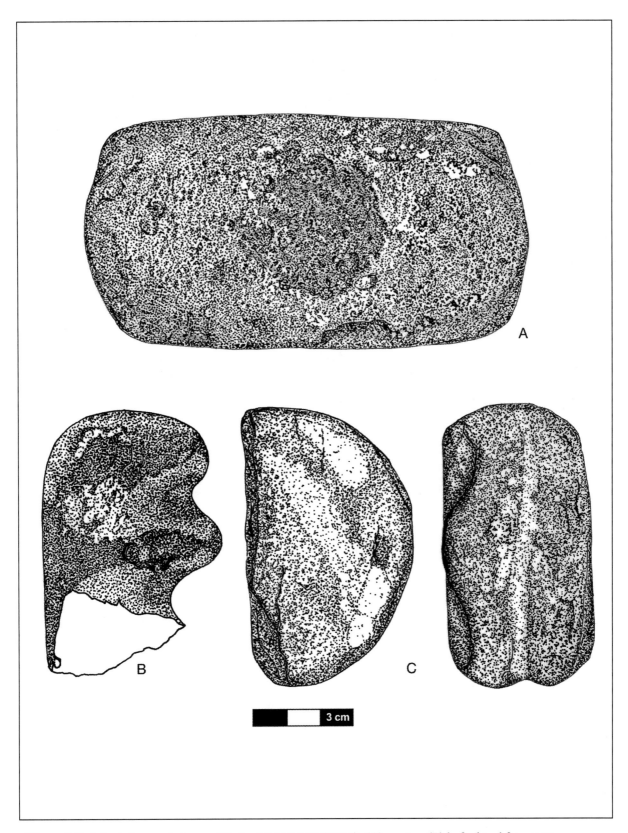

Figure 5.2. Selected ground stone artifacts, AZ N:7:155 (ASM): (A) mortar; (B) hafted tool fragment; (C) grooved handstone.

Dawn M. Greenwald

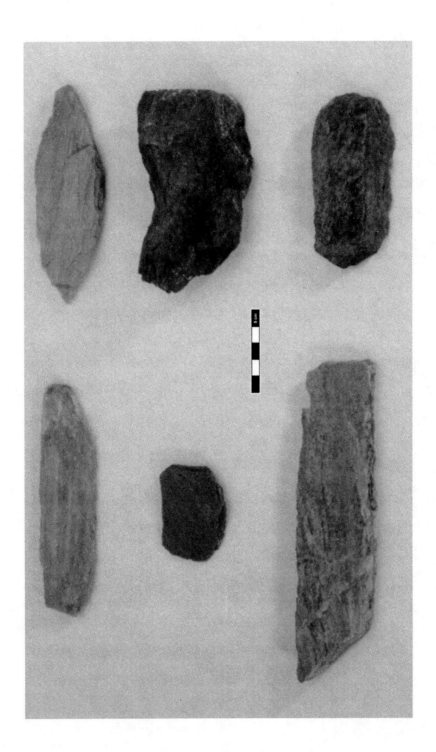

Figure 5.3. Complete tabular tools, AZ N:7:155 (ASM). (5-cm scale)

Thirteen of the 18 tabular tools that were complete enough for evaluation of production investment were well shaped or completely shaped, one was shaped, and four were unmodified. Fifty-four (93 percent) of the 58 tools exhibited traces of manufacturing techniques such as flaking, grinding, or incising, indicating that their preparation involved a fair amount of time and effort.

The 45 mineral specimens recovered from this site were found in structures and middens. Most were raw and unworked (15 azurite, 9 malachite, 6 hematite, 3 azurite and malachite combined, 3 possible arsenopyrite, 1 limonite, 1 indeterminate). Seven pieces of hematite had evidence of grinding/abrading use. Hematite is a widely occurring brownish-red iron oxide. Earthy, ocherous specimens, like those from AZ N:7:155 (ASM), were deposited under sedimentary conditions (Hurlbut 1970:197). Limonite, a natural yellow or brown pigment, is a mixture of hydrous iron oxides that may be produced by the weathering of iron minerals. Malachite and azurite often occur together in the same nodule. Both are copper carbonates, and they are so chemically similar that just a small variation in moisture can cause one to change to the other (Hurlbut 1970:172).

Malachite is green and can occur in spherical aggregates, like most of the pieces found on the site. Azurite, azure blue in color, usually occurs in crystalline form. Three small crystalline minerals that produced a silver-gray streak were tentatively identified as arsenopyrite, an iron ar-senide sulfide (Chesterman 1978:377). Arsenopyrite has a distinct crystalline structure and cleavage and occurs in large masses, by itself or with native gold (Hurlbut 1970:163). The specimens from AZ N:7:155 (ASM) may have been associated with Granite Creek deposits, which are known to contain placer gold (Chronic 1983:168).

Barnett documented hematite, malachite, and azurite at Lonesome Valley Ruin (Barnett 1973:10–15), at Las Vegas Ranch Ruin–East (Barnett 1978:39–40), and in large numbers at Fitzmaurice Ruin (Barnett 1974:55–56). These minerals probably were valued by the prehistoric inhabitants as pigments and were most likely locally available or easily accessible.

Stones that appeared to have been brought to the site, for use in tool making or perhaps as ceramic temper, but that showed no production modification were classified as raw material. Forty-four of these items were phyllite, two were pieces of micaceous quartzite, and one was a piece of granite. Raw material was present in a variety of contexts and represented 12.4 percent of the ground stone assemblage.

Rare or unusual items made up five percent of the assemblage. Six were pieces of worked stone, five were other stones, and four were pieces of slag. The others were a grooved grinder, an abrader, a piece of notched architectural stone, a stone bowl, a stone ball, a figurine, and a pendant.

Worked stones in this analysis were artifacts that exhibited significant production but for which type or function could not be determined. The recovered specimens were two broken pieces of ground argillite with no particular form; three ground fragments of phyllite that might have represented tabular tools, ornaments, or other forms; and one complete, unfinished artifact of granite, possibly a mano blank.

The other stone category consisted of one anvil/grooved abrader that was a recycled mano and four large granite items similar in shape and size but of unknown function. The recycled mano, found in Feature 1, originally had two use surfaces. One surface was flat, with a pitted center; a groove with grinding wear was pecked across the entire width of the opposite surface. The artifact measured 14.5 by 11.6 by 6.8 cm, and the groove was 10.0 cm long, 1 cm wide, and 0.3 cm deep.

The four granite artifacts were more or less oval or circular, with one or both ends flattened or truncated. These items easily stood on their flattened ends and may have been used as trivets or pot rests, but only one specimen had evidence of abrasion on the end opposite the flat surface (Figure 5.4). Seven items with similar descriptions were identified as floor smoothers by Barnett (1974:79), but the specimens from AZ N:7:155 (ASM) showed no evidence of polish or heavy abrasion. They may have served some ceremonial function. Large

Dawn M. Greenwald

Figure 5.4. Similar indeterminate ground stone artifacts, AZ N:7:155 (ASM). (5-cm scale)

and small specimens of shaped stone, rounded or conical in form with a flat surface to rest on, have been described as symbols of gods and goddesses and are associated with kivas and altars in the Zuni and Hopi areas (Adams 1979:96; Morris 1939:129–130; Woodbury 1954:184, 186). The four artifacts from AZ N:7:155 (ASM) were between 13.5 cm and 16.4 cm long, 12.4 cm and 15.8 cm wide, and 9.5 cm and 15.7 cm high. All specimens were recovered from structures: one from floor fill in Feature 2, one from floor fill in Feature 17, and two (similar in size) from Feature 3 fill.

A round grinding stone from Feature 5 fill had a narrow, shallow groove pecked around most of its circumference (Figure 5.2c). Both surfaces were ground, and one had two adjacent small grinding facets along the edge. Barnett (1974:75, Figure 42) illustrated and described similar artifacts from Fitzmaurice Ruin and referred to them as anvils used in ceramic production. However, the specimen from AZ N:7:155 (ASM) showed clear evidence of grinding use, and the small facets on one face suggested grinding of hard, dense material. Grooved grinders, referred to as grooved handstones, have been documented in the Hohokam region (Sayles 1965:Plate 45). At the large Hohokam site of Snaketown, along the Gila River in south-central Arizona, grooved handstones were associated with levels dating to approximately A.D. 850–1050.

A grooved abrader recovered from the fill of Feature 3 was ground on both sides. The specimen was a small, irregular sandstone slab measuring 6.7 by 4.1 by 0.9 cm. A narrow, shallow, roughly U-shaped groove 5.5 cm long and 0.4 cm wide had been ground into one side.

The notched stone, found in the backdirt during mechanical stripping of Feature 18 fill, was a rectangular fragment of sandstone that was well shaped by flaking, pecking, and grinding. A notch 9 cm wide and 2 cm deep on the intact end suggested an architectural function. The stone was 22.7 cm long (incomplete), 18.6 cm wide, and 3.5 cm thick.

The vesicular basalt bowl (Figure 5.5a) was from the fill of Feature 10. The vessel was small and round, with an off-center orifice. It measured 6.5 by 6.2 by 5.0 cm, had an interior diameter of 4.0–4.5 cm, and was 2.1 cm deep. A small portion of the exterior had been discolored by heat.

The stone ball was ovoid rather than spherical, measuring 15.0 by 14.0 by 12.5 cm. It was a natural cobble of porphyritic igneous material, with pecking on only a small portion of the surface, and was very heavy (4000.0 g). Wear patterns indicated that the ball had been rolled; it may have been used for games or sport or as a ceremonial thunderstone (Di Peso et al. 1974:284– 285).

An argillite figurine (Figure 5.5b) recovered from the fill of Feature 4 was a complete specimen but had been damaged by heat and exhibited spalling and discoloration. The head, torso, and legs were discrete. The head area was misshapen from apparent regrinding. The figurine measured 2.1 by 1.0 by 0.6 cm and was completely shaped by grinding and incising.

A complete turquoise pendant (Figure 5.5c) found in the floor fill of Feature 17 was more or less square, with rounded corners, and measured 1.5 by 1.4 by 0.3 cm. The entire artifact was ground and polished, with a biconically drilled perforation.

Four pieces of slag, recovered from Features 4, 5, and 10, were shiny and blistered from heat damage. Material type could not be identified because of alteration by high temperatures.

Small fragments of stone with evidence of grinding or pecking constituted the ground stone NFS category. Because of the fragmentary condition of these specimens, neither function nor form could be identified. The 51 artifacts in this category occurred in many features and represented a number of material types.

AZ N:7:156 (ASM)

The 337 items of flaked stone from AZ N:7:156 (ASM) represented a wide range of tools and core types. All but eight of the 51 artifacts in the ground stone assemblage were various types of grinding equipment, including standardized milling stones (round/oval or rectangular manos and slab or trough metates) and generalized grinders (handstones and a grinding slab).

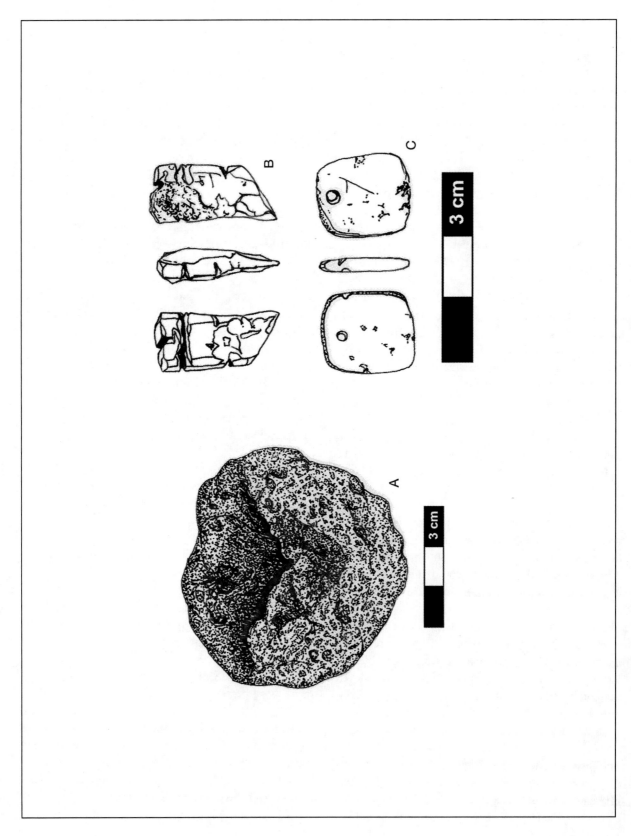

Figure 5.5. Selected ground stone artifacts, AZ N:7:155 (ASM): (A) stone bowl; (B) argillite figurine; (C) turquoise pendant.

The flaked stone assemblage comprised debitage, cores, hammerstones, a cobble tool, and unretouched and retouched flakes, including one projectile point. Although local material types dominated, a substantial number of items were of chert and other nonlocal material such as jasper and obsidian. Most of these microcrystalline materials were in the form of debitage, although some also occurred as cores and flake tools.

Whole flakes and flake fragments occurred in similar numbers. Most of the debitage was in the size 2 category and consisted of flake fragments, suggesting that trampling contributed to flake size and condition. Thus, site use may have been long term or recurring.

Five tertiary flakes identified as used flakes represented five different materials: chert, obsidian, chalcedony, basalt, and igneous NFS. Only one, the chert flake, was complete. Used flakes were generally small (sizes 1–3) and exhibited cutting/sawing wear. One specimen, the basalt flake, had both cutting/sawing and scraping wear.

Ten flaked stone artifacts were cores, two were core tools, and seven were core/hammerstones. Sixteen of these specimens were complete. One core tool had shaving/planing wear and another exhibited chopping wear. Three cores without use wear were basalt, two were igneous NFS material, and there was one specimen each of dacite, quartzite, quartz, chert, and jasper. Core/hammerstones, on the other hand, were restricted to hard, dense igneous materials such as basalt and diorite. Most modified and unmodified cores retained 50 percent or more cortex. The three exceptions were of chert, jasper, and quartz, all non-igneous materials. On 10 specimens core reduction was accomplished with a single platform; multiple, unsymmetrical platforms occurred on six.

All five of the non-flaked hammerstones were of igneous NFS materials. Four were complete specimens.

The retouched tool category (3.3 percent of the flaked stone assemblage) consisted of one cobble uniface, one flake uniface, six flake bifaces, one projectile point, and two indeterminate tools. The quartzite cobble uniface was retouched along less than one-half of its margin and was complete, measuring 7.9 by 6.7 by 3.3 cm, with cut-ting/sawing use wear. The chert flake uniface was incomplete; its intact edges did not show any wear. Four of the six flake bifaces were complete. They were generally poorly thinned, with retouch mostly on the edges. Two flake bifaces were chert, and the others were obsidian, igneous NFS material, phyllite, and orthoquartzite. Complete lengths ranged from 4.5 cm to 6.5 cm, widths from 0.9 cm to 4.7 cm, and thicknesses from 0.5 cm to 2.0 cm. Three of the six flake bifaces exhibited cutting/sawing use wear, one had scraping wear, one had no use wear, and one exhibited an indeterminate type of wear (possibly a combination of scraping, cutting, and drilling) at the worn, rounded junction of two edges. The two indeterminate tools were too fragmentary to determine form or technology; neither exhibited use wear.

The projectile point was oolitic orthoquartzite and had shallow side notches and a straight base (Figure 5.1j). The point was biconvex in cross section, but it was not quite symmetrical and was not well produced. The specimen was complete and measured 2.5 by 1.5 by 0.5 cm. A small impact fracture on the distal tip was evidence of projectile use.

Identifiable manos were almost evenly divided between round/oval (5) and rectangular (6) types; three manos were too fragmentary for type to be determined. Round/oval manos were generally narrower and thicker than rectangular forms (Table 5.12). Since no complete rectangular specimens were in the assemblage, lengths could not be compared, but in samples from other excavations in the region, round/oval manos tend to be shorter than rectangular types (Barnett 1973:Figure 13, 1974:Figures 44 and 45), in line with mano assemblages throughout the Southwest. Both mano categories were of similar materials, such as granite and dense, fine-grained igneous rock, although rectangular mano materials were more diverse and included vesicular basalt and schist. Manos exhibited various degrees of production investment, from none (natural cobble forms) to complete reshaping (by pecking and flaking).

Four of the five round/oval manos had fine-textured surfaces, most of them convex, and four of the six rectangular manos had coarse surfaces, most of them flat. In the Hohokam region, fine-textured round/oval manos

Table 5.12. Dimensional Data for Complete Grinding Implements, AZ N:7:156 (ASM)

Artifact Type/FS No.	Complete Dimensions (cm)		
	Length	Width	Thickness
Slab Metate			
FS 35	38.5	22.6	12.7
FS 53	51.5	30.2	15.0
FS 59	32.4	24.9	16.0
FS 70	44.7	32.0	5.6
FS 71	38.6	28.2	15.8
FS 129	38.5	20.3	12.5
FS 153	41.0	29.0	18.9
FS 154	26.0	31.0	22.4
FS 157	40.4	25.0	11.3
Mean	*39.1*	*27.0*	*14.5*
Round/Oval Mano			
FS 51	9.8	7.1	4.8
FS 54	13.2	12.6	6.8
FS 106	11.6	9.3	5.4
Mean	*11.5*	*9.7*	*5.7*
Rectangular Mano*			
FS 145		9.2	3.1
FS 145		9.6	3.1
FS 78			2.2
FS 150		9.6	3.3
Mean		*9.5*	*2.9*
Handstone			
FS 163	7.2	5.4	3.2
FS 164	9.8	7.0	2.2
FS 160	8.6	5.0	3.1
Mean	*8.5*	*5.8*	*2.8*

*Includes fragments

were used with fine-grained slab and basin metates to grind small seeds such as those from Cheno-ams and grasses. Rectangular manos were used with trough metates; both the manos and the metates had coarse-textured surfaces, and they were used to grind large seeds and buds such as corn and cholla (Greenwald 1990). Prescott Culture manos generally had these same attributes, although with more variation. One of the round/oval manos in the AZ N:7:156 (ASM) assemblage had a coarse-textured surface, one rectangular mano had a fine-textured surface, and another had a medium-grained surface.

Handstones are either irregular in shape or smaller than typical manos and may have been used to grind substances other than food. The four recovered handstones had fine-textured surfaces.

Of the 20 recovered metates and metate fragments, all of granite, 14 were the slab type, three were trough metates, and three were indeterminate. All but eight metates came from the modern ground surface; one slab metate fragment was found in the floor fill of Feature 1, and seven metates were in overburden. Nine of the slab metates were complete, but trough metates were represented only by fragments. Eleven slab metates were unmodified granite boulders that averaged 39 by 27 by 15 cm in size, with fine-textured (6) or medium-textured (5) surfaces. Most exhibited grinding wear over much of the surface, with no wear on the edges and most wear in the central area, often with a slight (0.1–0.5 cm deep) central depression.

A single broken grinding slab was smaller than the metates, measuring 20.2 by 20.3 by 6.3 cm. The wear pattern, however, was similar to that on slab metates: grinding covered most of the surface, but most of the wear, including bidirectional striations, was in the center.

The remainder of the ground stone assemblage from AZ N:7:156 (ASM) consisted of four netherstone fragments, seven indeterminate fragments, and a piece of "slatey" phyllite raw material. A bedrock grinding slick (Feature 9) at the site, measuring 54 cm long by 33 cm wide, was not analyzed.

Conclusions

All of the six Hassayampa project stone artifact assemblages represent occupations by Ceramic period people. Beyond that, one stands out from the rest. Assemblages from five of the sites suggest limited utilitarian activities, mostly resource processing. However, the artifacts from AZ N:7:155 (ASM) indicate long-term, year-round occupation. The occupants used the site for habitation, and both utilitarian and nonutilitarian activities are defined by the artifacts.

AZ N:6:9 (ASM) and AZ N:6:13 (ASM) yielded strong evidence for processing of plant resources: AZ N:6:9 (ASM) had a high frequency of hammerstones, while tabular knives, a metate, and a scraper plane dominated the ground stone tool kit from AZ N:6:13 (ASM), indicating that agave had been processed there. The small number of flaked stone artifacts and the attributes of the debitage at these sites, and at Site AZ N:6:19 (ASM) as well, are characteristic of short-term occupations. At AZ N:6:19 (ASM), plant processing could not be inferred from the stone artifact assemblages alone but was probably a primary activity. Grinding equipment was the only type of ground stone found at this site, and these implements were fine- and medium-grained cobbles, bedrock mortars and grinding slicks, and slab netherstones with little or no production modification. Although the quantity of flaked stone at AZ N:6:19 (ASM) was small, the presence of several large netherstones indicates that the site may have been used repeatedly. However, the high proportion of flaked stone tools relative to debitage suggests short visits with no opportunity for buildup of refuse.

Site AZ N:6:20 (ASM) exhibited evidence of habitation in the form of notched structural support stones and a wide range of artifact types. Although the stone artifact assemblage indicated that food processing was the primary site function, evidence of other activities was also present, such as core reduction (cores and debitage), ceramic production (polishing stones), animal procurement (projectile point), ornamentation/aesthetics (minerals), and agave processing (tabular tools). Rectangular manos and an incipient trough metate suggest that maize was one of the foodstuffs being processed. The small number of artifacts in general, and of special-purpose tools in particular, suggests that the site was not occupied for long or was not occupied year-round.

Evidence from AZ N:7:156 (ASM) indicates long-term occupation and repeated use, from the Archaic period into the Ceramic period. The stone assemblage recovered from the modern ground surface, which included most of the lithic artifacts from the site, appeared to represent two different sets of technological attributes. Most of the surface artifacts were similar to Ceramic period flaked stone from the other sites: microcrystalline materials were limited to white cherts, Perkinsville chert, jasper, chalcedony, and obsidian; biface thinning flakes were absent; and debitage was medium sized. However, part of the surface assemblage included a variety of microcrystalline materials (especially cherts), some biface thinning flakes, and small debitage. The differences indicate an Archaic period bifacial reduction technology and a Ceramic period general core reduction technology. The evidence was mixed on the surface of the site, and discrete loci could not be identified, but the differences were distinctive enough to suggest that the site was used by both Archaic and Ceramic period groups. The large number of complete slab metates (9) found at the site argues for long-term use as well. As eight metates were associated with a masonry room (Feature 1), it seems that the longest site use was during the Ceramic period. The ground stone assemblage from this site suggested primarily wild-plant processing, although some maize grinding was also indicated.

Artifacts from AZ N:7:155 (ASM) represented a myriad of activities, including grinding of wild plants and maize, pottery making, woodworking, timber cutting, agave procurement and processing, ornamentation, core reduction, ground stone and flaked stone tool production, animal procurement, and probably ceremony. Because of the lack of an appropriate typology for this part of the Southwest, the projectile points could not be used to narrow the occupation span for the site. In general terms, the projectile points indicated that the site was occupied during the Ceramic period. The single dart point that was recovered had been reused, probably also during the Ceramic period.

Unfortunately, artifacts that have been used as temporal markers in other regions, notably the Hohokam culture

area, cannot be associated with a particular period in the Prescott area, and establishing such an association would require extensive research with large collections of dated material. The 3/4-grooved and ridged axe from the floor of Feature 17 and the grooved grinder from the fill of Feature 5 are artifact types with restricted spans of use in the Hohokam region (A.D. 400–850 and A.D. 850–1050), but those date ranges may not apply to the Prescott area.

The dominant flaked stone technology exhibited at the six Hassayampa Country Club sites is best described as a generalized core reduction strategy. Tool makers removed flakes from cores in the most expedient way possible, by using natural core geometry to select convenient and appropriate platforms, and produced tools with the least possible effort. The most common tools were large, unmodified flakes. Retouching of flakes and cobbles for tool use involved little edge modification. Few tools were thinned; the exceptions included projectile points, a drill, and a few flake bifaces. Most of the flaked stone was of local materials. Just over 15 percent of the project assemblage was of nonlocal materials, but the small amount of energy expended on tool production suggests that nonlocal materials were relatively easy to acquire during the Ceramic period.

For the most part, ground stone tool technology also reflected expedient behavior. Most artifacts were natural cobbles or slabs without production modification, and most raw materials were locally available. Rectangular manos, hafted implements, tabular knives, and nonutilitarian artifacts were the only items with substantial amounts of energy invested in their manufacture and made of nonlocal materials. Based on data from the Ancestral Puebloan and Hohokam regions, rectangular manos and tabular knives were carefully made because they were used in the processing of two culturally significant food resources, maize and agave. High frequencies of the two tool types at AZ N:7:155 (ASM) confirm the importance of these food items in the prehistoric diet.

Endnote

1. Eight ground stone artifacts from Feature 10 were not made available to the analyst.

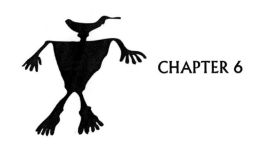

CHAPTER 6

Faunal Remains from Site AZ N:7:155 (ASM)

Dee A. Jones, Richard A. Anduze, John D. Goodman II, and James M. Potter

AZ N:7:155 (ASM) was the only Hassayampa project site to yield faunal remains. The assemblage consisted of 311 bones and bone fragments, nearly two-thirds (63.0 percent) identifiable to order or better. All of the analyzed remains were from midden deposits (Features 4 and 5), with the exception of a bone awl recovered from Feature 6, a burial.

Recovery Techniques and Analytical Methods

The quarter-inch mesh used to screen fill yielded most of the archaeofaunal remains. A small amount of bone material came from burial fill, which was screened through eighth-inch mesh to ensure recovery of very small fragments. As all of the human burials were in midden deposits, and midden soil constituted the fill of the burial pits, the analyzed assemblage included the faunal bone from both burial and non-burial contexts.

Analysis of the faunal material was by standard zooarchaeological methods. Taxonomic identifications were based on comparisons with specimens at the Arizona State University zooarchaeological laboratory, supplemented by literature sources as necessary (Gilbert 1980; Gilbert et al. 1981; McKusick 1976; Olsen 1964, 1968, 1979). Identifications were to the most specific level possible; the abbreviation *cf.* (compares favorably with) followed by the genus and/or species name indicates an approximate identification. Table 6.1 lists the recovered taxa by scientific and common names.

Attributes and conditions recorded for elements identifiable at least to order were species, element, side, degree of epiphyseal fusion, evidence of cooking or butchering, carnivore or rodent gnawing, other modifications, and

number of fragments. Class sizes for unidentifiable mammal and bird remains, based on cortex thickness and bone shape, are shown in Table 6.2.

To quantify faunal assemblages, zooarchaeologists most commonly use the number of identified specimens (NISP) rather than the minimum number of individuals (MNI). Although fragmentation, interdependence of elements, and differential preservation can affect specimen counts, NISP still provides the best estimate of the relative abundance of a given species in an assemblage (Grayson 1984) and is the basis for this analysis (Table 6.1). MNI values are provided in the table for information only.

The Faunal Assemblage

Of the 196 faunal specimens identified to order or better, eight identifications were to genus level and five were to species level: one canid, three lagomorph, three rodent, three artiodactyl, and three bird taxa. The identified remains represented leporids and artiodactyls in nearly equal numbers. The three lagomorph genera—cottontail (*Sylvilagus* sp.), black-tailed jackrabbit (*Lepus californicus*), and antelope jackrabbit (*L. alleni*)—accounted for 80 (40.8 percent) of the identifiable remains and all but one of the lagomorph remains. Fifty-four percent were black-tailed jackrabbit, 27.2 percent were cottontail, and 3.7 percent were antelope jackrabbit. The 79 artiodactyl remains constituted 40.3 percent of the identifiable bone. Deer bones (*Odocoileus* sp.) made up 13.9 percent of the artiodactyl assemblage, pronghorn (*Antilocapra americana*) 3.8 percent, and elk (*Cervus elaphus*) 2.5 percent. Eighty percent of these bones were indeterminate deer, elk, or pronghorn.

Dee A. Jones, Richard A. Anduze, John D. Goodman II, and James M. Potter

Table 6.1. Summary of Faunal Remains, AZ N:7:155 (ASM)

Taxon (Common/Scientific Name)	MNI	NISP	Percent*
Identified Remains			
Mammals (Class Mammalia)			
Carnivores (Order Carnivora)			
Indeterminate carnivore (not canid)		5	
Indeterminate dog/wolf (cf. *Canis* sp.)	1	2	
Total Carnivores		*7*	*3.6*
Lagomorphs (Order Lagomorpha)			
Indeterminate lagomorph (cf. Leporidae)		1	
Cottontail (*Sylvilagus* sp.)	3	22	
Black-tailed jackrabbit (*Lepus californicus*)	4	44	
Leporid (*Sylvilagus* sp. or *Lepus californicus*)		11	
cf. Antelope jackrabbit (*Lepus alleni*)	1	3	
Total Lagomorphs		*81*	*41.3*
Rodents (Order Rodentia)			
Indeterminate rodent (Rodentia)		3	
Indeterminate ground squirrel (Sciuridae)	1	1	
Prairie dog (*Cynomys* sp.)	2	7	
Indeterminate prairie dog (cf. *Cynomys* sp.)		2	
Indeterminate pocket gopher (cf. Geomyidae)		1	
Pocket gopher (*Thomomys* sp.)	2	8	
Wood rat (*Neotoma* sp.)	2	4	
Total Rodents		*26*	*13.3*
Ungulates (Order Artiodactyla)			
Indeterminate deer/elk/pronghorn (Cervidae or Antilocapridae)		27	
Indeterminate deer/pronghorn (*Odocoileus* sp. or *Antilocapra americana*)		36	
Deer (*Odocoileus* sp.)	2	11	
Elk (*Cervus elaphus*)	1	2	
Pronghorn (*Antilocapra americana*)	2	3	
Total Ungulates		*79*	*40.3*
Birds (Class Aves)			
Hawks/Falcons (Order Falconiformes)			
Hawks (*Buteo* sp.)	1	1	
Falcons (*Falco* sp.)		1	
cf. *Falco sparvarius*	1	1	
Total Birds		*3*	*1.5*
Total Identified Remains		**196**	**100.0**

Table 6.1. Summary of Faunal Remains, AZ N:7:155 (ASM), continued

Taxon (Common/Scientific Name)	MNI	NISP	Percent*
Unidentified Remains			
Mammals (Class Mammalia)			
Small		27	23.5
Small-medium		2	1.7
Medium		5	4.3
Medium-large		2	1.7
Large		55	47.8
Indeterminate		16	13.9
Total Mammals		*107*	*93.0*
Birds (Class Aves)			
Small		0	0.0
Small-medium		1	0.9
Medium		6	5.2
Medium-large		0	0.0
Large		0	0.0
Indeterminate		1	0.9
Total Birds		*8*	*7.0*
Total Unidentified Remains		115	100.0
Site Total		311	

MNI=Minimum Number of Individuals
NISP=Number of Identified Specimens
*Percent of total identified or unidentified NISP

Table 6.2. Size Categories for Faunal Remains not Identifiable to Taxon

Size	Mammal	Bird
Small	rabbit or smaller	dove or smaller
Small-medium	between rabbit and canid	between dove and Swainson's hawk
Medium	canid	Swainson's hawk
Medium-large	between canid and deer	between Swainson's hawk and turkey
Large	deer or larger	turkey or larger

The remainder of the identifiable portion of the assemblage consisted of rodent (13.3 percent), indeterminate small carnivore (2.6 percent), bird (1.5 percent), and canid (1.0 percent) remains. Rodent remains were mainly prairie dog (*Cynomys* sp.) (34.6 percent) and pocket gopher (Geomyidae and *Thomomys* sp.) (34.6 percent). Bird taxa represented were hawk (*Buteo* sp.) and falcon (*Falco* sp. and *F. sparvarius*).

Burning

Table 6.3 lists the frequencies of bones exhibiting evidence of burning, including charring and calcination. Jackrabbit is the most common taxon in this category, followed by artiodactyl. The virtual lack of burning on rodent bones suggests that many of these specimens represented post-abandonment intrusion. The lack of burning associated with identifiable bird bones suggests a non-subsistence use for these species.

Modified Bone

Thirteen recovered fragments were worked bone, including awls (Table 6.4). A bone hairpin or awl (Figure 6.1) recovered from Feature 6, an inhumation, was fashioned from a split artiodactyl metapodial; portions of the vascular groove had not been ground away. This specimen was 9.7 cm long and 1.1 cm wide on the proximal end. All edges of the piece except the proximal end exhibited grinding striations and shaping. This artifact was yellowish and may have been slightly affected by fire.

Summary and Conclusions

Given the small size of the faunal assemblage, drawing any substantial conclusions about Prescott Culture subsistence from these remains is difficult. However, several patterns in the data suggest some interesting possibilities. The first is the predominance of large game in the assemblage, especially artiodactyls, contrary to the pattern observed in most sites south of the project area (e.g., in the Phoenix Basin), as well as sites in the mountainous region to the north, such as Elden Pueblo (Quirt-Booth and Cruz-Uribe 1997) and the Starlight Pines site (Potter 1999). Furthermore, the assemblage represents a fairly diverse suite of artiodactyl species, including mule deer, pronghorn, and elk. The high relative frequency and diversity of artiodactyl remains may relate to the proximity of the Hassayampa project area to multiple environmental zones, including the open grasslands preferred by pronghorn and the mountainous regions preferred by elk and deer. It is also likely that the sites are close to seasonal game trails, and their location in prime artiodactyl-hunting territory certainly would have encouraged long-term occupation, as at AZ N:7:155 (ASM).

Another interesting pattern to emerge from the analysis is the high frequency of jackrabbits relative to cottontails. This pattern suggests an open, sparsely vegetated environment, due to either intensive clearing for agriculture or natural environmental factors. A greater abundance of jackrabbit remains also suggests the possibility of communal hunting as a technique for acquiring small game. Unlike cottontail rabbits, which hide and burrow when chased, jackrabbits attempt to outrun predators, making communal hunting with nets particularly effective for procuring these animals.

Among remains from identifiable species, jackrabbit and artiodactyl bones exhibited the highest incidence of burning. These were also the most common species in the assemblage, accounting for about 70 percent of the identifiable specimens, and are good sources of bone marrow. Post-depositional midden burning or the incidental burning of bones in hearths should be more evenly distributed among species. Heating bones, especially from large mammals, is a common means of facilitating breakage for the extraction of marrow and grease (Potter 1995). The paucity of burning evident on rodent and cottontail remains suggests either that these animals were intrusive or that they were not exploited for marrow and grease because of their small size.

The lack of burning associated with wild-bird remains suggests a non-subsistence use for these animals. Their feathers, especially those of raptors such as hawks and falcons, may have been used in ritual paraphernalia, a common practice among historical Puebloan groups (Potter 1997).

Table 6.3. Burning Pattern, Faunal Remains from AZ N:7:155 (ASM)

Taxon	Unburned	Burned	Total	Percent Burned
Identified Remains				
Indeterminate carnivore	5	0	5	0.0
cf. dog/wolf	2	0	2	0.0
Indeterminate leporid	1	0	1	0.0
Cottontail	21	1	22	4.5
Jackrabbit	36	8	44	18.2
Cottontail or Jackrabbit	8	3	11	27.3
Antelope jackrabbit	3	0	3	0.0
Indeterminate rodent	2	1	3	33.3
Indeterminate squirrel	1	0	1	0.0
Prairie dog	9	0	9	0.0
Pocket gopher	9	0	9	0.0
Woodrat	4	0	4	0.0
Indeterminate ungulate	14	13	27	48.1
Indeterminate deer/pronghorn	27	9	36	25.0
Deer	11	0	1	0.0
Elk	2	0	2	0.0
Pronghorn	2	1	3	33.3
Hawk	1	0	1	0.0
Falcon	2	0	2	0.0
Total Identified Remains	*160*	*36*	*196*	*18.4*
Unidentified Remains				
Small mammal	11	16	27	59.3
Small-medium mammal	2	0	2	0.0
Medium mammal	5	0	5	0.0
Medium-large mammal	1	1	2	50.0
Large mammal	41	14	55	25.5
Indeterminate mammal	14	2	16	12.5
Small-medium bird	1	0	1	0.0
Medium bird	4	2	6	33.3
Indeterminate bird	1	0	1	0.0
Total Unidentified Remains	*80*	*35*	*115*	*30.4*
Site Total	**240**	**71**	**311**	**22.8**

Table 6.4. Modified Bone, AZ N:7:155 (ASM)

Feature	Specimen	Dimensions (mm)		Comments	Count
		Length	Width		
4	awl fragment	102.0	14.5	artiodactyl long-bone sliver, proximal portion	1
4	awl fragment?	42.0	7.0	lateral fragment? fire-affected, high polish	1
4	awl distal tip	33.0	7.5	artiodactyl metapodial fragment, calcined	1
4	half of bead?	11.0	7.0	lagomorph? fire-affected, central incised cut	1
4	awl medial fragment	61.5	14.5	indeterminate large-mammal bone	1
4	bone bead	15.5	6.0	lagomorph tibia? fire-affected	1
5	possible hairpin fragments	27.0 21.0	5.5 4.8	indeterminate large-mammal bone, rectangular, high polish, fire-affected	2
5	awl fragments	42.5 36.5	8.5 10.0	artiodactyl long-bone sliver, tip and mid-tip of one awl	2
5	half of tube bead	52.0	19.5	indeterminate large-mammal bone, tapered cut ends, high polish, fire-affected	1
6	hairpin or awl	97.0	11.0	split artiodactyl metapodial	1
?	bone tube fragment	22.0	16.0	indeterminate large-mammal bone, high polish, fire-affected	1
Total					**13**

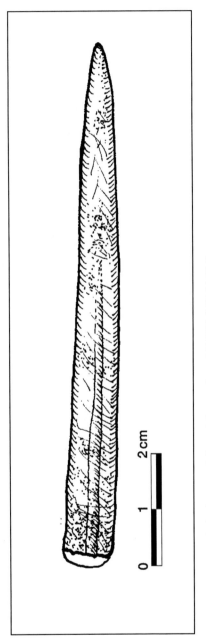

Figure 6.1. Bone hairpin or awl from inhumation, AZ N:7:155 (ASM).

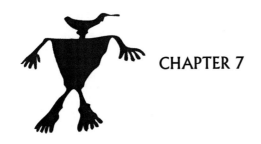

CHAPTER 7

Shell Artifacts

John D. Goodman II

The Hassayampa project shell assemblage consisted of 17 shells or shell fragments, all but one from AZ N:7:155 (ASM). All specimens were marine shell taxa that occur along the Pacific Coast of Southern California and in the Gulf of Mexico. The analysis included taxonomic identification, documentation of the presence or absence of cultural modifications, and classification of modified specimens, based on the typology originally developed by Haury (1937b) for the Snaketown material, as Prescott Culture sites have not yielded much shell.

Findings

Of the 16 marine shells or shell fragments collected from AZ N:7:155 (ASM), field personnel recovered nine specimens from three middens near the central habitation area and seven from three inhumations (Table 7.1). The shell from the middens consisted of three *Glycymeris* sp. bracelet fragments, three *Laevicardium elatum* valve pieces, one *Argopecten circularis* valve fragment, one indeterminate bivalve fragment, and one univalve piece from a large gastropod (probably *Strombus galeatus*). The shell specimens found with the inhumations were four small *Glycymeris* sp. valves with umbo-hole perforations, possibly for stringing as beads or pendants (Figure 7.1a), one *Glycymeris* sp. bracelet fragment (Figure 7.1b), and two indeterminate gastropod fragments (probably *Strombus galeatus*) (Figure 7.1c).

Five shell specimens, the greatest number from a single area of the site, came from Feature 4, a midden in the eastern portion of the site. One *Glycymeris* sp. bracelet

Table 7.1. Summary of Shell Artifacts, AZ N:7:155 (ASM)

Feature	Feature Type	Taxon/Specimen	Count
4	midden in eastern site area	*Glycymeris* sp. bracelet fragments, fire-affected	2
		Laevicardium elatum valve piece, worn, fire-affected	1
		Argopecten circularis valve fragment, fire-affected	1
		Indeterminate* bivalve fragment, fire-affected	1
5	midden in northern site area	*Glycymeris* sp. bracelet piece, gracile, fire-affected *Laevicardium*	1
		elatum fragment, fire-affected indeterminate univalve piece	1
		(*Strombus galeatus*?), fire-affected	1
7	inhumation in Feature 5	indeterminate univalve pieces (*Strombus galeatus*?), fire-affected	2
10	midden in northern site area	*Laevicardium elatum* fragment, worn and chalky	1
13	inhumation in Feature 4	*Glycymeris* sp. pendants/beads, small valves with holes	4
15	inhumation in Feature 4	*Glycymeris* sp. bracelet fragment, not fire-affected	1
Total			**16**

*Not taxonomically identifiable

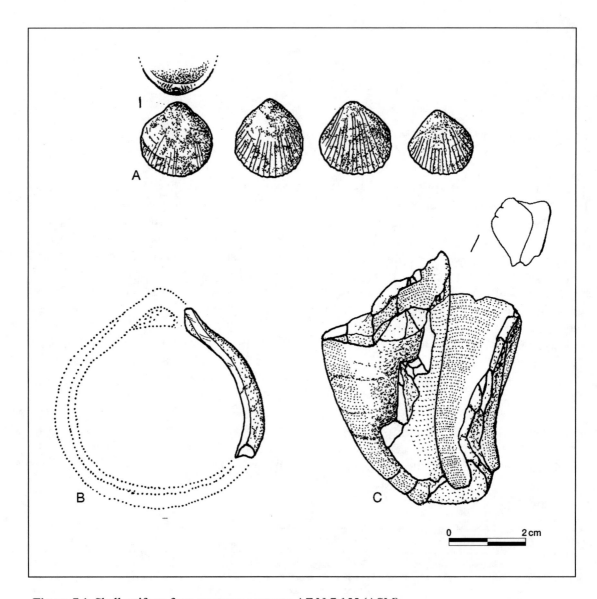

Figure 7.1. Shell artifacts from mortuary contexts, AZ N:7:155 (ASM).

fragment and one piece of *Argopecten circularis* were recovered from mechanically stripped fill. The *Glycymeris* sp. bracelet fragment was a split anterior margin piece with two remaining ground sides (two other sides/ facets were missing) and portions of a ventral muscle scar. The original morphology of this fragment could not be discerned. This specimen was cracked and fire-affected. The *Argopecten circularis* piece, also recovered from the mechanically stripped area, was a small posterior margin fragment that was worn and fire-affected. One *Glycymeris* sp. bracelet fragment (lateral margin) and one *Laevicardium elatum* piece were found in a control unit. The robust *Glycymeris* sp. bracelet fragment was fire-affected and ground on four sides. The *Laevicardium elatum* piece was a fire-affected central valve fragment, very worn and chalky. The fifth specimen from Feature 4, a small indeterminate bivalve fragment, was also retrieved from a control unit. This fire-affected specimen was a small central valve portion that could not be identified to genus.

Three shell specimens came from Feature 5, a midden in the northern portion of the site: one *Glycymeris* sp. bracelet fragment, one *Laevicardium elatum* piece, and one indeterminate univalve fragment. The fire-affected bracelet fragment was a fairly gracile lateral margin piece with three ground sides. A fire-affected indeterminate univalve fragment from the same control unit was a portion of a body whorl from a large gastropod (perhaps *Strombus galeatus*). A small, fire-affected *Laevicardium elatum* fragment from the midden fill around Feature 11, an inhumation, was a piece of a central valve.

Another *Laevicardium elatum* valve fragment was collected from a control unit in Feature 10, a midden in the southern area of the site. This specimen, a small central valve fragment, was very worn and chalky.

The three inhumations that contained shell specimens were in middens. Feature 7, within Feature 5, yielded two large indeterminate univalve fragments that probably were *Strombus galeatus*. These two recovered shell fragments were lower-end "conch" pieces with canals, outer lips, and columellae portions. Both of the specimens were burned and cracked and generally in poor condition. Feature 13, an inhumation in Feature 4, yielded four complete valves (beads?) of *Glycymeris* sp., possibly *G. maculata*. These valves were close together near the pelvic region of the interred individual

and may have been from a waist band or perhaps a wrist bracelet. All of these valves were weathered and had ground umbo perforation holes. A *Glycymeris* sp. bracelet fragment from Feature 15, another inhumation in Feature 4, was a relatively gracile upper margin piece with four ground edges, and portions of the posterior muscle scar on the ventral side.

A single shell artifact recovered from the surface of AZ N:6:14 (ASM), a historical site (Anduze et al. 1999), was a *Chione fluctifraga* valve fragment with the umbo and surrounding anterior margin portion. As this old, weathered valve was the only shell recovered from a historical context, it may have been scavenged from one of the nearby prehistoric sites.

Discussion

The shell specimens recovered from AZ N:7:155 (ASM) were similar to shell jewelry items recovered from other Prescott Culture sites in the general region. Shell jewelry is abundant on Hohokam sites and appears to have been an integral part of Hohokam material life. It is unfortunate that the pieces of *Glycymeris* sp. bracelets were too fragmentary to identify specific design types. The general lack of carving or ornateness suggests that they may have been contemporary with later Hohokam bracelet forms, which generally are uncarved.

At least two large gastropod shells, probably *Strombus galeatus*, were found at AZ N:7:155 (ASM). Barnett (1973b:109) documented the recovery of shells from numerous large gastropods such as *S. galeatus* from a number of Southwest sites and noted that prehistoric craftsmen sometimes abraded the apex of these shells to manufacture shell trumpets. According to Haury (1937b), shell trumpets generally occur in association with Classic period Hohokam sites or horizons.

The shell assemblage from the Hassayampa project supplements the small but growing database on Prescott Culture shell artifacts. Barnett recovered a single shell pendant (*Noetia ponderosa*) with a perforated umbo hole from Lonesome Valley Ruin (Barnett 1973a:16) and three shell pieces (indeterminate bivalve fragments) from Fitzmaurice Ruin (Barnett 1975:7). Two of the valve pieces had been abraded through the umbo to make holes for stringing as pendants or beads.

CHAPTER 8

Pollen and Macrofloral Analyses

Linda Scott Cummings, Kathryn Puseman, and Thomas E. Moutoux

PaleoResearch Laboratories analyzed pollen and macro-botanical remains from three prehistoric sites (AZ N:6:20, AZ N:7:155, and AZ N:7:156 [ASM]) and one historical site (AZ N:6:14 [ASM]) in the Hassayampa project area. This chapter, describing the prehistoric sites, has been condensed from the original report; for detailed methods, an ethnobotanic overview of utilized species, and the analysis of botanical remains from the historical site, please see Cummings et al. 1999.

Methods

A chemical extraction technique based on flotation is the standard procedure used in the PaleoResearch laboratory for the removal of pollen grains from the large volume of sand, silt, and clay with which they are mixed. The process was developed for extraction of pollen from soils where preservation has been less than ideal and pollen density is low. Sample preparation involves removal of calcium carbonates, clay, and other inorganic particles from the soil, and recovery of starch granules. A pollen wash from a metate, submitted by SWCA, was processed in a similar manner.

The pollen counts, made by light microscope at a magnification of 400–600X, include starch granules, pollen aggregates (clumps of a single type of pollen counted as single grains), and indeterminate pollen (pollen grains that are folded, mutilated, or otherwise distorted beyond recognition) but not pollen noted outside the regular count while scanning the remainder of the microscope slide. Comparative reference materials collected at the Intermountain Herbarium at Utah State University and the University of Colorado Herbarium were used to identify the pollen to the most specific level possible. Total counts per sample ranged from 7 to 203 pollen

grains. Only two samples yielded fewer than 75 grains, and percentages were not calculated for these samples. Pollen preservation in the samples varied from good to poor.

The flotation technique used for the macrofloral samples was a modification of procedures outlined by Matthews (1979). Identification of recovered remains was based on manuals (Martin and Barkley 1973; Musil 1978; Schopmeyer 1974) and comparison with modern and archaeological references. Larger charcoal pieces were separated from the rest of the light fraction and a representative sample was broken to expose fresh cross sections. Both the remainder of the light fraction and the charcoal were weighed and examined microscopically. The analysis also included examination of the coarse or heavy fractions. Estimates of frequencies were calculated from the sort of a portion of the total volume floated. The term *seed* is used for seeds, achenes, caryopses, and other disseminules. Remains from the light and heavy fractions were combined and recorded as charred or uncharred, whole or fragments. In accordance with the accepted standard for prehistoric sites, only charred seeds were considered in interpreting features and resource use (Minnis 1981). Some remains were identified as PET (processed edible tissue). This term, coined by Nancy Stenholm (1994), refers to soft tissue types such as starchy parenchymoid or fruity epithelial tissues. PET fruity tissues resemble sugar-laden fruit or berry tissue without the seeds.

Tables 8.1 and 8.2 list, by both scientific and common names, all taxa identified in pollen samples or as macrobotanical remains. Pollen and macrobotanical counts by site and feature are provided in Appendix C.

Table 8.1. Pollen Types Observed in Samples from AZ N:6:20 (ASM), AZ N:7:155 (ASM), and AZ N:7:156 (ASM)

Scientific Name	Common Name
Arboreal Pollen	
Fraxinus	ash
Juglans	walnut
Juniperus	juniper
Pinus	pine
Quercus	oak
Salix	willow
Ulmus	elm
Nonarboreal Pollen	
cf. *Abronia*	sand verbena
Apiaceae	parsley/carrot family
Asteraceae	sunflower family
Artemisia	sagebrush
High-spine	includes aster, rabbitbrush, snakeweed, sunflower, etc.
Low-spine	includes ragweed, cocklebur, etc.
Liguliflorae	includes dandelion and chicory
Brassicaceae	mustard family
Cheno-ams	includes amaranth and pigweed family
Cylindropuntia	cholla cactus
Cyperaceae	sedge family
Dodonaea	hopbush
Ephedra nevadensis-type	Mormon tea
Ephedra torreyana-type	Mormon tea
Ericaceae	heath family
Eriogonum	wild buckwheat
Erodium	heron-bill
Euphorbia	spurge
Fabaceae	bean or legume family
Lotus	birdfoot trefoil
Geraniaceae	geranium family
Kallstroemia	kallstroemia
Liliaceae	lily family
Brodiaea (*Dichelostemma*)	brodiaea, wild onion, wild hyacinth, bluedicks, covena, grass nuts
Malva	mallow

Table 8.1. Pollen Types Observed in Samples from AZ N:6:20 (ASM), AZ N:7:155 (ASM), and AZ N:7:156 (ASM), continued

Scientific Name	Common Name
Nyctaginaceae	four o'clock family
Mirabilis-type	four o'clock
Onagraceae	evening primrose family
Opuntia	prickly pear cactus
Poaceae	grass family
Polygonum sawatchense-type	sawatch knotweed
Portulaca	purslane
Rhamnaceae	buckthorn family
Rosaceae	rose family
Cercocarpus	mountain mahogany
cf. *Rosa woodsii*	wild rose
Sphaeralcea	globemallow
Typha angustifolia-type	cattail
Typha latifolia-type	cattail
Cultigens	
Cucurbita	squash, pumpkin, gourd
Zea mays	maize, corn
Starches	
Angular starch with hilum	
Dot starch	
Hollow starch	
Hordeum-type starch	little barley–type starch
Starch with hilum	
Zea-type starch	maize-type starch
Spores	
Selaginella	clubmoss
Sporormiella	
Thecaphora	
Trilete	
Other	
Asteraceae plate	sunflower family
Nicotiana seed epidermis	tobacco

Table 8.2. Macrofloral Remains Recovered from AZ N:6:20 (ASM), AZ N:7:155 (ASM), and AZ N:7:156 (ASM)

Scientific Name	Common Name
Floral Remains	
cf. *Agave*	agave
Alnus	alder
Arctostaphylos	manzanita, kinnikinnick
Asteraceae	sunflower family
Ambrosia	ragweed
Astragalus	milkvetch, rattleweed, locoweed
Brassicaceae	mustard family
Lepidium	pepperweed
Calandrinia	rock purslane, red maids
Celtis	hackberry
Cheno-am	includes goosefoot and amaranth families
Atriplex	saltbush
Chenopodium	goosefoot
Cleome	beeweed
Convolvulus	bindweed
Euphorbia	spurge
Juglans	walnut
Juniperus	juniper
Lamiaceae	mint family
Malva	mallow, cheeseweed
Mollugo	carpetweed
Oenothera	evening primrose, sundrops
Opuntia	prickly pear cactus
Phaseolus	common bean
Physalis	tomatillo, groundcherry
Pinus	pine
P. monophylla	piñon pine
P. ponderosa	ponderosa pine
Poaceae	grass family
Bouteloua	grama grass
Festuca	fescue
Sporobolus	dropseed
Polygonum	smartweed, knotweed

Table 8.2. Macrofloral Remains Recovered from AZ N:6:20 (ASM),
AZ N:7:155 (ASM), and AZ N:7:156 (ASM), continued

Scientific Name	Common Name
Portulaca	purslane
Prunus	cherry, plum
Quercus	oak
Sesuvium	sea purslane
Trifolium	clover
Vitis	grape
Zea mays	maize, corn
Charcoal/Wood	
Cercocarpus	mountain mahogany
Cowania	cliffrose
Juniperus	juniper
Pinus	pine
P. ponderosa	ponderosa pine
Prunus	plum/cherry, including chokecherry
Quercus	oak

Results

AZ N:6:20 (ASM)

Feature 1

Feature 1 was a large pit structure with an intrusive room (Feature 9) at its southwest end; both structures were outlined with upright granite stones. Pollen Sample 106 and Flotation Sample 107 were collected from floor contact adjacent to one of the tabular stones in the southwest quadrant of Feature 1.

Quercus pollen, accompanied by a few aggregates ranging in size from small to an anther fragment, dominated Sample 106. Moderately small to small quantities of *Juniperus*, *Pinus*, *Artemisia*, Low-spine and High-spine Asteraceae, Cheno-am, *Ephedra nevadensis*-type, *Erodium*, *Kallstroemia*, *Mirabilis*-type, Poaceae, Rosaceae (scabrate), and *Zea mays* pollen were present as well. At the time of occupation the local woodland appears to have been dominated by oak, with some juniper and pine. Local shrubby and herbaceous vegetation

appears to have included sagebrush, other members of the sunflower family, Cheno-ams, kallstroemia, four o'clock, and a member of the rose family. The heron-bill pollen may represent a native species or a species that was introduced into this sample through bioturbation. Grasses also were present. The only pollen that appears to represent economic activity in this pit structure is a small quantity of maize pollen recorded in the scan. An angular starch with hilum was also noted; these starch granules occur in maize but are not diagnostic. Small quantities of trilete spores, Asteraceae plates, and tobacco seed-coat fragments were present. Unburned tobacco seed coats probably represent relatively modern seeds that had been moved through the sediments through bioturbation.

Sample 107 contained a charred monocot stem fragment and moderate amounts of *Cercocarpus* and *Quercus* charcoal. Numerous uncharred seeds, insect fragments, rodent feces, and worm castings suggest significant disturbance from bioturbation. A single pottery fragment was in the sample.

Feature 2

Pollen Sample 89 and Flotation Sample 92 represent Level 2 of the control unit in Feature 2, a midden area northeast of Feature 1. Sample 89 was generally similar to the pollen samples from Features 1 and 9. This sample yielded nearly identical quantities of *Quercus*, *Artemisia*, and Cheno-am pollen and a few small Cheno-am aggregates. The Poaceae pollen frequency was high and accompanied by a few small aggregates. A small quantity of *Portulaca* pollen was present in the scan. *Zea mays* pollen was recovered, but not starch granules. The pollen record from this midden area indicates the possibility that Cheno-ams and purslane grew on the midden.

Sample 92 contained two charred *Arctostaphylos* seed fragments and a charred PET fragment, possibly represent use of manzanita berries or other fleshy fruit/berry resources or succulent plant remains such as cactus pads. Charred *Atriplex* seeds and seed fragments suggest use of saltbush seeds, perhaps to add a salty flavor to foods. Charred *Zea mays* cupules and cupule fragments may represent processing of maize and/or use of corn cobs as fuel. *Quercus* dominated the charcoal record; a few pieces of *Cercocarpus*, *Juniperus*, and *Pinus ponderosa* charcoal were also present.

Feature 3

Feature 3 was another midden, southwest of Feature 1. Pollen Sample 63 and Flotation Sample 64 were composite samples from Level 2 fill at the bottom of Unit 1 in the southeast corner of the midden. *Quercus* pollen dominated Sample 63. The Cheno-am frequency was not as large as in Feature 2, and no aggregates were present. The sample contained small quantities of *Opuntia* and Rosaceae (scabrate) pollen. In other ways the pollen record is similar to the record from Feature 2 and probably represents local natural vegetation.

Charred remains in Sample 64 were a *Juniperus* seed and a *Zea mays* cupule fragment. Uncharred seeds represent a variety of modern plants. The sample also contained pieces of *Quercus*, *Pinus*, and *Cercocarpus* charcoal, as well as a calcined bone fragment, insect remains, a moderate quantity of rodent feces, and numerous worm castings.

Feature 9

Pollen Sample 111 and Flotation Sample 109 were collected from floor contact in the northeast corner of Feature 9, the later room that intruded the southern portion of Feature 1. Like the pollen sample from Feature 1, Sample 111 was dominated by *Quercus* pollen accompanied by a few small aggregates. Other elements of the pollen record also were similar to those noted in Feature 1, with a few exceptions. Sample 111 contained small quantities of Cyperaceae, *Eriogonum*, and Rosaceae (psilate) pollen, which may represent natural vegetation. A small quantity of *Zea mays* pollen recorded during the scan of this sample probably represents processing/ storage of maize in this room. Small quantities of *Hordeum*-type starch and *Zea*-type starch granules were present as well, further suggesting processing of maize, as well as seeds from plants such as little barley grass.

Sample 109 contained a charred *Zea mays* cupule fragment and a charred monocot stem fragment. The maize cupule may represent shelled cobs that were burned as fuel. *Quercus* dominated the charcoal from this feature, with *Cercocarpus* and *Juniperus* charcoal present in lesser amounts. Uncharred seeds, insect fragments, and numerous rodent fecal pellets and worm castings reflect bioturbation in this area.

AZ N:7:155 (ASM)

Feature 2

Feature 2 was a subrectangular pit structure near the center of the site, northeast of the room block, with two occupation surfaces. Pollen Sample 184 and Flotation Samples 182 and 186 were collected from hearths in this feature.

Subfeature 2.01 was a circular hearth in the lower floor near the center of the structure. Sample 184, from fill in the western half of the hearth, yielded nearly equal quantities of *Pinus*, *Quercus*, and Low-spine and High-spine Asteraceae pollen. Small quantities of *Fraxinus*, *Artemisia*, Liguliflorae, Cheno-am, Cyperaceae, *Euphorbia*, and Poaceae pollen probably represent natural vegetation. Small quantities of *Opuntia* and *Zea mays* pollen likely represent processing of prickly pear cactus and maize in or near this hearth. A small quantity of starch granules with hila suggest processing of either maize or grass seeds.

Sample 182, also from the fill of Subfeature 2.01, contained a charred *Polygonum* seed fragment and charred *Zea mays* cupule and kernel fragments. Uncharred *Pinus ponderosa* needles and needle fragments represent modern ponderosa pine trees. A moderate amount of *Quercus* charcoal was also present.

Subfeature 2.02 was an unprepared hearth in the east-central portion of the pit structure, apparently associated with a later floor. Sample 186, taken from the hearth fill, contained two charred *Juglans* nutshell fragments, suggesting use of walnuts. Uncharred remains again represent modern plants. No charcoal pieces were large enough to be identified. Some insect fragments were in the sample.

Feature 3

Feature 3 was a rectangular pit structure with a clay floor and evidence of burning, northwest of the room block. Samples from this feature were associated with a metate found on the floor in the northeast corner of the structure.

Sample 540, from a wash of the metate, did not yield sufficient pollen for analysis. Pollen types observed were consistent with taxa identified in other samples from this site. Other than Cheno-ams and grasses, there was no hint of plants that may have been processed on this metate.

Sample 541, representing floor contact around the metate, contained a charred *Zea mays* cupule, a cupule fragment, and kernel fragments that indicate use of maize in the structure and perhaps processing of maize on the metate. Other economic remains were charred *Pinus*-type bark scale fragments, *P. ponderosa* charcoal, and smaller amounts of *Cercocarpus*, *Cowania*, and *Quercus* charcoal.

Feature 4

Feature 4 was a midden area on the east side of the site. Pollen Samples 336, 348, 383, and 438 and Flotation Samples 335, 347, 382, and 439 represent four levels of fill from a unit placed near the center of the midden area. The midden contained three primary inhumations, none of them in the excavation unit.

Most of the pollen noted in Sample 336 from Level 1, the top excavation level, was similar to pollen from other features at this site. *Quercus* pollen accompanied by a few small aggregates dominated the sample. Notable pollen types or frequencies include a relatively high Cheno-am count with a few small aggregates, as well as small quantities of *Cylindropuntia*, *Cucurbita*, and *Zea mays* pollen. *Dodonaea* pollen indicates the presence of hopbush. Dot starch and starch granules with hila recorded in this sample are forms that occur primarily in grass seeds and maize.

Charred remains from Sample 335 were a *Juglans* nutshell fragment, a *Zea mays* cupule fragment, and an unidentified seed fragment, possibly representing use of these resources and processing activities. Numerous uncharred plant remains represent modern plants at the site. The only charcoal was a few pieces of *Pinus*. Uncharred and calcined bone fragments, as well as charred and uncharred rodent tooth fragments, suggest processing/discard of animal remains. Other non-botanic remains in this sample were insect fragments, snails, and worm castings.

Sample 348 from Level 2 yielded an elevated Cheno-am pollen frequency accompanied by a few small aggregates. Other pollen types of note in this sample are small quantities of *Cylindropuntia*, Rosaceae (scabrate), and *Zea mays* pollen, the latter accompanied by a few small aggregates. These pollen types probably represent both remains discarded in the midden and the growth of weedy Cheno-ams.

Sample 347 contained a charred Cheno-am embryo and charred *Chenopodium* seed fragments. Other charred remains were *Arctostaphylos* seeds and seed fragments,

Juglans nutshell fragments, a *Juniperus* seed, *Vitis* seeds and seed fragments, and *Zea mays* cupules, cupule fragments, and kernel fragments. *Quercus* dominated the charcoal, with *Juniperus*, *Pinus ponderosa*, and *Prunus* charcoal present in smaller amounts. A canine tooth and charred, calcined, and uncharred bone fragments suggest use of faunal resources. Few insect fragments or worm castings were present in this sample.

Sample 383 from Level 3 displayed an elevated Cheno-am pollen frequency accompanied by a few small aggregates. The sample also included small quantities of *Cylindropuntia* pollen accompanied by a few small aggregates, *Dodonaea* pollen accompanied by a single small aggregate, *Portulaca* and Rosaceae (scabrate pollen), and an elevated *Zea mays* pollen frequency accompanied by a few small aggregates. This portion of the midden appears to have been used to discard a variety of plant remains, and Cheno-ams may have grown here as weedy plants.

Charred remains in Sample 382 included *Arctostaphylos* seeds and seed fragments, Cheno-am embryos, a *Chenopodium* seed, a *Cleome* seed, *Juglans* nutshell fragments, an *Opuntia* seed, and *Zea mays* cupules, cupule fragments, and kernel fragments. *Quercus* dominated the charcoal sample, which also contained moderate amounts of *Pinus ponderosa* charcoal and smaller amounts of *Cercocarpus*, *Cowania*, and *Pinus*. Unidentifiable vitrified charcoal, which has a glassy appearance caused by fusion, was also present. Non-botanic remains included charred and uncharred bone, calcined bone fragments, animal tooth fragments, insect remains, rodent fecal pellets, and snails.

Sample 438, from Level 4 fill of the midden, exhibited an elevated Cheno-am frequency and a few Cheno-am aggregates ranging in size from small to anther fragments. Small quantities of *Cylindropuntia*, *Cercocarpus*, *Rosa woodsii*, *Typha angustifolia*-type, and *Typha latifolia*-type pollen were observed. The *Zea mays* pollen frequency was elevated and included a few small aggregates. No starch granules were recorded. This area of the midden appears to have been used to discard the remains of a variety of plants.

Charred remains in Sample 439 from Level 4 included a possible *Agave* epidermis fragment, a *Physalis* seed, and a *Portulaca* seed. Charred *Pinus*-type bark scale fragments most likely represent use of pine wood as fuel. Other charred remains in this sample were typical of those found in the upper levels of fill and included *Arctostaphylos* seeds and seed fragments, a *Chenopodium* seed, four *Juglans* nutshell fragments, and *Zea mays* cupules, cupule fragments, and kernel fragments. A few uncharred plant remains represent modern plants. This lower level of fill yielded charcoal representing *Arctostaphylos*, *Cercocarpus*, *Pinus ponderosa*, and *Quercus*, as well as unidentifiable vitrified charcoal.

The samples from Feature 4 all displayed elevated Cheno-am pollen frequencies accompanied by aggregates of varying sizes. It is likely that weedy plants of this group grew in the midden areas, providing a concentrated and easily procured resource. Processed Cheno-am remains may have been discarded in the midden as well. Other plants in the pollen record that may represent discarded remains included cholla, hopsage, purslane, members of the rose family, cattail, maize, and possibly grasses.

The macrofloral record from Feature 4 includes charred evidence for the use of a variety of plant resources. Recovery of charred manzanita seeds, walnut shell fragments, and maize cupules and kernels from all four levels of fill suggests that these plants were important food resources. Calcined and uncharred bone also was recovered from all four levels of fill; charred goosefoot seeds, ponderosa pine charcoal, oak charcoal, and charred bone fragments were present in the three lower levels. Food-plant remains found in only one or two levels of fill include possible agave epidermis, Cheno-am embryos, a beeweed seed, a juniper seed, a prickly pear cactus seed, a tomatillo seed, a purslane seed, wild grape seeds, and an unidentified seed fragment. Identifiable charcoal types present in the midden samples were manzanita, mountain mahogany, cliffrose, juniper, pine, and plum/cherry; unidentifiable vitrified charcoal was also present.

Feature 5

Feature 5, a midden area at the north end of the site, contained four primary inhumations, none of them within the control unit. Pollen Samples 308, 316, and 328 and Flotation Samples 305, 317, and 327 were collected from three excavation levels.

Sample 308 from Level 1 contained nearly equal quantities of *Pinus, Quercus*, and High-spine Asteraceae pollen, probably introduced through wind transport and representing local vegetation, although High-spine Asteraceae pollen may represent growth of members of the sunflower family on or near the midden. Small quantities of pollen from Cheno-ams (accompanied by a few small aggregates), *Cylindropuntia*, Liliaceae *Brodiaea*-type, Rhamnaceae, and *Zea mays* (accompanied by a single small aggregate) may represent discarded plant remains. A single starch granule with hilum may represent grass seeds or maize.

Sample 305 from Level 1 contained a charred *Juglans* nutshell fragment and charred *Zea mays* cupule and kernel fragments, suggesting use of walnuts and maize. Uncharred seeds in this sample reflect a variety of modern plants at the site. A few pieces of *Pinus, Quercus*, and unidentified charcoal most likely represent woods burned as fuel. Charred, calcined, and uncharred bone fragments suggest processing and discard of animal remains. The sample also contained insect remains and a moderate amount of rodent fecal pellets and worm castings.

Sample 316 from Level 2 of Feature 5 contained an elevated amount of Cheno-am pollen accompanied by a few small aggregates. The *Cylindropuntia* pollen frequency was elevated in this sample as well, and *Zea mays* pollen and a small quantity of Apiaceae pollen were present. A single starch granule with hilum noted in this sample may represent deterioration of grass seeds and/or maize.

Charred remains found in Sample 317 from Level 2 included *Arctostaphylos* seed fragments, *Juglans* nutshell fragments, *Pinus ponderosa* seeds, and *Zea mays* cupules, cupule fragments, and kernel fragments. Few uncharred seeds were present. The sample contained

moderate amounts of *Arctostaphylos, Pinus ponderosa*, and *Quercus* charcoal, and smaller amounts of *Cercocarpus* and *Prunus* charcoal. Single pieces of charred and calcined faunal bone fragments and a few insect fragments and snails were also present.

Cheno-am pollen dominated Sample 328 from Level 3 and was accompanied by a few aggregates ranging in size from small to large, indicating weedy growth as well as probable discard of Cheno-am remains. Small quantities of *Cylindropuntia* pollen accompanied by a single small aggregate and *Portulaca*, Rosaceae (scabrate), *Typha latifolia*-type, *Cucurbita*, and *Zea mays* pollen probably represent processed resource remains discarded in the midden.

Sample 327 from Level 3 contained charred *Arctostaphylos* seeds and seed fragments, charred *Juglans* nutshell fragments, and charred *Zea mays* cupules, cupule fragments, and kernel fragments. Other charred plant remains from this lower level of midden fill included Cheno-am embryos, *Chenopodium* seeds, an *Opuntia* seed fragment, *Phaseolus* seed fragments, and a *Vitis* seed fragment. Most of the charcoal recovered from this sample was vitrified and unidentifiable. Identified charcoal types present were *Arctostaphylos, Cercocarpus, Pinus ponderosa, Prunus*, and *Quercus*. Charred, calcined, and uncharred bone fragments suggest processing or discard of animal remains. The sample also contained an animal tooth fragment, one insect fragment, and two snails.

The lower levels of fill from Feature 5 contained larger quantities of Cheno-am pollen than the top level, indicating subsurface disturbance. Cholla and maize remains appear to have been discarded regularly in this midden. The occasional presence of pollen representing purslane, squash/pumpkin, cattail, and the rose family indicates the probability that portions of these plants were discarded as well.

The macrofloral record from Feature 5 contained charred remains similar to those recovered from Feature 4, the eastern midden, including manzanita seeds, Cheno-am embryos, goosefoot seeds, walnut shell fragments, a prickly pear seed, a wild grape seed fragment, and maize cupules and kernel fragments. Walnut shell fragments and maize remains again were present in all levels of midden fill, as was oak charcoal, charred bone, and calcined bone. Manzanita seeds and charcoal, mountain mahogany charcoal, ponderosa pine charcoal, wild plum/cherry charcoal, vitrified charcoal, and uncharred bone fragments were present in two of the midden levels. Charred *Phaseolus* cotyledon fragments and charred *Pinus ponderosa* seeds also were recovered from this midden, suggesting use of cultivated beans and ponderosa pine nuts.

Feature 10

Feature 10 was a midden area in the southern portion of the site. Pollen Samples 357 and 367 and Flotation Samples 356 and 366 were collected from two excavation levels.

Quercus pollen dominated Sample 357 from Level 1, probably representing proximity of an oak woodland. This sample also contained small quantities of Cheno-am pollen, *Cylindropuntia* pollen accompanied by a single moderate-sized aggregate, elevated Poaceae pollen accompanied by a few small aggregates, and *Zea mays* pollen accompanied by a single small aggregate.

Sample 356 from Level 1 contained a charred Cheno-am seed, a charred *Juglans* nutshell fragment, and a charred *Zea mays* cupule fragment. A large quantity of uncharred seeds represented a variety of modern plants. *Juniperus* was the only charcoal type present. Numerous insect fragments, rodent feces, and worm castings indicate some disturbance from bioturbation.

Sample 367 from Level 2 displayed an elevated Cheno-am pollen frequency accompanied by a few small aggregates. Small quantities of *Cylindropuntia* pollen, an elevated Poaceae pollen frequency accompanied by a single small aggregate, and Rhamnaceae, *Vitis*, *Cucurbita*, and *Zea mays* pollen were present as well. This sample contained the only *Vitis* pollen found at this site.

A charred *Chenopodium* seed and two charred Lamiaceae seeds were present in Sample 366 from Level 2. A charred *Pinus* needle fragment may represent use of pine needles as tinder or a medicinal resource, although needles may simply have been on pine branches or logs

that were burned, as evidenced by charred *Pinus*-type bark scale fragments. A few pieces of *Juniperus* and *Quercus* charcoal were present. Non-botanic remains in this sample included an uncharred bone fragment, two snails, and numerous insect fragments and worm castings.

AZ N:7:156 (ASM)

Feature 1

Feature 1 was an activity area consisting of an occupation surface with a hearth. Subfeature 1.01, the circular, clay-lined hearth, was near the center of the occupation surface. Pollen Sample 152 from fill in the north half of the hearth did not yield sufficient pollen for analysis. Pollen types identified were present in trace amounts and appeared to represent natural local vegetation.

Flotation Sample 151 from the hearth fill contained a charred *Arctostaphylos* seed fragment, four charred *Chenopodium* seed fragments, a moderate amount of *Quercus* charcoal, and a calcined bone fragment. The sample also contained insect fragments, numerous rodent fecal pellets, and a moderate amount of worm castings.

Feature 4

Feature 4, a probable check dam, consisted of a linear concentration of granite rock extending across a drainage. Pollen Sample 63, collected from the packed, decomposed granite alluvium on the upstream side of the feature, was dominated by *Juniperus* pollen, indicating that this feature likely was built in an open juniper woodland. Small quantities of *Pinus*, *Quercus*, *Artemisia*, Low-spine and High-spine Asteraceae, Cheno-am, Cyperaceae, *Dodonaea*, Ericaceae, *Eriogonum*, Poaceae, and *Polygonum sawatchense*-type pollen probably represent local vegetation.

Summary and Conclusions

The pollen and macrofloral data from Sites AZ N:6:20, AZ N:7:155, and AZ N:7:156 (ASM) indicate exploitation of both wild and cultivated plant resources by the occupants of these sites. Inhabitants of AZ N:6:20

(ASM) utilized maize and appear to have exploited manzanita, saltbush and other Cheno-am plants, juniper berries, prickly pear cactus, grasses, purslane, members of the rose family, and possibly other fleshy fruit/berry resources. Charred monocot stem fragments from pit structure fill may represent use of monocots as roof-closing material, for weaving, or in processing other foods. Recovery of mountain mahogany charcoal from all four features at this site suggests common use of this local wood. Other charcoal types indicate use of juniper and pine, including ponderosa pine, as fuel or building material.

Examination of data from two pit structures and three middens at AZ N:7:155 (ASM) yielded abundant evidence for use of plant resources. The macrofloral record from the structures suggests processing or use of smart-weed/knotweed, walnuts, and maize in these structures. Fill from the midden areas contained both pollen and macrofloral evidence for the use of maize, as well as pollen from squash or pumpkin and charred macrofloral remains from beans. Native plants that appear to have been used include a member of the parsley/carrot family, manzanita, saltbush, goosefoot, beeweed, cholla, prickly pear cactus, walnut, juniper, a member of the mint family, a member of the lily family such as brodi-aea, tomatillo/groundcherry, ponderosa pine, piñon pine, grasses, purslane, members of the buckthorn and rose families, cattail, wild grape, and possibly agave, other Cheno-am plants, and hopbush. Plants represented by charcoal from this site included manzanita, mountain mahogany, cliffrose, juniper, pine (including ponderosa pine), wild cherry/plum, and oak. These trees and shrubs would have provided edible and medicinal resources, as well as wood for construction and for fuel. Larger quantities of Cheno-am pollen in the lower levels of Feature 4 suggest increased disturbance, followed by a reduction in use of this area. The pollen and charred macrofloral remains from AZ N:7:155 (ASM) represent use of plants from both of the local plant communities, as well as from riparian habitats along local watercourses.

Analysis of a pollen sample from a hearth (Subfeature 1.01) in an activity area at AZ N:7:156 (ASM) did not provide evidence of economic activity. The macrofloral record from this feature suggests processing of manzanita berries and goosefoot seeds; goosefoot also may have been used to process other foods. Oak charcoal recovered from the hearth suggests use of local oak wood as fuel. The hearth also contained a calcined bone fragment, suggesting processing/discard of animal remains. The sample from the check dam did not contain pollen that would indicate what, if any, crops were planted there. This feature appears to have been located in an open juniper woodland.

CHAPTER 9

Human Remains

Dee A. Jones

SWCA's field personnel recovered the remains of nine individuals (eight primary inhumations, one secondary cremation) and five isolated deposits of human remains from eight burial features at Site AZ N:7:155 (ASM), as well as another 11 deposits of isolated human remains. The inhumation burials, located during mechanical trenching of midden deposits, contained the remains of six adults (one female, three males, two whose gender could not be determined), one child, and one infant. The cremated remains, recovered during the excavation of Feature 18, an extramural activity area, represented one adult of undetermined gender. The analyst identified these remains as human in the laboratory.

The 16 deposits of isolated bone, two of them from Site AZ N:6:20 (ASM), represented at least one more infant and one more adult of indeterminate age. Because of the fragmentary nature of these remains and their questionable contexts, they were not included in the osteological analysis and are discussed separately.

The description of the Hassayampa skeletal series in this chapter focuses on age, gender, and pathologies. Individual osteological summaries are provided in Appendix D.

Excavation and Laboratory Methods

Field personnel exposed the inhumation features during backhoe trenching and surface scraping and gave each one a unique feature number. As each feature was identified, the crews removed overburden with the backhoe and by hand. Three inhumation burial features had distinct pit outlines. No pit outline could be discerned in the other four, and arbitrary excavation units were dug over these burials. Each burial was within a midden

(Feature 4 or Feature 5), in a pit or crevice extending at least partly into the bedrock. The first step in excavation was exposing the skeletal remains and removing the pit fill, which was screened through eighth-inch mesh to recover all loose bone fragments. Field crews also screened backdirt from areas of known features to recover human bone and associated grave goods and mapped each inhumation prior to analysis and removal. Most of the inhumations appeared to have been disturbed by rodents.

In the field, the analyst carefully removed the remains from their soil matrix, with the assistance of Yavapai tribal elder Stan Rice, Sr., and Tribal Archaeologist Linda Blan. The burials and associated artifacts were then transported to SWCA's Flagstaff office for storage and analysis. Human remains and artifacts recovered from the screens were bagged separately but stored together, with juniper boughs, as requested by the Yavapai tribal representatives. The remains and the artifacts were then given specimen numbers and entered on the burial bag list.

The remains from each feature were examined separately. The analyst removed sediments adhering to the bones with a fine brush to facilitate analysis, washing them only when deposits could not be loosened with the brush. Attempts to refit skeletal elements to obtain more osteological information identified few conjoining pieces due to the fragmentary condition of the remains. Refits were not glued. When a second individual was identified in a set of remains, the analyst retained the original feature number for both individuals and distinguished them by adding an A for the individual identified in the field and a B for the individual identified in the laboratory.

Age and gender estimations were based on standard osteological methods (Bass 1987; Black 1978; Gustafson and Koch 1974; Hoffman 1979; Iscan and Loth 1986; Katz and Suchey 1986; Krogman and Iscan 1986; McKern and Stewart 1957; Phenice 1969; Steele and Brambett 1988; Stewart 1979; Suchey et al. 1986; Todd 1920; Ubelaker 1989; Webb and Suchey 1985). The pubic bone is the element favored for determination of both age and gender; however, portions of the pubic symphysis were present for only one individual. For the other burials, the analyst relied on cranial morphology and overall robusticity for sexing, and on epiphyseal union, dental development, and changes to the sternal end of the fourth rib for determining age at time of death. Most of the inhumations were otherwise relatively complete and in good condition; age estimations were possible for all individuals, and sex estimations were possible for four of the seven interred adults. The cremated remains were fragmentary, and this individual could be identified only as an adult of indeterminate sex.

Methods for estimating the biological age of a skeleton vary with developmental maturation. Ages of children (3–12 years) and adolescents (13–18 years) can be assigned with greater accuracy than can ages of adults, because techniques based on dental development (Gustafson and Koch 1974; Ubelaker 1989), bone growth (Hoffman 1979), and epiphyseal union (Krogman and Iscan 1986) offer fairly reliable indications of age. With the cessation of the growth process in adults, age estimation becomes less precise. Age estimates in adults based on morphological changes to the pubic bones (Suchey et al.1988) and the metamorphosis of the sternal end of the fourth rib (Iscan and Loth 1986) are currently considered to be fairly accurate when used together. Unfortunately, in most of the Hassayampa burials these elements were not preserved, and less precise methods were necessary. These techniques included examination of the fusion of the medial end of the clavicle (Webb and Suchey 1985), development of osteophytic growth around the vertebral bodies and other articular surfaces (Steele and Brambett 1988), and tooth loss/attrition (Brothwell 1965).

For the adult individuals lacking the pubic bone, the bases for gender determination were other pelvic char-

acteristics, cranial morphology, and overall size and robustness. No attempt was made to estimate gender in juveniles, as secondary sex characteristics do not manifest until puberty.

Intact long bones provided evidence of stature; estimates were based on multiple elements when possible. The standard reference was Trotter and Gleser's (1952) study of stature in Caucasian and African-American populations in the United States. A cross check of stature results derived from the Caucasian estimates against estimates derived using Genoves's (1967) method yielded a roughly similar set of figures. These estimates represent skeletal stature; living stature could have been slightly different due to factors such as age and posture.

Visual examination of the remains for pathological conditions revealed porotic pitting and osteoarthritis in this burial group (Ortner and Putschar 1985; White 1991). Dental pathologies, including antemortem tooth loss, caries, abscesses, and enamel hypoplasia, were present on 100 percent of the remains with dentition present.

Results

Age and Gender

Age at death could be estimated for all individuals in this population and ranged from under 2 years to 43–55 years. (Table 9.1). Although 78 percent of the remains were of adults, the distribution represented all age groups. This burial group was not representative of a living population. Any inferences that could be drawn from this analysis are biased by the small sample size and are limited to the context at hand.

The gender distribution for the seven adult burials is one female, three males, and three adults of indeterminate sex. The males in this population tended to be fairly robust. The female was more gracile but had moderately strong muscle markings. No major differences in health were apparent between the genders, but this could be due to sample size. The only incidence of trauma observed was in an older adult male.

Table 9.1. Age and Gender, Burials from AZ N:7:155 (ASM)

Feature	Age (years)	Sex
Inhumation		
6	43–55	Male
7	30+	Male
11A	25–35	Female
11B	>2	Indeterminate
12	Adult	Indeterminate
13	9 ± 2.5	Indeterminate
15	Adult	Male
16	18–23	Indeterminate
Cremation		
8	Adult	Indeterminate

Stature

Stature estimations were possible for four of the seven adults in this burial group (Table 9.2) Whether stature in this population was similar to that of individuals in the few other Prescott Culture inhumations that have been excavated is not known, as information from the reported burials is meager. The only stature estimate available was 167 cm for a male from the Copper Basin site (Smith et al. 1977).

Pathological Conditions

The incidence of pathological conditions was low in this skeletal series. Pathologies primarily took the form of porotic pitting and osteoarthritis.

No active cases of porotic hyperostosis or cribra orbitalia were present in this population. Porotic scarring, the remnants of healed porotic lesions, occurred in three adults (Table 9.3), suggesting the presence of a hematopoietic disorder. The exact cause of these anematic disorders is debatable, although their rates were high in formative cultures throughout the Southwest. Until recently, these conditions were thought to be symptomatic of an iron-deficient diet. However, El-Najjar et al. (1975) claim that chronic iron-deficiency anemia probably resulted from a combination of factors, including the low iron content in maize and the practice of preparing maize by alkali soaking. Recent research has shown a range of other variables that could cause iron-deficiency anemia, such as parasitism, poor sanitary conditions, diarrheal diseases, infection, and metabolic diseases (Fink 1986; Kent 1987; Mensforth et al. 1978; Walker 1986). Stuart-Macadam (1987) has downplayed the role of diet in the occurrence of this anemia and suggests that porotic hyperostosis indicates a high incidence of parasitism in the environment.

Porotic hyperostosis (lesions of the frontal, parietal, and occipital vault) and cribra orbitalia (lesions of the superior border of the orbits) "are manifest as the widening of the spongy diploe with a corresponding thinning of

Table 9.2. Stature Data, Inhumations from AZ N:7:155 (ASM)

Feature	Sex	Elements Used	Length (cm)	Estimated Height (cm)*
6	M	Humerus, femur	33.1, 46.4	172
7	M	Humerus, tibia	30.6, 37.8	168
11A	F	Humerus, femur, tibia	29.7, 41.5, 35.7	160
15	M	Femur, tibia	45.9, 39.8	171

*From Trotter and Gleser (1952)

Dee A. Jones

Table 9.3. Pathological Conditions, Burials from AZ N:7:155 (ASM)

Feature	Age	Sex	Porotic Pitting			Osteo-arthritis	TMJ	Periostitis
			F	P	O			
6	43-55	male				X	X	
7	30+	male			M	X	X	X
15	adult	male	H	H		X		
16	adult	?		L				

F=frontal; P=parietal; O=occipital
L=light pitting; M=moderate pitting; H=heavy pitting; X=present

the dense cortical bone resulting in the appearance of surface porosity" (Goodman et al. 1984). In cases where the bone has been heavily remodeled, vestigial pitting is present. This porotic scarring is evident as small, light to heavy funnel-shaped pinhole lesions on the outer table of the cranial vault and indicates childhood episodes of porotic hyperostosis (Fink 1989).

The pinhole pitting, the only remaining evidence of the lesions in this skeletal group, ranged from light to heavy. Feature 7, an older male, had moderate pitting of the occipital bone. Feature 15, an adult male, had extensive pitting of the frontal and parietal regions. Feature 16, an adult of indeterminate gender, had light pitting on the parietal bones.

Arthritic changes had occurred in three of the six adults from inhumations. Degenerative arthritis of the amphiarthrodial vertebral joints occurs in two forms: marginal development of osteophytes and degeneration of the vertebral disks (Ortner and Putschar 1985). Degeneration of the vertebral disk may lead to its herniation, causing pressure on the vertebral body, and the eburnation eventually leads to erosion of the vertebral body's articular surface. These focal-pressure erosion lesions are called Schmorl's nodes. The three individuals with arthritic changes had vertebral bodies with marginal lipping, and one also exhibited Schmorl's nodes.

Feature 6, a male between the ages of 43 and 55, had a series of arthritic changes on the vertebrae. This individual had slight to moderate (0.9 cm) marginal lipping projecting posteriorly and superiorly on the bodies of the ninth through eleventh thoracic vertebrae and the

first and second lumbar vertebrae. The sixth, seventh, ninth, tenth, and twelfth thoracic and the first lumbar also exhibited Schmorl's nodes on the superior surface of the vertebral bodies. Feature 7, a male over 30 years of age, had severe osteophytic growths on the thoracic and lumbar vertebrae. The seventh through twelfth thoracic vertebrae had slight marginal lipping. This individual had diffuse idiopathic skeletal hyperostosis (DISH) on the lumbar and first sacral vertebrae. DISH is typified by ossification of the anterior longitudinal ligament and is characterized by a continuous flow of dense bone growth that has sometimes been described as a "dripping candle wax" pattern (Arriaza et al. 1993). The second and third lumbar vertebrae had extensive marginal lipping approximately 1.5 cm wide that projected superiorly approximately 2 cm from the middle of the vertebral body. The fifth lumbar and the first sacral vertebrae demonstrated massive bone hypertrophy that had partially fused the two vertebrae. The lack of diarthrodial joint involvement (costal and sacroiliac joints) suggests that the fusion was not due to rheumatoid arthritis or ankylosing spondylitis (Ortner and Putschar 1985). The only other joints with slight arthritic lipping were the olecranon fossa of the right ulna and both temporal mandibular joints (see below). Feature 15, an adult male, had a mild case of marginal lipping on the first sacral vertebra.

Only one case of periosteal infection occurred in the inhumations from AZ N:7:155 (ASM). Feature 15, an adult male, had well-healed periosteal lesions on the right tibia between 27 cm and 32 cm from the proximal end of the shaft along the anterior surface. The infection appeared to be local, with no evidence of any breakage of the tibia. The healed surface was irregular, which could be due to trauma or to the healing process. In terms of bone infections, these individuals were relatively healthy.

Feature 7, an older male, exhibited the only case of perimortem trauma (trauma occurring around the time of death) in this collection and the first case of perimortem trauma identified in Prescott Culture people. Two of the three injuries noted on this individual's remains were serious enough to have caused death; there was no way of discerning the exact progression of these injuries or whether any of them actually killed him. The least serious of the injuries was the severing of the left gonial angle of the left mandible. The other two injuries were much more severe. On the vertebral column, the spinous processes of the fourth and fifth cervical vertebrae had been cut off, and there was a cut mark in the left side of the spinous process of the sixth cervical vertebra. The individual's head was probably angled slightly down and to the right at the moment of impact, and he received what appeared to have been a glancing blow that was not intended to decapitate him. The third injury was blunt-object trauma near the middle of the left temporal-occipital suture. The resulting ovoid, pond-like depression is typical of blunt trauma to green cranial bone. Death could have been caused by either of the more serious injuries. See Appendix D for a more complete description.

Temporal mandibular joint (TMJ) anomalies appeared only in Features 6 and 7. The exact causes and byproducts of deformation of the temporal mandibular joint are not known. Joint anomalies cause flattened or misshaped mandibular condyles with mirrored deformation of the glenoid fossa of the temporal bone. Deformation can be due to a congenital defect of the joint or fossa, occupational stress, bruxism, irregular occlusion, or any number of factors leading to abnormal stressing of the joint. The TMJ deformation in this burial population took the form of a flattened mandibular condyle that formed a flat and mostly angular articulation with the cranium at the temporal mandibular joint.

The dentition of the inhumed skeletal series from the Hassayampa project displayed a range of pathologies (Table 9.4). Besides the two cases of degenerative changes to the temporal mandibular joint, one instance of enamel hypoplasia, three instances of antemortem tooth loss, one instance of caries, and two abscesses were also present. Detailed descriptions of the dental anomalies are in Appendix D.

Enamel hypoplasia affected one of the four individuals with observable dentition. Enamel hypoplasia is characterized by transverse lines, pits, and grooves from the disruption of dental development due to metabolic disturbances (White 1991). Degree of enamel hypoplasia can range from faint ridging to deep grooves. The specific stress causing the cessation of enamel formation is variable; thus, the exact cause of hypoplastic lines cannot be specified. The individual with enamel hypoplasia, Feature 15, exhibited a mild case, with only one cessation line on all present dentition.

Table 9.4. Dental Pathologies, Burials from AZ N:7:155 (ASM)

Feature	Age	Sex	Enamel Hypoplasia	Antemortem Tooth Loss	Caries	Abscess
6	Adult	Male	0	15	0	2
7	43-55	Male	0	1	0	5
11A	25-35	Female	0	2	10	0
15	Adult	Male	14	0	0	0

Note: Counts represent number of teeth displaying the condition.

The amount of antemortem tooth loss in the inhumations was fairly extensive, particularly in one individual. Antemortem loss of teeth can be attributed to a variety of factors, including attrition due to age and coarse diet and infection (caries, abscesses, or periodontal disease). Once a tooth is lost, and especially after remodeling has occurred, the cause of the loss cannot be discerned. Three of the four inhumations with observable mandibles and maxillae had antemortem loss of teeth.

Feature 11A, an adult female, had the only caries observed. Of the 10 caries present, six had eroded away the top half of the crown. Two individuals had suffered from abscesses. In Feature 7, an older male, five abscesses had eroded three large holes in the maxilla and one small hole in the mandible at the apex of the right central incisor. The most extensive of this individual's maxillary abscesses, above the left incisors, was approximately 1.2 by 2.2 cm in size and had eroded a hole through the palate nearly to the nasal septum. There was no evidence of healing.

Two individuals, Features 11A and 15, had developmental dental anomalies. Feature 11A had a supernumerary tooth posterior to the left maxillary lateral incisor. Feature 15, an adult male, had retained the right maxillary deciduous canine.

Multiple Burials

One burial in this skeletal series contained two individuals. Excavators identified Feature 11 in the field as one inhumation, an adult female. In examining these remains in the laboratory, the analyst found portions of the cranium, the right scapula, and the innominates of an infant under 2 years of age. Based on the relatively undisturbed context of Feature 11, the difference in age between the two sets of remains, and the amount of bone present, the infant was identified as a separate individual and designated Feature 11B; the adult female was designated as Feature 11A. It was clear that Feature 11B was a different individual from the isolated remains found with Feature 6, since both included a right petrous portion of the temporal bone (see below).

Miscellaneous Bone

The analyst found five of the 16 miscellaneous deposits of human bone (Table 9.5) in the laboratory: the petrous portion of the right temporal of an infant, with Feature 6, an older male; a fragmented right tibia with a complete proximal end, most likely from an adult, with Feature 7, an older male; a middle phalanx of an adult with Feature 12, an adult; and a fibula shaft fragment and a cremated radius shaft fragment of indeterminate side, both from an adult, with Feature 13, a child.

A zygomatic and a portion of a maxilla of an adult were found in Feature 9, a small rock-lined room, at AZ N:6:20 (ASM). These bones exhibited hematite stains. The 10 other isolated remains were identified during analysis of midden material from AZ N:7:155 (ASM). Given the midden context of the burials, it was not surprising to find isolated remains mixed in with the midden matrix and with the burials themselves, perhaps representing disturbance to previous burials. These miscellaneous remains represented at least one infant and one adult of indeterminate gender.

Summary

The Hassayampa skeletal series comprised one adult female, three adult males, three adults of indeterminate sex, one child, one infant, and 16 sets of miscellaneous bone. While this is a small skeletal series, there were no indications that the distribution of the burial population was not normal. The quantity and severity of pathological conditions were low. Unfortunately, no further inferences from this collection are possible. Prior to this analysis, the Copper Basin project skeletal series of five individuals (Smith et al. 1977) was the best-documented collection of remains from the Prescott area; reports from Lonesome Valley Ruin and Fitzmaurice Ruin (Barnett 1973a, 1975) are cursory and lack the detail necessary for adequate comparison. Nevertheless, the sample sizes of the Hassayampa and Copper Basin collections are too small for any meaningful analysis of biological affinities or disease patterns. With further excavations in the Prescott area and larger databases, researchers may hope to learn more about the cultural and biological affinities of the Prescott Culture people.

Table 9.5. Miscellaneous Human Bone

Feature	Bag No.	Cremated	Non-Cremated	Remains
AZ N:7:155 (ASM)				
Burials				
6	B1030		X	1 petrous portion of right temporal (infant <2 yrs)
7	B1032		X	5 proximal right tibia fragments (adult)
12	531		X	1 middle phalanx (adult)
13	B1031		X	1 fibula shaft fragment (adult)
13	B1031	X		1 radius shaft fragment (adult?)
Midden				
4	87		X	1 femur shaft fragment, broken post-mortem (adult?)
4	139		X	1 left rib fragment (indeterminate)
4	212		X	1 right rib fragment, costal articulation with transverse process arthritic, possibly part of Feature 15 (adult, possibly older)
4	389		X	1 left clavicle lateral half, 1 right ulna olecranon fossa and half shaft, 4 indeterminate radial shaft fragments, 2 left rib fragments, 3 lateral temporal condyle fragments, 4 indeterminate vertebral fragments (probably adult); ulnar, radial bones osteoporotic
4	428		X	1 left maxillary lateral incisor with extensive wear, 1 middle phalanx (adult)
4	372		X	2 thoracic/lumbar vertebral fragments, 1 right patella, 1 sternal fragment, 1 acetabulum fragment, 2 rib proximal portions (adult)
5	204		X	1 right rib fragment (indeterminate)
5	321		X	1 left distal end of fibula, 1 indeterminate shaft fragment, 1 left scaphoid, 1 distal phalanx, 1 fragment of distal femoral condyle (adult)
5	333		X	1 left metatarsal, lunate, third cuneiform (adult)
5	324		X	1 proximal end of middle phalanx, 5 distal tibia fragments (indeterminate)
AZ N:6:20 (ASM)				
Rock-Lined Feature				
9	92		X	1 right zygomatic and portion of maxilla near zygomaxillary suture, with hematite staining (adult)

CHAPTER 10

Summary

James M. Potter

Investigation of seven sites with Prescott Culture components on the Hassayampa Country Club property cast some new light on a prehistoric Southwest culture about which little is known. In this chapter we summarize the project results within the context of the problem domains identified in the research design—site function, community patterning and regional interaction, subsistence, and chronology—and discuss the broader implications of this study for understanding the prehistory of the Prescott area.

Site Function

The prehistoric sites in the project area were of three types: resource procurement and processing, long-term and short-term habitation, and, possibly, communal ceremonial. Two habitation sites had evidence of resource procurement and processing as well.

Sites used strictly for resource procurement and processing were AZ N:6:9 (ASM) and AZ N:6:19 (ASM), plus the prehistoric component of AZ N:6:13 (ASM). AZ N:6:16 (ASM) was primarily a processing site with evidence of seasonal occupation. These were fairly isolated sites at elevations at or above 5,600 feet (1,705 m).

AZ N:6:9 (ASM) consisted of several rock alignments/ concentrations and an associated artifact scatter. It lacked structural features and artifacts were preponderantly lithic, especially cores and hammerstones. Resources exploited at this site may have included lithic materials and plant resources requiring pounding.

A group of artifact concentrations with no architectural features made up the prehistoric component of AZ N:6:13 (ASM). Tabular tools in the artifact assemblage

suggested agave processing, and several rock concentrations/piles at the site may have been related to agricultural production, especially of agave.

A rock pile and several stone alignments at AZ N:6:16 (ASM) probably were related to agricultural production, and two bedrock mortars at the site were undoubtedly related to plant processing. Few artifacts were recovered from this site, which was not excavated. Collapsed masonry suggested seasonal habitation.

AZ N:6:19 (ASM) was a multi-component plant processing site with several bedrock grinding slicks, a petroglyph, and a plethora of ground stone artifacts, including manos, metates, and grinding slabs. At 5,590 feet (1,735 m), it was the lowest of the processing sites and was probably associated with habitation site AZ N:7:156 (ASM), a short distance to the east above Aspen Creek.

The primary habitation sites identified were AZ N:6:20 (ASM), AZ N:7:155 (ASM), and AZ N:7:156 (ASM). AZ N:6:20 (ASM) was on a ridge at 5,725 feet (1,745 m); the other two sites were at the lowest elevations of the seven sites investigated. The botanical evidence suggests that corn and a variety of wild plants were processed at each of these sites.

AZ N:6:20(ASM) consisted of nine features, including structures, middens, check dams, and a bedrock grinding slick. The substantial habitation architecture on the site and the diversity of artifacts and features indicate long-term habitation.

More than 20 structures, middens, burials, rock alignments, and extramural features made up AZ N:7:155

(ASM), the most substantial of the long-term habitation sites. This site also produced the largest number and greatest diversity of artifacts in the project area.

Although habitation architecture at AZ N:7:156 (ASM) was less substantial than at the other two sites of this type, the site covered a much larger area. AZ N:7:156 (ASM) consisted of an activity area with an associated hearth, multiple rock features, five petroglyphs with an associated grinding slick, and various artifact concentrations. The dense concentration of ground stone in the activity area and the many rock features present suggest agricultural production and processing. The large quantity of artifacts and the variety of types indicate a wide range of activities, suggesting habitation. This site may have been a farmstead supporting maize agriculture, a communal ceremonial gathering place, or both.

AZ N:7:155 (ASM) and AZ N:7:156 (ASM) were close to Aspen Creek, on the eastern (downstream) end of the project area. AZ N:6:20 (ASM), on the other hand, was near the center of the project area, at a much higher elevation. The presence of a habitation site in this location is interesting; the site may also have functioned as, or may have originated as, a lithic core reduction site. The large quantity and diversity of ground stone artifacts at this site suggest intensive processing of both wild and domestic plants.

Five petroglyphs were associated with AZ N:7:156 (ASM). Given that this was the only habitation site with rock art, more than domestic or economic activities may have occurred here. The very large area encompassed by this site may in fact represent repeated, short-term communal ritual use rather than long-term habitation by a small number of people.

Community Patterning and Regional Interaction

The size of the project area and the number of sites investigated afforded the researchers the opportunity to consider at least part of a prehistoric community and the nature of that community's interactions with surrounding areas. Jeter's (1977) "permanent base/temporary exploitation site model" appears to fit quite well with the data from the project area. AZ N:7:1:155 ASM) was a habitation/agricultural site at a fairly low elevation

(below 5,600 feet/1,705 m), while AZ N:6:9 (ASM), AZ N:6:16 (ASM), AZ N:6:19(ASM), and the prehistoric component of AZ N:6:13 (ASM) appeared to have been plant and lithic resource procurement and processing sites at higher elevations. AZ N:6:20 (ASM), which was both a substantial habitation site and a resource procurement and processing site, was also at a higher elevation. As suggested above, the function of AZ N:6:20 (ASM) may have changed over time, from a camp for resource procurement and processing to a more permanent habitation. The one site that did not fit Jeter's (1977) model was AZ N:7:156 (ASM), which lacked substantial evidence of permanent habitation but was much too extensive in area and had too diverse an artifact assemblage to be simply a "temporary exploitation site." It may have been a locus of repeated communal gatherings, which is not one of Jeter's site types.

In terms of a definable site hierarchy, there is no evidence to suggest that occupants of any site had political or economic influence over the occupants of any other site. AZ N:7:1:155 (ASM) did have a greater variety of economic goods, including exotic pottery and shell, than the other habitation sites. However, the richer assemblage from this site is undoubtedly due, at least in part, to the fact that the artifact assemblage was substantially larger than the samples from other sites.

Local and regional social and economic interactions can be examined using a combination of data sources, including ceramic sourcing, the distribution of known exotics such as shell and decorated ceramics, and stylistic differences and similarities among communities. One of the unique aspects of the Prescott Culture area is a distinctive pottery tradition defined by the presence of Prescott Gray Wares. Both decorated and undecorated Prescott Gray Ware sherds are found in great abundance at most Chino phase (A.D. 1000–1350) sites in the area. Since they are abundant on sites in the Prescott area and are called "Prescott" Gray Wares, archaeologists tend to assume that they were all locally produced. This is especially the case for undecorated vessels, which are usually assumed to have been produced, used, and consumed at the same site. Petrographic analysis of temper in sherds recovered during the Hassayampa project indicates that while undecorated Prescott Gray Ware vessels were produced locally, it is possible that some were imported from outside the project area. Ceramic samples from Site AZ N:7:155 (ASM), for example, consist not only of sherds tempered with the alluvial sands from nearby Aspen and Butte Creeks, but also of sherds tempered with potassium feldspars that are unlike any of the sand or bedrock sources in the region (Appendix A). These data suggest exchange of at least some Prescott Gray Wares over long distances. Unfortunately, the small size of the analyzed sample precludes drawing any conclusions about the proportions of local and nonlocal sherds at Site AZ N:7:155 (ASM) or exploring the potential variation in pottery among sites in the project area.

Exotic artifacts identified in the project area were shell, decorated buffware and whiteware pottery, and obsidian. Of the 17 shells or shell fragments recovered, 16 were from AZ N:7:155 (ASM), all of them marine shell from southern California or the Sea of Cortez. Exotic decorated sherds constituted less than 1 percent of the total ceramic assemblage. Twenty-three were recovered from AZ N:7:155 (ASM); one Tusayan White Ware sherd and two Hohokam Buff Ware sherds were recovered from AZ N:1:156 (ASM). The marine shell and buffware pottery were probably obtained directly from the Hohokam through long-distance exchange, or indirectly through down-the-line exchange. The whiteware sherds indicate contacts with groups to the northeast. Obsidian, which made up 2 percent of the lithic artifact assemblage, was not sourced but probably came from Government Mountain or Partridge Creek.

One of the most intriguing aspects of AZ N:7:155 (ASM) is the assemblage of fragments of small, crude, ceramic human and animal forms associated with this site. Motsinger (2000) summarizes the data on these figurines and notes several interesting patterns. First is the strong pattern of breakage of the figurines and their association with middens. Only one of 39 specimens from the site was recovered intact. Motsinger (2000:152) suggests that this consistent fragmentation is the result of intentional mutilation of these artifacts and is consistent with the pattern reported by Simmons (n.d.:9) for the Groom Creek figurines. Motsinger also notes that the distributional range of ceramic figurines is generally restricted to an area of about 80 km² of ponderosa forest south of Prescott, specifically the Groom

Creek area and the Hassayampa River drainage. He suggests that this pattern is associated with an ethnic split that developed after about A.D. 1000 between the "pit house–figurine" group in the wooded uplands of the Hassayampa area and the puebloans in the grasslands and chaparral to the north. Motsinger further suggests that these figurines were used for ritual purposes and involved a figurine "cult" (Motsinger 2000:152–153).

While these artifacts may indeed have been used for ritual purposes, they may also have played an important role in establishing social identity and maintaining social boundaries. In dealing with social identity as established through stylistic messages, Southwest archaeologists usually think of decorated and colorfully slipped ceramic vessels (Braun and Plog 1982; Crown 1994), but a plausible possibility is that the Prescott area inhabitants adopted and elaborated an alternative medium: ceramic figurines. Wobst (1977) predicted that artifacts used to transmit stylistic messages would be highly visible and a regular part of social contexts. This prediction fits well with what is known about the figurines. That 38 of the 39 specimens from AZ N:7:155 (ASM) were fragments recovered from middens indicates that they were discarded after being broken (deliberately or accidentally) during actual use, rather than made for inclusion in hidden, non-visible contexts such as inhumations, secret shrines, or ritual caches.

Why it would have been necessary for Prescott Culture peoples to actively communicate social identity and establish social boundaries is not known. Given that the Prescott people were surrounded by culturally dominant groups to the south, north, and east, it is possible that such behavior was part of establishing access and rights to economic and social resources, including land and marriage partners (Wiessner 1983).

Subsistence

Useful botanical and faunal data were limited to one site, AZ N:7:155 (ASM), though feature and artifact data from several other sites provided some information. Evidence of plant procurement and processing was recovered from higher-elevation sites within the project area. Tabular stone tools recovered from AZ N:6:13 (ASM) suggest the procurement of agave, while rock piles and bedrock mortars at AZ N:6:16 (ASM) and bedrock grinding slicks and the large number of grinding implements recovered from AZ N:6:19 (ASM) suggest not only the procurement and processing of wild plant resources, but the cultivation of domesticates (probably corn). The preponderance of manos and metates associated with Feature 1 at AZ N:7:156 (ASM) suggests corn processing at this site, possibly for periodic communal feasts.

The inhabitants of AZ N:7:155 (ASM) exploited a variety of wild plants, at least three domesticated plants, and an assortment of large game. Wild plant resources included prickly pear cactus, walnuts, manzanita berries, juniper berries, wild grapes, cholla, and agave. Domesticates recovered were maize, beans, and squash. Hunted animals included deer, antelope, and elk. Thus, the inhabitants of the site had access to a wide range of resources, including large game, which undoubtedly contributed to the long-term success of the settlement.

Prehistoric Chronology

All seven of the prehistoric sites had evidence of use and/or occupation during the Chino phase. This broad temporal span ranges from about A.D. 1000 to 1350. Most of the sites were dated by the presence of Prescott Gray Ware and a few intrusive ceramics. Radiocarbon dates from two sites supported a Formative period assignment but did little to narrow the date. The single radiocarbon date from AZ N:6:20 (ASM) yielded a two-sigma calibrated date range of A.D. 1045–1415, a wide range to say the least. The two radiocarbon samples from AZ N:7:155 (ASM) generated non-overlapping two-sigma confidence intervals of A.D. 1025–1260 and A.D. 1275–1410. None of the tree-ring samples submitted from the site proved datable. It was therefore not possible to date these sites more precisely than their ceramic assemblages indicated.

The project sites also yielded some indirect evidence of Archaic occupation. AZ N:6:19 (ASM) and AZ N:7:156 (ASM) both had rock art that may have dated to Archaic times (pre–A.D. 700). In addition, AZ N:6:19 (ASM) had no ceramics, a high ratio of flaked stone tools to

debitage, and a diversity of lithic raw material types, all attributes consistent with an Archaic hunter-gatherer adaptation. The rock art at AZ N:7:156 (ASM), if it does date to earlier Archaic times, may have persisted as an important ritual gathering place during the Prescott Culture phase. Such use would explain why the characteristics of this site are not consistent with what is expected of either a habitation site or a resource procurement and processing site during the Formative period occupation.

Concluding Remarks

The Prescott Culture was not simply an extension of or mix of attributes from other areas in the Southwest. It is distinguished by a unique array of culture traits, such as a decorated grayware tradition, hilltop forts, and stone-lined pit houses. Moreover, these traits co-occur within and develop along a historical trajectory that is particular to the region.

One of these historical developments occurs at about A.D. 1000, in the form of a substantial cultural divide between the northern "puebloan" Prescott groups and a southern "pit house–figurine" group, within which the Hassayampa project sites appear to belong. These groups dwelled primarily in pit house hamlets, some with masonry structures such as the Hassayampa Ruin (AZ N:7:155 [ASM]), made and used animal figurines, and traded for pottery and other exotic goods. Their subsistence strategy was based on the diversity of natural resources in the region, including large game, and their settlement system included sites for habitation, resource procurement and processing, and communal ceremonies.

Like other regions in the Southwest, the Prescott region has its own history, which is more than simply a set of environmental adaptations. The reuse of Archaic rock art sites as communal ritual sites may be an example of behavior structured by the area's past as well as by the local environment. Future research in the area has the potential to test the conclusions reached here, and thus broaden our understanding of the unique history of the Prescott Culture Area.

APPENDIX A

Petrographic Analysis of Sand and Sherd Samples

Andrew L. Christenson

Studies in the Tucson, Phoenix, and Tonto basins have demonstrated that fairly small ceramic production areas can be defined by matching ceramic temper to mineralogically distinct areas of sand and bedrock (petrofacies) (Lombard 1987; Miksa 1992; Miksa and Heidke 1995; Schaller 1994). The thin-sectioning and analysis of a number of stream-sand samples and prehistoric sherds described here were part of a pilot program to determine the feasibility of such studies on Prescott area pottery. These samples, when added to those previously analyzed from the Neural and Sundown sites (Christenson 1995), provide a baseline for assessing the method and directing future research.

The Sample

The ceramic sample consisted of nine sherds from AZ N:7:155 (ASM) and two from AZ N:7:156 (ASM). Eight of the specimens from AZ N:7:155 (ASM) were rim sherds—one Wingfield Plain and seven Prescott Gray—from mechanical stripping of Feature 4, a midden. The ninth was a Prescott Gray sherd from floor fill of Feature 2, a pit house. The two sherds from AZ N:7:156 (ASM) were Prescott Gray, both from Feature 1, an activity area. The goal of the selection, done early in the analysis, was to cover some of the variation observed in the temper, but no claim can be made for the representativeness of the chosen sherds. Basic information on the sample sherds and on three others included for comparative purposes appears in Table A.1.

The sherds from other sites, chosen to provide additional information on the range of variation in ceramic mineralogy in the project area, were a single Prescott Gray sherd from the Sandretto Site (N:7:163 [ASM])

and two partial Prescott Black-on-gray bowls, excavated by J. W. Simmons, from King's Ruin (NA 1587). This site is particularly important because it is the type site for Prescott (formerly Verde) Black-on-gray (Colton and Hargrave 1937:185).

The analyst collected a number of samples from streams in the region: Butte Creek northwest of AZ N:7:155 (ASM), Aspen Creek near AZ N:7:156 (ASM), Mint Wash about 1.6 km (1 mile) south of the Sundown site, Lynx Creek below Fitzmaurice Ruin, Big Chino Wash 1.6 km (1 mile) from King's Ruin, and Willow Creek below the Sandretto site. Six of these sand samples were analyzed, and those data and data from a previously analyzed sand sample from a tributary of Willow Creek were included in the study.

Methods

Samples from sherds were cut to size (about 30 × 20 mm) with a lapidary saw. Quality Thin Sections of Tucson prepared the samples by impregnating them with epoxy, staining them for potassium and plagioclase feldspar, and thin-sectioning them parallel to the vessel wall.

Each sand sample was collected with a trowel at appropriate intervals across a stream bed to obtain about 1/2 cup to 1 cup of material. The samples were divided into approximately 1 tablespoon portions and submitted to Quality Thin Sections for preparation in the same manner as the sherds.

Initial scanning of the thin sections was at 40X to record the minerals and rocks present and to make general

Table A.1. Description of Sherds in Petrographic Analysis

Site/ Sample No.	Provenience	Ware/Type	Vessel Form	Description
AZ N:7:155				
1	Feature 4	Wingfield Plain	Bowl	Oxidized paste and surface, wiped interior
4	Feature 4	Prescott Gray	Bowl	Reduced paste and surface, minimal silver mica, medium-coarse texture, abundant temper
6	Feature 4	Prescott Gray	Bowl	Oxidized exterior, reduced paste, no mica, medium-coarse texture, abundant temper
8	Feature 4	Prescott Gray	Jar	Reduced paste and surface, no mica, medium texture, moderate temper, smudged and polished
11	Feature 4	Prescott Gray	Jar	Reduced paste and surface, moderate silver mica, medium-coarse texture, abundant temper
14	Feature 4	Prescott Gray	Jar	Reduced paste and exterior, oxidized interior, moderate silver mica, medium-coarse texture, moderate temper
17	Feature 2	Prescott Gray	Jar	Oxidized paste and surface, abundant gold mica, medium-coarse texture, abundant temper
20	Feature 4	Prescott Gray	Jar	Reduced paste, oxidized exterior, minimal silver mica, medium-coarse texture, abundant temper
22	Feature 4	Prescott Gray	Jar	Reduced paste and interior, oxidized exterior, abundant silver mica, medium-coarse texture, abundant temper
AZ N:7:156				
34	Feature 1	Prescott Gray	Jar	Reduced paste and surface, abundant silver mica, abundant dark minerals, fine-medium texture, fine-moderate temper
35	Feature 1	Prescott Gray	Bowl	Oxidized paste and surface, minimal silver mica, medium-coarse texture, abundant temper
AZ N:7:163				
1	Unit T1, 50-75 cm	Prescott Gray	Jar (?)	Reduced paste and surface, abundant silver mica, medium-coarse texture, abundant temper
NA 1587				
2	23.B	Prescott Black-on-gray	Bowl	Oxidized paste, reduced surface, abundant silver mica, medium-coarse texture, abundant temper
1	H.No.I, B.No.2	Prescott Black-on-gray	Bowl	Reduced paste and exterior, oxidized interior, no mica, medium texture, moderate-abundant temper

observations. Point-counting was at 100X using a Meiji petrographic microscope with a point-count stage set at intervals of 0.6 to 0.9 mm to ensure a total count of between 350 and 400 points, following the technique developed by Gazzi and Dickinson (Dickinson 1970) for sedimentary rocks. Sand-size or larger (>0.065 mm) minerals were counted as the mineral, whether they were alone or part of a rock fragment. Minerals smaller than sand size but part of a rock fragment were counted as volcanic, plutonic, sedimentary, or metamorphic fragments, as appropriate. Mineral or rock fragments smaller than 0.065 mm (i.e., silt size) were not counted. Unidentified minerals and rocks were counted as unknown. For samples that had not cracked badly in grinding, a single linear sample of 100 points at 0.3-mm intervals was counted to obtain the frequency of voids, sand-size rock, and matrix (silt and clay).

Results

Tables A.2 through A.4 contain the point-count data for the sherd and sand samples. Minerals or rock seen in the initial scan but not present in the point-counted sample are indicated by a + (plus). Looking first at the sand samples (Table A.2), we see a fair amount of variation in basic quartz and feldspar frequencies. Accessory minerals such as pyroxenes, epidote, and opaque minerals show some variation that may be of use in provenience studies. Rock types show fairly dramatic differences, with abundant volcanic and metamorphic rock in the Willow Creek tributary and abundant carbonaceous sedimentary rock fragments (mostly limestone) in the Big Chino Wash sample. All of the sands, except perhaps the Willow Creek tributary sample, are derived primarily from granitic rock. Because mineral grains in plutonic rocks, such as granite, are by definition mostly larger than sand size, fragments of these rocks are rarely counted under rock type. Virtually all of the feldspar and most of the quartz in Tables A.2 through A.4 are derived from plutonic (mostly granitic) rocks.

The sherd samples from Site AZ N:7:155 (ASM) (Table A.3) fall into two categories: Group A, plagioclase-dominated samples (4, 6, 8, and 14); and Group B, potassium feldspar–dominated samples (11, 17, 20, and 22). The Group B samples also have about twice as much mica and more hematite and opaque minerals than the samples in Group A; the Group A samples, on the other hand, are more likely to have epidote. The Group A samples are very similar to the alluvial sands from Aspen and Butte creeks nearby, but the Group B samples are unlike any of the sand samples or any granitic bedrock in the region.

The two sherds from AZ N:7:156 (ASM) differ in the same way. One is slightly potassium feldspar–dominated, with abundant mica, hematite, and opaques, while the other is strongly plagioclase dominant, with much epidote (Table A.4). This latter sample is unusual in having abundant amphiboles. The Sandretto site sample also falls into the high potassium feldspar group, which is quite different from the sand sample collected nearby in Willow Creek. The King's Ruin samples are fairly similar to one another except for the superabundance of mica in one, but they are radically different from the other sherd samples in the abundance of quartz present. They also differ dramatically from the sand sample collected nearby in Big Chino Wash.

Figure A.1 is a ternary diagram plotting the percentages of quartz, plagioclase, and potassium feldspar for all of the samples considered, as well as for some local granitic bedrock types. The different sites show some clustering, although they do not always match the sand sample from the nearest stream. This plot is deceptive because it includes only three minerals and none of the rocks, and it is in the accessory minerals and rocks that a different story may be told. Just a cursory comparison of Table A.1 with Tables A.2 and A.3 reveals a fairly dramatic difference between all the sand samples and all the sherd samples. Sand samples are more diverse in both minerals and rock types present, and all of the sand samples include volcanic rock, which was found in only one sherd (not in the point-count sample).

A simple plot of mineral diversity (richness) versus rock diversity shows the difference clearly (Figure A.2). No sand sample has less than three rock types, and no sherd sample has more than two. The sand samples have a mean of 7.4 minerals, while the sherd samples have a mean of only 5.6. These data suggest that alluvial sands were not used to temper the ceramic samples analyzed

Table A.2. Point-Count Data, Sand Samples

Mineral/Rock	Source (Sample Number)						
	Willow Creek Tributary (1)	Mint Wash (5)	Aspen Creek (7)	Butte Creek (8)	Lynx Creek (10)	Big Chino Wash (11)	Willow Creek (13)
Mineral							
Quartz	122	205	139	113	46	206	122
K feldspar	66	138	49	47	12	107	44
Plagioclase	80	136	220	214	132	58	210
Unknown feldspar		2		1	1		2
Muscovite			1			2	
Biotite		3	4	1			1
Unknown mica							3
Amphibole	1		1	4	2		3
Pyroxene	19					1	
Epidote	13	1	8	16	30	1	16
Olivine	6			+(?)		1[a]	
Carbonate						3	
Hematite	1	1			2		
Other opaque		2	3	4	9	3	7
Unknown	55	8	10	23	44	5	11
Rock Type							
Volcanic	77	20	1	1	3	33	5
Plutonic	2	2	6	5	2	9	7
Sedimentary	1					34	
Metamorphic	50	4	4	3	11	2	1
Unknown	36	5	2	10	45	45	10

K=potassium
+=mineral seen in original examination but not encountered in point counting
[a]altered to iddingsite

Table A.3. Point-Count Data, Sherd Samples, AZ N:7:155 (ASM)

Mineral/Rock	Group (Sample Number)							
	Group A				Group B			
	(4)	*(6)*	*(8)*	*(14)*	*(11)*	*(17)*	*(20)*	*(22)*
Mineral								
Quartz	117	111	116	154	175	188	156	198
K feldspar	17	49	54	61	120	159	101	176
Plagioclase	245	175	232	153	85	73	69	43
Unknown feldspar	7	2	4				1	2
Muscovite		1	+	1	3	5	6	7
Biotite	3				1	1		
Unknown mica		2	2		2		2	1
Amphibole								
Pyroxene								
Epidote	26	1	2	1	1			
Olivine								
Carbonate								
Hematite						2	2	+
Other opaque	1				5	6	6	
Unknown	5	6	7	2		2	8	7
Rock Type								
Volcanic								
Plutonic	+	+	3	3	4	3	2	4
Sedimentary								
Metamorphic		1					3	1
Unknown	4	3	1	3	1	2	1	1
Matrix (%)	56	64	48	60	48		63	
Temper (%)	41	32	38	30	30		29	
Void (%)	4	6	14	9	21		7	

K=potassium
+=mineral seen in original examination but not encountered in point counting

Andrew L. Christenson

Table A.4. Point-Count Data, Sherd Samples, Other Sites

Mineral/Rock	Site (Sample Number)				
	Aspen Creek AZ N:7:156		Sandretto AZ N:7:163		King's Ruin NA 1587
	(34)	*(35)*	*(1)*	*(1)*	*(2)*
Mineral					
Quartz	147	114	190	193	266
K feldspar	111	9	139	38	19
Plagioclase	99	188	44	83	38
Unknown feldspar		6	2		
Muscovite	9		5		25
Biotite	+	1		+	+
Unknown mica			12		27
Amphibole		15			
Pyroxene					+
Epidote		15			
Olivine					
Carbonate					
Hematite	5	2	1	5	2
Other opaque	6	6		6	23
Unknown	22	52	3	61	23
Rock Type					
Volcanic					+
Plutonic	2	13	2	3	4
Sedimentary					
Metamorphic		1			
Unknown	5	14	1	6	1
Matrix (%)	54				
Temper (%)	38				
Void (%)	8				

K=potassium
+=mineral seen in original examination but not encountered in point counting

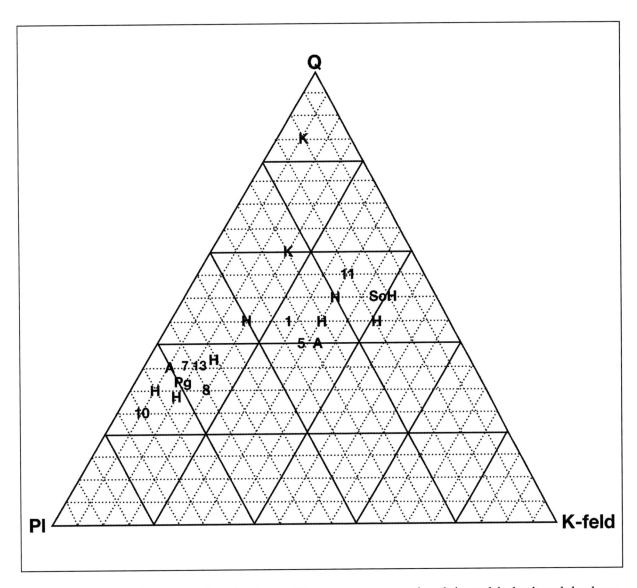

Figure A.1. Ternary diagram showing abundance of three most common minerals in sand, bedrock, and sherd samples. Sands: (1) Willow Creek tributary; (5) Mint Wash; (7) Aspen Creek; (8) Butte Creek; (10) Lynx Creek; (11) Big Chino Wash; (13) Willow Creek. Bedrock: (Pg) Prescott mass, Prescott Granodiorite. Sherds: (A) Site AZ N:7:156 (ASM); (H) Site AZ N:7:155 (ASM); (K) King's Ruin; (So) Sandretto Site.

Number of Minerals	Number of Rocks			
	1	*2*	*3*	*4*
4	155-8			
5	163-1 1587-1	155-6 155-20 155-22		
6	155-4 155-11 155-14 155-17 156-34		Sand 5 Sand 10	
7		156-35 1587-2	Sand 13	
8			Sand 7 Sand 8	Sand 1
9				Sand 11

Figure A.2. Rock and mineral diversity of petrographic samples.

here. Table A.5 compares the local bedrock mineralogy with that of the two AZ N:7:155 (ASM) ceramic clusters and the Aspen Creek and Butte Creek sand samples. There is little difference between the stream sands, the bedrock, and Cluster A of the sherds. The mica frequency is higher in the bedrock, probably because sericite (fine-grained muscovite) was counted. As this mineral does not usually occur in sand-size grains, it is not counted in the method used here. The alluvial sand samples are distinguished by the presence of accessory minerals and by the presence of volcanic and metamorphic rock fragments.

For many archaeologists, the finding that crushed rock, or at least residual sands, may be the primary source of temper in Prescott pottery is confirmation of what has always been believed. Colton and Hargrave (1937:184) defined Prescott Gray Ware temper as "quartz sand, crushed rock, and mica." Later analysts have also noted that this ware seems to be tempered with crushed granitic rock that "appears to have been greatly decomposed when obtained, sometimes resembling a coarse sand" (Keller 1993:67). It is unclear whether a coarse sand obtained near the bedrock source could easily be distinguished from a crushed rock. Certainly angular-

Table A.5. Mineralogy of Bedrock, Alluvial Sands, and Ceramic Temper

Locus	Mineral						Number of Samples
	Quartz	K Feldspar	Plagio-clase	Mica	Epidote	Other	
Bedrock[1]	28	10	54	6	2	tr	7
Butte Creek	28	12	54	0	4	2	1
Aspen Creek	33	9	52	1	2	1	1
AZ N:7:155							
Group A	33	12	53	1	2	tr	4
Group B	45	35	17	2	t	1	4

[1]Prescott mass, Prescott Granodiorite (from Krieger 1965:29); K=potassium; tr=trace (<0.5%)

If a potter from AZ N:7:155 (ASM) had stepped outside her dwelling, broken off a piece of bedrock, crushed it, and used it as temper, the resulting material would have had a composition similar to what was found in the Cluster A sherds: about five mineral types and only one rock type (plutonic). Presumably, residual sands around the bedrock outcrops would be similar. The fact that even the alluvial sands in the area have the characteristics of the local bedrock indicates that they originate from the breakdown of the Prescott mass of the Prescott Granodiorite, with small inputs of rock fragments from other remnant volcanic and metamorphic sources upstream.

The Cluster B sherds are an enigma, because no granitic bedrock in the Prescott area has a similar mineralogy (Krieger 1965:Table 7). Perhaps the temper in these sherds represents a granitic source outside the area studied by Krieger, or perhaps there is variation within the area that was not covered by her samples.

ity of the temper is probably not an adequate indicator by itself (Rice 1987:410).

This finding, based as it is on a small sample, should not be viewed as a reason for abandoning the collection of alluvial sand samples. There is evidence that some ceramics from the Neural site (NA 20788) were tempered with alluvial sands or made with self-tempered alluvial clays (Christenson 1996, 2000). Many more sites need to be examined before the relative importance of the two sources can be estimated. Krieger (1965) has sampled granitic rocks in the Prescott area (Prescott and Paulden, Arizona, 15 minute USGS quadrangles), but work needs to be done to the south and west.

A finding not in accord with the standard definition of Prescott Gray Ware is the low temper density in the sherds analyzed for this value (Tables A.3 and A.4). The range of values is from 30 to 41 percent, even though many of the sherds counted were estimated visually to have abundant temper (Table A.1). This discrepancy demonstrates that visual estimates of temper abundance on broken sherd surfaces are probably consistently high.

Oxidation Analysis

Mary-Ellen Walsh

Analysts undertake ceramic oxidation studies to characterize the composition of clays and ceramic pastes by color. The underlying principal of this technique is that certain clays will fire to only a specific range of colors (Shepard 1980). Because the approach is not quantitative, it is not as precise as a chemical analysis; the results can, however, be used to define the range of variation within a single ceramic type and among wares. Further, we can evaluate whether sherds of one or more types may have been produced with similar or different clays.

For the Hassayampa project analysis, the sample consisted of 104 sherds: 62 Prescott Gray, 2 Prescott Black-on-gray, 2 Prescott Red, 2 Prescott Red-on-gray, 1 possible Prescott Buff, 3 Tsegi Red-on-orange (possibly local), 20 Verde Brown, 1 Tuzigoot Brown, 5 Wingfield Plain, 1 Deadmans Black-on-gray, 3 untyped San Francisco Mountain Gray, and 2 untyped (one a brownware, one a possible buffware). Twelve of the Prescott Gray sherds had surface finish characteristics of Alameda Brown Ware; three other Prescott Gray sherds and the possible Prescott Buff sherd were similar in surface finish to San Francisco Mountain Gray Ware. The sherds represent at least 14 sites in the Prescott region and the Verde Valley.

Four clay samples were fired for comparative purposes, one each from Watson Lake and AZ N:7:163, AZ N:7:165, and AZ N:7:166 (ASM), all in the Prescott area. The sample from Watson Lake was a very fine paste silty clay with no obvious inclusions, and the sample from AZ N:7:163 (ASM) was a fine silty clay with fine sand inclusions. The samples from AZ N:7:165 (ASM) and AZ N:7:166 (ASM) were very sandy, particularly the one from AZ N:7:165 (ASM). No mica inclu-

sions were visible in the selected samples, but fine flecks of gold mica appeared in all four after firing.

Prior to firing, wet and dry Munsell colors were recorded for all samples under a 40-watt incandescent bulb. The clay samples were soaked in water for a few days, then worked by hand and formed into small, pie-shaped disks. After air-drying for three days, the samples were heated in a toaster oven at a temperature of about 100°F (38°C) for 30 minutes. The sherds and the completely cooled clay samples were placed in an electric kiln, and the temperature was gradually brought up to 950°F (520°C) and held constant for half an hour. After firing, colors were again recorded under a 40-watt incandescent bulb.

Table B.1 lists all samples with their Munsell colors after firing. Numbers in the "Group" column represent color groups identified by Bubemyre and Mills (1993:237) in oxidation studies for the Transwestern Pipeline Expansion project. Over 80% of the sherds and all of the clay samples in the current analysis oxidized to Group 6, red. Within this group were all of the Verde Brown sherds, the Tuzigoot Brown sherd, most Prescott Gray Ware sherds, two of the five Wingfield Plain sherds, the two untyped sherds, and one of the Tsegi Red-on-orange sherds. Eight sherds—three Prescott Gray, three Wingfield Plain, and the other two Tsegi Red-on-orange—fired to Group 7, a deeper red. The 11 sherds in Group 5, yellow-red, were one Prescott Red-on-gray, the possible Prescott Buff, five Prescott Gray, the Deadmans Black-on-gray, and the three San Francisco Mountain Gray Ware.

Bubemyre and Mills (1993:274) found that most of their Prescott Gray Ware sherds oxidized to Group 5, yellow-

Table B.1. Results of Oxidation Analysis by Munsell Color Groups

Sample	Site	Color	Group	Type
13	Sandretto Site	5YR 6/6	5	Prescott Gray
32	AZ N:7:155	5YR 6/6	5	Deadmans Black-on-gray
43	AZ N:7:155	5YR 6/6	5	Prescott Gray (SFM)
48	AZ N:7:155	5YR 6/6	5	untyped San Francisco Mountain Gray Ware
6	Bonnie Site	5YR 6/8	5	Prescott Gray
26	AZ N:7:155	5YR 6/8	5	Prescott Gray
40	AZ N:7:155	5YR 6/8	5	Untyped San Francisco Mountain Gray Ware
57	AZ N:7:155	5YR 6.6/8	5	Prescott Red-on-gray
49	AZ N:7:155	5YR 7/8	5	Untyped San Francisco Mountain Gray Ware
62	AZ N:7:155	7.5YR 7/4	5	Prescott Buff? (SFM)
67	AZ N:7:155	7.5YR 7/4	5	Prescott Gray (SFM)
33	AZ N:7:155	2.5YR 3/6	6	Tuzigoot Brown
17	no provenience	2.5YR 4/8	6	Verde Brown
35	AZ N:7:155	2.5YR 4/8	6	Prescott Gray (A)
38	AZ N:7:155	2.5YR 4/8	6	Prescott Gray (A)
68	AR-03-04-01-101	2.5YR 4/8	6	Verde Brown
69	AR-03-04-01-101	2.5YR 4/8	6	Verde Brown
70	AR-03-04-01-207	2.5YR 4/8	6	Verde Brown
71	AR-03-04-01-207	2.5YR 4/8	6	Verde Brown
74	AR-03-04-01-418	2.5YR 4/8	6	Verde Brown
75	AR-03-04-01-418	2.5YR 4/8	6	Verde Brown
93	AZ N:7:166	2.5YR 4/8	6	Prescott Gray
101	AZ N:7:166	2.5YR 4/8	6	Wingfield Plain
106	Clay - 165	2.5YR 4/8	6	Clay
44	AZ N:7:155	2.5YR 4.5/8	6	Prescott Gray
47	AZ N:7:155	2.5YR 4.5/8	6	Prescott Gray (A)[1]
65	AZ N:7:155	2.5YR 4.5/8	6	Prescott Gray (A)
5	Bonnie Site	2.5YR 5/6	6	Prescott Gray
60	AZ N:7:155	2.5YR 5/6	6	Prescott Gray (SFM)[2]
2	King's Ruin	2.5YR 5/8	6	Prescott Gray
3	King's Ruin	2.5YR 5/8	6	Prescott Gray
14	no provenience	2.5YR 5/8	6	Verde Brown
15	no provenience	2.5YR 5/8	6	Verde Brown
16	no provenience	2.5YR 5/8	6	Verde Brown
19	no provenience	2.5YR 5/8	6	Verde Brown
20	no provenience	2.5YR 5/8	6	Verde Brown
34	AZ N:7:155	2.5YR 5/8	6	Prescott Gray (A)
37	AZ N:7:155	2.5YR 5/8	6	Prescott Gray (A)
39	AZ N:7:155	2.5YR 5/8	6	Prescott Gray (A)
41	AZ N:7:155	2.5YR 5/8	6	Prescott Gray
42	AZ N:7:155	2.5YR 5/8	6	Prescott Gray (A)
45	AZ N:7:155	2.5YR 5/8	6	Prescott Gray
46	AZ N:7:155	2.5YR 5/8	6	Prescott Gray
50	AZ N:7:155	2.5YR 5/8	6	Prescott Gray
51	AZ N:7:155	2.5YR 5/8	6	untyped
52	AZ N:7:155	2.5YR 5/8	6	Prescott Red
54	AZ N:7:155	2.5YR 5/8	6	Prescott Red
55	AZ N:7:155	2.5YR 5/8	6	Prescott Gray (A)

Table B.1. Results of Oxidation Analysis by Munsell Color Groups, continued

Sample	Site	Color	Group	Type
56	AZ N:7:155	2.5YR 5/8	6	Prescott Gray
58	AZ N:7:155	2.5YR 5/8	6	Prescott Gray (A)
59	AZ N:7:155	2.5YR 5/8	6	Prescott Gray (A)
61	AZ N:7:155	2.5YR 5/8	6	Prescott Gray
66	AZ N:7:155	2.5YR 5/8	6	Prescott Gray
72	AR-03-04-01-266	2.5YR 5/8	6	Verde Brown
73	AR-03-04-01-266	2.5YR 5/8	6	Verde Brown
76	AR-03-04-01-505	2.5YR 5/8	6	Verde Brown
77	AR-03-04-01-505	2.5YR 5/8	6	Verde Brown
78	AR-03-04-01-521	2.5YR 5/8	6	Verde Brown
79	A1-03-04-01-521	2.5YR 5/8	6	Verde Brown
83	AZ N:7:165	2.5YR 5/8	6	Prescott Gray
84	AZ N:7:165	2.5YR 5/8	6	untyped brownware
89	AZ N:7:165	2.5YR 5/8	6	Prescott Gray
90	AZ N:7:165	2.5YR 5/8	6	Prescott Gray
92	AZ N:7:166	2.5YR 5/8	6	Prescott Gray
94	AZ N:7:166	2.5YR 5/8	6	Prescott Gray
95	AZ N:7:166	2.5YR 5/8	6	Prescott Gray
104	AZ N:7:166	2.5YR 5/8	6	Prescott Gray
105	clay - 163	2.5YR 5/8	6	clay
107	clay - 166	2.5YR 5/8	6	clay
108	clay - Watson Lake	2.5YR 5/8	6	clay
8	Bonnie Site	2.5YR 5.6/8	6	Prescott Gray
18	no provenience	2.5YR 5.6/8	6	Verde Brown
30	AZ N:7:155	2.5YR 5.6/8	6	Prescott Gray
36	AZ N:7:155	2.5YR 5.6/8	6	Prescott Red-on-gray
63	AZ N:7:155	2.5YR 5.6/8	6	Prescott Gray (A)
1	NA 26573	2.5YR 6/6	6	Prescott Gray
22	AZ N:7:155	2.5YR 6/6	6	Prescott Gray
24	AZ N:7:155	2.5YR 6/6	6	Prescott Gray
25	AZ N:7:155	2.5YR 6/6	6	Prescott Gray
9	Sandretto Site	2.5YR 6/6.8	6	Wingfield Plain
23	AZ N:7:155	2.5YR 6/6.8	6	Prescott Gray
4	Bonnie Site	2.5YR 6/8	6	Verde Brown
7	Bonnie Site	2.5YR 6/8	6	Prescott Gray
10	Sandretto Site	2.5YR 6/8	6	Prescott Gray
11	Sandretto Site	2.5YR 6/8	6	Prescott Gray
12	Sandretto Site	2.5YR 6/8	6	Prescott Gray
27	AZ N:7:155	2.5YR 6/8	6	Prescott Gray
28	AZ N:7:155	2.5YR 6/8	6	Prescott Gray
53	AZ N:7:155	2.5YR 6/8	6	Prescott Gray (SFM)
64	AZ N:7:155	2.5YR 6/8	6	Prescott Gray
88	AZ N:7:165	2.5YR 6/8	6	Prescott Gray
91	AZ N:7:165	2.5YR 6/8	6	Prescott Gray
96	AZ N:7:166	2.5YR 6/8	6	Prescott Gray
98	AZ N:7:166	2.5YR 6/8	6	Tsegi Red-on-orange
100	AZ N:7:166	2.5YR 6/8	6	Prescott Black-on-gray
101	AZ N:7:166	2.5YR 6/8	6	Prescott Gray

Table B.1. Results of Oxidation Analysis by Munsell Color Groups, continued

Sample	Site	Color	Group	Type
103	AZ N:7:166	2.5YR 6/8	6	Prescott Black-on-gray
29	AZ N:7:155	2.5YR 6.8/6	6	Prescott Gray
21	AZ N:7:156	2.5YR 6.8/8	6	Prescott Gray
31	AZ N:7:155	2.5YR 6.8/8	6	Prescott Gray
80	AZ N:7:165	10R 5/8	7	Prescott Gray
81	AZ N:7:165	10R 5/8	7	Prescott Gray
82	AZ N:7:165	10R 5/8	7	Prescott Gray
85	AZ N:7:165	10R 5/8	7	Wingfield Plain
86	AZ N:7:165	10R 5/8	7	Wingfield Plain
87	AZ N:7:165	10R 5/8	7	Wingfield Plain
97	AZ N:7:166	10R 6/8	7	Tsegi Red-on-orange
99	AZ N:7:166	10R 6/8	7	Tsegi Red-on-orange

[1]looks like (southern) Alameda Brown Ware
[2]looks like San Francisco Mountain Gray Ware

red. The results, they suggested, indicated compositionally similar pottery with differences in firing. Most samples of Alameda Brown Ware from their project area oxidized to Groups 4 and 5, yellow-red, although some sherds were in Group 6, red (Bubemyre and Mills 1993:275). Bubemyre and Mills (1993:275) also found that San Francisco Mountain Gray Ware oxidized to the same colors as Alameda Brown Ware (and Prescott Gray Ware), but they suggested different sources of production for the two wares.

In the present study, the yellow-red-firing clays of the San Francisco Mountain Gray Ware are distinct from the red-firing clays of Alameda Brown Ware and Prescott Gray Ware. Among the latter two groups, clays were apparently similar, though not necessarily derived from the same source or sources. However, the results of the analysis suggest as many as three sources of clay for the Prescott Gray Ware in the sample but a single source for the Verde Brown.

The results of the oxidation analysis cannot be used to suggest that Verde Brown pottery was made with the same clay as much of the Prescott Gray Ware (Group 6, Table B.1). However, the similarities in the types of clay used may reflect a sharing of ideas about ceramic production by the Prescott and the southern Sinagua. Similarly, although the small number of Prescott Gray sherds in Group 5, yellow-red, may indicate a misclassification of the sherds, another plausible explanation is that Prescott potters tried to imitate the production of San Francisco Mountain Gray Ware by using similar clays. The source of these clays is uncertain.

Note

This report is revised from a paper presented at the 1996 Arizona Archaeological Council meetings in Prescott.

Pollen and Macrobotanical Data

Linda Scott Cummings, Kathryn Puseman, and Thomas E. Moutoux

The following diagrams and tables provide the incidence of pollen taxa and counts of macrobotanical remains by feature for Sites AZ N:6:20 (ASM), AZ N:7:155 (ASM), and AZ N:7:156 (ASM).

Total pollen counts per sample range from 7 to 203. Pollen counts include starch granules, pollen aggregates as individual grains, and indeterminate pollen (pollen grains folded, mutilated, or otherwise distorted beyond recognition). Pollen aggregates are denoted on the pollen diagrams by an *A*. A plus (+) indicates either a pollen type observed outside the regular count while scanning the remainder of the microscope slide or pollen recorded in an amount too small for a percentage to be calculated.

Macrofloral identifications include taxon, plant part, and whether the specimen was charred or uncharred. In most instances only charred macrofloral remains are considered in interpreting prehistoric sites. Interpretation of uncharred seeds as presence in the prehistoric record is considered on a sample-by-sample basis and generally depends on extraordinary conditions for preservation.

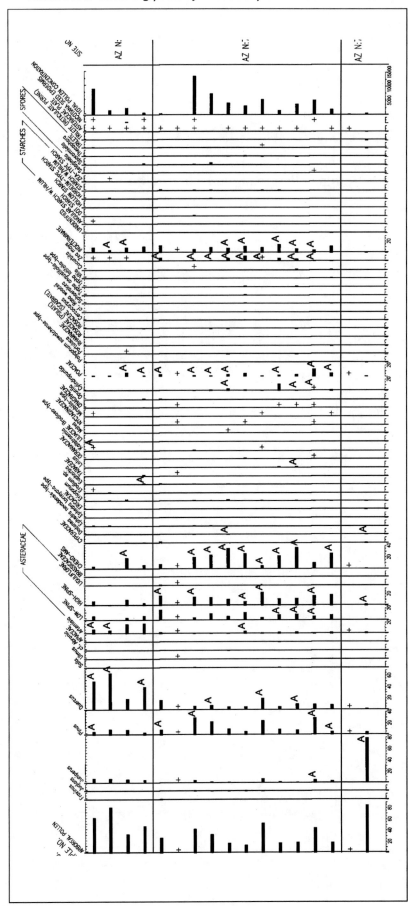

Figure C.1. Pollen diagram, AZ N:6:20 (ASM), AZ N:7:155 (ASM), and AZ N:7:156 (ASM).

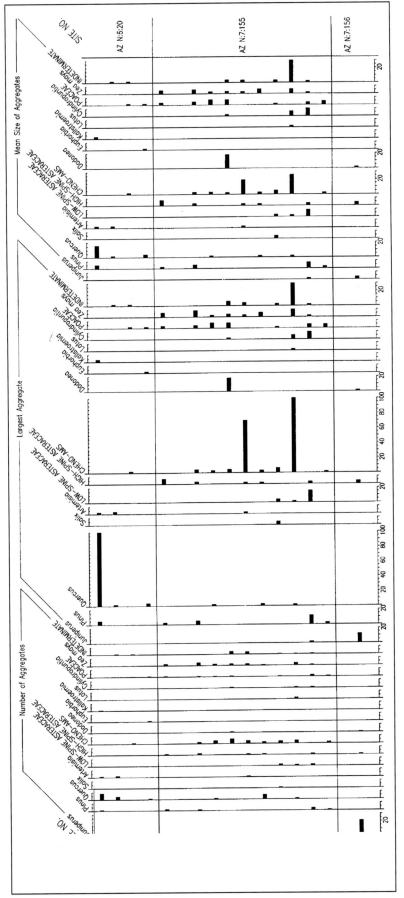

Figure C.2. Pollen aggregates diagram, AZ N:6:20 (ASM), AZ N:7:155 (ASM), and AZ N:7:156 (ASM).

Table C.1. Macrofloral Remains, AZ N:6:20 (ASM)

Sample (Feature)	Identification	Part	Charred		Uncharred		Weight/ Comments
			W	F	W	F	
107 (1)	Liters Floated						4.2
	LF Weight						61.85 g
	Floral Remains						
	Monocot	Stem		1			
	Chenopodium	Seed			1		
	Lamiaceae	Seed			1		
	Mollugo	Seed			780*		
	Pinus monophylla	Needle			1		
	Portulaca	Seed			90*		
	Sesuvium	Seed			2		
	Rootlets					X	Numerous
	Sclerotia				X		Moderate
	Charcoal/Wood						
	Total charcoal ≥ 2 mm						0.07 g
	Cercocarpus	Moderate		4			0.03 g
	Quercus	Moderate		4			0.02 g
	Nonfloral Remains						
	Insect					21	
	Rodent feces				X		Numerous
	Worm castings				X		Numerous
92 (2)	Liters Floated						3.8
	LF Weight						43.37 g
	Floral Remains						
	Arctostaphylos	Seed		2			
	Atriplex	Seed	3	3			
	Zea mays	Cupule	3	4			
	PET Fruity	Tissue		1			
	Pinus monophylla	Needle			1	X	Moderate
	Rootlets					X	Numerous
	Sclerotia				X		Numerous
	Charcoal/Wood						
	Total charcoal ≥ 2 mm						0.66 g
	Cercocarpus	Present		3			0.03 g
	Juniperus	Present		1			<0.01 g
	Pinus ponderosa	Present		1			0.01 g
	Quercus	Dominant		6			0.25 g
	Nonfloral Remains						
	Insect	Puparia			1		
	Insect					13	
	Beetle				2		
	Worm castings				X		Numerous

Table C.1. Macrofloral Remains, AZ N:6:20 (ASM), continued

Sample (Feature)	Identification	Part	Charred		Uncharred		Weight/ Comments
			W	F	W	F	
64 (3)	Liters Floated						2
	LF Weight						24.30 g
	Floral Remains						
	Juniperus	Seed	1				
	Zea mays	Cupule		1			
	Atriplex	Seed			7		
	Chenopodium	Seed			1	4	
	Euphorbia	Seed			2		
	Lamiaceae	Seed			1		
	Mollugo	Seed			12		
	Pinus monophylla	Needle				1	
	Portulaca	Seed			2		
	Rootlets					X	Numerous
	Charcoal/Wood						
	Total charcoal ≥ 2 mm						0.13 g
	Cercocarpus	Present		1			0.01 g
	Pinus	Sub-Dominant		5			0.05 g
	Quercus	Dominant		7			0.05 g
	Nonfloral Remains						
	Calcined bone			1			
	Insect					32	
	Rodent feces				X		Moderate
	Worm castings				X		Numerous
109 (9)	Liters Floated						4.5
	LF Weight						45.03 g
	Floral Remains						
	Zea mays	Cupule		1			
	Monocot	Stem		1			
	Astragalus	Seed			1		
	Atriplex	Seed			1		
	Chenopodium	Seed			1	5	
	Lamiaceae	Seed			1	2	
	Mollugo	Seed			160*		
	Pinus	Needle				1	
	Pinus	Seed			2		
	Portulaca	Seed			32*		
	Sesuvium	Seed			1		
	Trifolium	Seed			1		
	Rootlets					X	Numerous
	Sclerotia				X		Moderate

Table C.1. Macrofloral Remains, AZ N:6:20 (ASM), continued

Sample (Feature)	Identification	Part	Charred		Uncharred		Weight/ Comments
			W	F	W	F	
109 (9) cont.	**Charcoal/Wood**						
	Total charcoal ≥ 2 mm						0.06 g
	Cercocarpus	Present		1			<0.01 g
	Juniperus	Present		2			0.01 g
	Quercus	Dominant		6			0.03 g
	Nonfloral Remains						
	Insect					48*	
	Rodent feces				X		Numerous
	Worm castings				X		Numerous

W=whole
F=fragment
X=presence noted in sample
LF=light fraction
*Estimated frequency based on sort of portion of total volume floated

Table C.2. Macrofloral Remains, AZ N:7:155 (ASM)

Sample (Feature)	Identification	Part	Charred		Uncharred		Weight/ Comments
			W	F	W	F	
182 (2-1)	Liters Floated						2.2
	LF Weight						16.48 g
	Floral Remains						
	Polygonum	Seed		1			
	Zea mays	Cupule		3			
	Zea mays	Kernel embryo	1				
	Pinus ponderosa	Needle			3	6	
	Rootlets					X	Numerous
	Charcoal/Wood						
	Total charcoal ≥ 2 mm						0.01 g
	Quercus	Moderate		7			0.01 g
186 (2-2)	Liters Floated						1.3
	LF Weight						32.25 g
	Floral Remains						
	Juglans	Nutshell		2			
	Mollugo	Seed			2		
	Pinus	Needle				3	
	Rootlets					X	Numerous
	Nonfloral Remains						
	Insect				2	1	
541 (3)	Liters Floated						2.6
	LF Weight						25.65 g
	Floral Remains						
	Pinus-type	Bark scale		7			
	Zea mays	Cupule	1	1			
	Zea mays	Kernel		4			
	Rootlets					X	Moderate
	Sclerotia				1		
	Charcoal/Wood						
	Total charcoal	≥ 2 mm					0.49 g
	Cercocarpus	Present		1			<0.01 g
	Cowania	Present		1			<0.01 g
	Pinus ponderosa	Dominant		10			0.34 g
	Quercus	Present		3			<0.01 g
	Nonfloral Remains						
	Insect					1	

Linda Scott Cummings, Kathryn Puseman, and Thomas E. Moutoux

Table C.2. Macrofloral Remains, AZ N:7:155 (ASM), continued

Sample (Feature)	Identification	Part	Charred		Uncharred		Weight/ Comments
			W	F	W	F	
335 (4)	Liters Floated						5.3
	LF Weight						85.65 g
	Floral Remains						
	Juglans	Nutshell		1			
	Zea mays	Cupule		1			
	Unidentified	Seed		1	4	7	
	Alnus	Seed			1		
	Asteraceae	Seed			5	1	
	Ambrosia	Seed			7	3	
	Brassicaceae	Seed			40*		
	Chenopodium	Seed			2		
	Euphorbia	Seed			2		
	Lamiaceae	Seed			1		
	Malva	Fruit			1		
	Mollugo	Seed			2		
	Pinus ponderosa	Needle				X	Numerous
	Pinus ponderosa	Cone scale				2	
	Pinus ponderosa	Seed			3		
	Poaceae	Stem base				X	Numerous
	Poaceae	Leaf/Stem				X	Moderate
	Poaceae	Seed			3	2	
	Bouteloua	Inflorescence			4		
	Bouteloua	Seed			51		
	Festuca	Seed			1		
	Sporobolus	Seed			1		
	Portulaca	Seed			2		
	Quercus	Acorn			1		
	Dicot	Leaf			1		
	Rootlets					X	Numerous
	Charcoal/Wood						
	Total charcoal ≥ 1 mm						0.03 g
	Pinus	Present		3			0.03 g
	Nonfloral Remains						
	Bone					21	
	Calcined bone			1			
	Rodent tooth			1		3	
	Insect					102	
	Snail				3		
	Worm castings				X		Moderate

Table C.2. Macrofloral Remains, AZ N:7:155 (ASM), continued

Sample (Feature)	Identification	Part	Charred		Uncharred		Weight/ Comments
			W	F	W	F	
347 (4)	Liters Floated						5
	LF Weight						39.76 g
	Floral Remains						
	Arctostaphylos	Seed	15	15			
	Cheno-am	Embryo	1				
	Chenopodium	Seed		2			
	Juglans	Nutshell		14			
	Juniperus	Seed	1				
	Vitis	Seed	2	3			
	Zea mays	Cupule	3	23			
	Zea mays	Kernel		5			
	Mollugo	Seed			6		
	Pinus ponderosa	Needle				2	
	Sesuvium	Seed				1	
	Rootlets					X	Numerous
	Charcoal/Wood						
	Total charcoal ≥ 2 mm						0.62 g
	Juniperus	Present		1			0.01 g
	Pinus ponderosa	Present		3			0.07 g
	Prunus	Present		3			0.07 g
	Quercus	Dominant		13			0.26 g
	Nonfloral Remains						
	Bone			5		23	
	Calcined bone			5			
	Canine tooth				1		
	Insect					30	
	Snail				6		
	Worm castings				X		Few
382 (4)	Liters Floated						3.9
	LF Weight						21.78 g
	Floral Remains						
	Arctostaphylos	Seed	15	21			
	Cheno-am	Embryo	2	1			
	Chenopodium	Seed	1				
	Cleome	Seed	1				
	Juglans	Nutshell		37		2	
	Opuntia	Seed	1				
	Zea mays	Cupule	3	51			
	Zea mays	Kernel		23			
	Mollugo	Seed			2		
	Rootlets					X	Moderate

Table C.2. Macrofloral Remains, AZ N:7:155 (ASM), continued

Sample (Feature)	Identification	Part	Charred		Uncharred		Weight/ Comments
			W	F	W	F	
382 (4) cont.	**Charcoal/Wood**						
	Total charcoal ≥ 2 mm						1.23 g
	Cercocarpus	Present		2			<0.01 g
	Cowania	Present		2			0.01 g
	Pinus	Moderate		7			0.30 g
	Quercus	Dominant		9			0.12 g
	Unidentifiable (vitrified)	Present		1			0.07 g
	Nonfloral Remains						
	Bone			3	1	31	
	Calcined bone			4			
	Tooth					3	
	Insect					190	
	Rodent feces					X	Few
	Snail				4	1	
439 (4)	Liters Floated						3.8
	LF Weight						26.12 g
	Floral Remains						
	cf. *Agave*	Epidermis	1				
	Arctostaphylos	Seed	15	21			
	Chenopodium	Seed	1				
	Juglans	Nutshell		4			
	Physalis	Seed	1				
	Pinus-type	Bark scale		3			
	Portulaca	Seed	1				
	Zea mays	Cupule	3	15			
	Zea mays	Kernel		8			
	Celtis	Seed				2	
	Pinus	Needle				1	
	Poaceae	Inflorescence			1		
	Bouteloua	Seed			2		
	Rootlets					X	Numerous
	Charcoal/Wood						
	Total charcoal ≥ 2 mm						1.06 g
	Arctostaphylos	Present		1			<0.01 g
	Cercocarpus	Present		4			0.09 g
	Pinus ponderosa	Present		1			0.02 g
	Quercus	Dominant		10			0.27 g
	Unidentifiable (vitrified)	Present		4			0.11 g

Table C.2. Macrofloral Remains, AZ N:7:155 (ASM), continued

Sample (Feature)	Identification	Part	Charred		Uncharred		Weight/ Comments
			W	F	W	F	
439 (4) cont.	**Nonfloral Remains**						
	Bone			1		35	
	Calcined bone			2			
	Tooth					1	
	Insect					9	
	Snail				4		
305 (5)	Liters Floated						5
	LF Weight						56.51 g
	Floral Remains						
	Juglans	Nutshell		1			
	Zea mays	Cupule		5			
	Zea mays	Kernel		1			
	Asteraceae	Seed			29		
	Ambrosia	Seed			7		
	Brassicaceae	Seed			14		
	Lepidium	Seed			1		
	Calandrinia	Seed			1		
	Celtis	Seed				1	
	Chenopodium	Seed			4	1	
	Euphorbia	Seed			5		
	Lamiaceae	Seed			1		
	Mollugo	Seed			20		
	Pinus	Needle				X	Few
	Poaceae	Stem				X	Few
	Poaceae	Seed			9	2	
	Bouteloua	Seed			1		
	Festuca	Seed			1		
	Sporobolus	Seed			10		
	Polygonum	Seed			2		
	Portulaca	Seed			2		
	Sesuvium	Seed			3	1	
	Rootlets					X	Numerous
	Charcoal/Wood						
	Total charcoal ≥ 2 mm						0.06 g
	Pinus	Present		1			0.01 g
	Quercus	Moderate		5			0.02 g
	Unidentified	Moderate		4			0.02 g

Table C.2. Macrofloral Remains, AZ N:7:155 (ASM), continued

Sample (Feature)	Identification	Part	Charred		Uncharred		Weight/ Comments
			W	F	W	F	
305 (5) cont.	**Nonfloral Remains**						
	Bone			3		9	
	Calcined bone			5			
	Insect				7	153	
	Rodent feces				X		Moderate
	Worm castings				X		Moderate
317 (5)	Liters Floated						5.1
	LF Weight						31.38 g
	Floral Remains						
	Arctostaphylos	Seed		10			
	Juglans	Nutshell		15			
	Pinus ponderosa	Seed	2				
	Zea mays	Cupule	4	22			
	Zea mays	Kernel		8			
	Asteraceae	Seed				1	
	Festuca	Seed			1		
	Mollugo	Seed			3		
	Portulaca	Seed			1		
	Rootlets					X	Moderate
	Charcoal/Wood						
	Total charcoal ≥ 2 mm						0.46 g
	Arctostaphylos	Moderate		5			0.05 g
	Cercocarpus	Present		1			0.01 g
	Pinus ponderosa	Moderate		6			0.08 g
	Prunus	Present		2			0.03 g
	Quercus	Moderate		6			0.05 g
	Nonfloral Remains						
	Bone			1			
	Calcined bone			1			
	Insect					2	
	Snail				2	1	
327 (5)	Liters Floated						4.3
	LF Weight						29.87 g
	Floral Remains						
	Arctostaphylos	Seed	11	8			
	Cheno-am	Embryo	2				
	Chenopodium	Seed	6	1			
	Juglans	Nutshell		7			
	Opuntia	Seed		1			
	Phaseolus	Seed		4			

Table C.2. Macrofloral Remains, AZ N:7:155 (ASM), continued

Sample (Feature)	Identification	Part	Charred		Uncharred		Weight/ Comments
			W	F	W	F	
327 (5) cont.	*Vitis*	Seed		1			
	Zea mays	Cupule	2	16			
	Zea may	Kernel		2			
	Mollugo	Seed			1		
	Portulaca	Seed			7		
	Rootlets					X	Moderate
	Charcoal/Wood						
	Total charcoal ≥ 2 mm						3.84 g
	Arctostaphylos	Moderate		6			0.03 g
	Cercocarpus	Present		2			<0.01 g
	Pinus ponderosa	Present		2			0.01 g
	Prunus	Present		1			0.01 g
	Quercus	Present		2			0.02 g
	Unidentifiable (vitrified)	Dominant		17			3.10 g
	Nonfloral Remains						
	Bone			8		30	
	Calcined bone			3			
	Tooth					1	
	Insect					1	
	Snail				2		
356 (10)	Liters Floated						4.5
	LF Weight						48.12 g
	Floral Remains						
	Cheno-am	Seed	1				
	Juglans	Nutshell		1			
	Zea mays	Cupule		1			
	Arctostaphylos	Seed			2		
	Asteraceae	Seed			3	5	
	Brassicaceae	Seed			1		
	Chenopodium	Seed			1		
	Convolvulus	Seed			2		
	Lamiaceae	Seed			31		
	Mollugo	Seed			915*	20*	
	Oenothera	Seed			3		
	Pinus ponderosa	Needle				X	Moderate
	Pinus ponderosa	Cone scale				2	
	Pinus ponderosa	Seed				1	
	Poaceae	Stem base				X	Moderate
	Poaceae	Seed			4	5	
	Bouteloua	Inflorescence				2	
	Bouteloua	Seed			80		

Table C.2. Macrofloral Remains, AZ N:7:155 (ASM), continued

Sample (Feature)	Identification	Part	Charred		Uncharred		Weight/ Comments
			W	F	W	F	
356 (10) cont.	*Festuca*	Seed			2		
	Polygonum	Seed			10		
	Portulaca	Seed			176*		
	Sesuvium	Seed			6		
	Trifolium	Seed			1		
	Unidentified	Seed			2		
	Dicot	Leaf			1		
	Rootlets					X	Numerous
	Charcoal/Wood						
	Total charcoal ≥ 2 mm						0.11 g
	Juniperus	Dominant					0.08 g
	Nonfloral Remains						
	Insect				3	1755*	
	Rodent feces				X		Moderate
	Worm castings				X		Numerous
366 (10)	Liters Floated						4.9
	LF Weight						10.40 g
	Floral Remains						
	Chenopodium	Seed	1				
	Pinus	Needle		1		1	
	Pinus-type	Bark scale		2			
	Lamiaceae	Seed	2				
	Mollugo	Seed			374*		
	Poaceae	Seed			2		
	Portulaca	Seed			160*	6	
	Sesuvium	Seed			1		
	Unidentified	Seed				1	
	Rootlets					X	Numerous
	Charcoal/Wood						
	Total charcoal ≥ 1 mm						<0.01 g
	Juniperus	Present		2			<0.01 g
	Quercus	Present		2			<0.01 g
	Nonfloral Remains						
	Bone					1	
	Insect					395*	
	Snail				2		
	Worm castings				X		Numerous

W=whole, F=fragment, X=presence noted in sample, LF=light fraction
*Estimated frequency based on sort of a portion of total volume floated

Table C.3. Macrofloral Remains, AZ N:7:156(ASM)

Sample (Feature)	Identification	Part	Charred		Uncharred		Weights/ Comments
			W	F	W	F	
151 (1-1)	Liters Floated						3.6
	LF Weight						52.13 g
	Floral Remains						
	Arctostaphylos	Seed		1			
	Chenopodium	Seed		4			
	Juniperus	Leaf/Twig				1	
	Rootlets					X	Numerous
	Sclerotia				212*		
	Charcoal/Wood						
	Total charcoal ≥ 2 mm						0.07 g
	Quercus	Moderate		4			0.07 g
	Nonfloral Remains						
	Calcined bone			1			
	Insect					106	
	Rodent feces				X		Numerous
	Worm castings				X		Moderate

W=whole
F=fragment
X=presence noted in sample
LF=light fraction
*Estimated frequency based on sort of a portion of total volume floated

Osteological Description of Burial Features from AZ N:7:155 (ASM)

Dee A. Jones

Eight burial features at Site AZ N:7:155 (ASM) contained the remains of nine individuals. Features 6, 7, 11A, 11B, 12, 13, 15, and 16 were inhumations; Feature 8 was a cremation.

Feature 6

Age: 43–55 years
Sex: male

Feature 6 was the fragmentary remains of an older adult male. Backhoe trenching removed the hands, innominates, femora, and left patella, and the proximal portion of the right tibia. Except for the missing patella, portions of all these elements appeared during backdirt screening. The left tibia was stained with hematite.

Male gender identification was based on pelvic and cranial characteristics along with overall robustness. The pelvis had a somewhat narrow sciatic notch with a raised auricular surface and a pre-auricular sulcus. The body of the sacrum was larger than its ala. This individual's cranium displayed a retreating forehead, blunt superior orbit borders, and suprameatal crests. The mandible had a square mental eminence. This individual was generally robust, with maximum humeral and femoral head diameters well into the male range (50 mm for the right humerus and 53 mm for the right femur). The midshaft circumferences of the femora were also large, at 89 mm.

Age at death was determined from the sternal end of the fourth rib and the epiphyseal union. The sternal end of the right fourth rib was clearly a Phase 6 (43--55 years). All epiphyses were fused, including the medial end of the clavicle (30+ years). Arthritic lipping of the thoracic

and lumbar vertebrae and the presence of Schmorl's nodes supported the older-adult designation.

The dentition was also consistent with an older adult. This individual had lost 15 teeth antemortem: the maxillary R:CI through P1 and L:M1 and the mandibular R:CI, LI, P2, M1, M3, L:CI, and P1 through M1. All areas with antemortem tooth loss also demonstrated extensive remodeling of the alveolar surface. The maxillary R:P2 and the mandibular R:C, P1, L:LI, and C were present, with extensive wear. The maxillary L:LI through P2 were damaged postmortem, precluding observations of these teeth. Several other teeth were missing postmortem: the maxillary R:M2, L:M2, and M3 and the mandibular R:M2, L:M2, and M3. Two apical abscesses were present, one at the base of the right canine and one at the base of the first premolar.

Pathological conditions also affected the temporal mandibular joint and the vertebrae of this individual. The right mandibular condyle exhibited an extremely flattened superior surface with slight arthritic growth on the condyle. The left condyle was only slightly flattened. Arthritis of the vertebral column ranged from slight to a 0.9-cm projection posteriorly and superiorly from the vertebral bodies of the ninth through eleventh thoracic vertebrae and the first and second lumbar. The sixth, seventh, ninth, tenth, and twelfth thoracic and the first lumbar vertebrae also exhibited Schmorl's nodes on the superior surface of the vertebral bodies. The right patella showed slight lipping on the superior border of the articular surface.

Nonpathological anomalies were also present. The trochanteric fossae of the femora exhibited exostosis. The ilia had pronounced anterior gluteal lines, almost a canal rather than simply a roughening on the lateral ilial surface. Finally, the mental foramen were much larger than normal.

Feature 7

Age: 30+ years
Sex: male

This remains of this male were well preserved and relatively complete. Feature 7 was in the older age range, with many arthritic growths, and was the only individual in this collection who had experienced perimortem trauma. Hematite staining was present on the distal half of each tibia.

The gender of this individual was determined by pelvic and cranial characteristics. The pelvis had a narrow sciatic notch, an acute sub-pubic angle, a flat auricular surface, and no pre-auricular sulcus. The sacrum was curved, with a sacral body larger than its ala. The cranium displayed pronounced supraorbital ridges, a retreating forehead, blunt superior orbit borders, a moderately developed external occipital protuberance, a developed suprameatal crest, and medium mastoid processes. The mandible had a square mental eminence and a gonial angle that was close to 90 degrees. Overall this individual was robust and muscular, with the maximum head diameters of the humerus (53 cm) and femora (51 cm and 52 cm) well within the male range.

Estimation of age at death was based primarily on epiphyseal union. All epiphyses were fused, including the medial end of the clavicle (30+ years). The number of arthritic changes that affected this individual and the presence of ossified thyroid cartilage also supported the designation of older adult.

The dentition was either worn to dentine, with the majority of the cusps worn away, or completely worn to root stumps (the maxillary R:LI, C, P1, M1, L:C through M2). All of the mandibular teeth were worn to dentine, with the exception of the R:M3, which still had identifiable cusps with only moderate wear. The upper right M2 was missing antemortem, and the alveolar surface was totally remodeled. The mandible had a small apical abscess at the right central incisor. The maxilla

exhibited four abscesses. One large abscess, above the left second molar, was approximately 1.6 cm in diameter. The edges were rough, with no healing present in the abscess itself. A smaller apical abscess, posterior to and slightly above the third molar, was in the process of being subsumed by the larger one at the time of this individual's death. The most extensive of the maxillary abscesses was above the left incisors. This abscess measured 2.2 by 1.2 cm and had eroded a hole through the palate, nearly to the nasal septum. No evidence of healing was present. The fourth abscess, above the right central incisor, was a small apical abscess that was starting to heal and remodel.

Extensive arthritic osteophytosis had affected this male's vertebral column. The seventh through twelfth thoracic vertebrae had slight arthritic lipping of the marginal border of the body. The second, third, and fifth lumbar vertebrae exhibited diffuse idiopathic skeletal hyperostosis (DISH), with projections measuring approximately 2 by 1.5 cm rising superiorly and posteriorly from the midbody of the vertebrae. The fifth lumbar and the sacrum demonstrated the same exostosis, but the left side of these projections had fused the two elements. As there was no involvement of the costal and sacral joints, this individual did not have ankylosing spondylitis. Both mandibular condyles were slightly flattened superiorly. The olecranon fossa of the right ulna demonstrated slight arthritic lipping of the articular surface.

The most interesting aspect of this burial was the presence of unhealed trauma. First, the spinous processes of the fourth and fifth cervical vertebrae had been cut off by a sharp-edged object, leaving a cut mark on the left side of the spinous process of the sixth cervical vertebra. Second, the left gonial angle of the mandible was cut off in an anterior inferior angle. Lastly, slightly posterior to the middle of the left temporal-occipital suture was a depression from blunt-object trauma. The object that induced the trauma had a small edge, roughly 1–3 cm. A pond fracture approximately 10 cm long and 5 cm wide surrounded the depression, and a large, open crack fissured superiorly through the left parietal and into the right. An ovoid, pond-like depression occurs only when blunt trauma has been applied to green cranial bone; dry bone usually cracks or breaks in a non-uniform manner.

The absence of healing indicates that these traumas occurred around the time of death and more than likely were the cause of this individual's death.

Feature 8

Age: adult
Sex: indeterminate

Feature 8 was the only cremation found at the site. These adult remains were well preserved but fragmentary. The bone was white and porcelainized, with moderate warping.

Due to the fragmented nature of these remains, the gender of the individual could not be determined. Estimated age at death was based on epiphyseal union. The radial head was fused (18–19+ years). There were no other indicators of age, and all fragments were consistent with adult skeletal morphology.

Weight of Determinate Bones	6.0 g
Weight of Indeterminate Bones	7.0 g
Total Bone Weight	**13.0 g**
Identifiable Fragments	11
Unidentifiable Fragments	35
Total Number of Fragments	**46**

Feature 11A

Age: 25–35 years
Sex: female

Feature 11A was the fragmented but relatively complete and very well preserved remains of a female. Hematite staining was present on the midshaft of the femora, and the cranium exhibited extreme artificial occipital deformation.

The gender of this individual was determined by examination of the pelvis and cranium. The pelvis had very strong female characteristics: a wide sciatic notch, an obtuse sub-pubic angle, a raised pre-auricular surface, a pinched ischio-pubic ramus, and dorsal pitting of the pubis. The sacrum was flat, with the body nearly the same size as the ala. The cranium had small mastoid processes and a small suprameatal crest. The mandible had a round mental eminence.

Estimated age at death was based on changes to the pubic symphysial face and epiphyseal closure. The pubic symphysis was a Phase VI by the Todd (1920) method (30–35 years) and a Phase IV by the Suchey-Brooks (1988) method (25–50 years). All present epiphyses were fused; the medial end of the clavicle was not present. The small amount of wear on the dentition and the lack of arthritic changes place this individual at the lower end of the age range given by the two pubic symphysis methods.

The dentition exhibited light to moderate wear. The maxillary R:CI, C, P1, P2, M3, L:CI, C, P2, P2, and M2 and the mandibular R:CI through P2 and L:CI through C demonstrated light wear with no dentine exposed. The maxillary R:M1, M2, and L:M1 were worn to the dentine. The mandibular R:M2, and L:P1 through M3 cusps were eroded away by extensive occlusal caries. The mandibular right first premolar also had a distal interproximal caries, and the maxillary R:M1, M2, and L:M2 had small occlusal caries. The maxillary R:LI, L:LI, and M3 were missing postmortem. The mandibular R:M1 and M3 were missing antemortem, with only slight remodeling present. This individual also had a supernumerary tooth posterior to the left maxillary lateral incisor.

This young adult female had a few non-pathological skeletal anomalies. The vertebrae demonstrated cranial shifting, as the first sacral vertebra had lumbar-like characteristics. The lamina of the spinous process and the articular facets (with the second sacral vertebra) were unfused. This individual still had traces of a bipartite Mendoza suture on the occipital bone.

Feature 11B

Age: <2 years
Sex: indeterminate

Feature 11B, an infant, was identified in the laboratory during analysis of Feature 11A. The remains of this individual were fairly well preserved and consisted of the right scapula with unfused glenoid fossa and medial border, a piece of unfused ischium, a petrous portion of the temporal, a portion of the condyloid fossa, an unfused posterior portion of the occipital, and three parietal fragments.

Estimated age at death was based on skeletal development and the size of the remains. There were no fused elements, and all portions were small. The best estimate is under 2 years. Gender identification is not possible in an individual this young.

Feature 12

Age: adult
Sex: indeterminate

The remains of this adult were moderately well preserved but incomplete, consisting of fragmented portions of the occipitals, temporals, right ulna, innominates, femora, fibulae, and left tibia, five ribs, the right calcaneus, the tenth through twelfth thoracic vertebrae, and two other thoracic vertebrae. Two phalanges, the right talus, and the left maxillary lateral incisor were present and complete. The distal portion of the tibia exhibited slight hematite staining.

Appropriate elements for determining the gender of this individual were not present. Estimated age at the time of death was based on skeletal development. The distal tibia and femur were fused, indicating that this individual was an adult.

The one tooth present, the left lateral incisor, was found in the pit fill. The cusps were worn, and secondary dentine was exposed. The talus and calcaneus had squatting facets, and moderate rodent gnawing was observed on the femoral shafts and the anterior crest of the fibulae.

Feature 13

Age: 9 ± 2.5 years
Sex: indeterminate

Feature 13 represented the fragmentary and incomplete but well-preserved remains of a child. Elements present were fragmented portions of both parietals, the left temporal, the right maxilla, the left mandible, both scapulae,

the right radius, the left ulna, the right tibia, one thoracic vertebra, and three lumbar vertebrae. The ilium, ischium, femur, left tibia, and four ribs were present and complete.

Age at death was determined by dental eruption. The left maxillary lateral incisor had erupted and was missing postmortem. The left maxillary canine was soon to erupt but was still in the crypt. The left maxillary second or third molar was still in the crypt; the state of preservation did not allow more exact identification. The dental eruption pattern and overall skeletal development supported an age range of 9 ± 2.5 years. Gender cannot be determined in an individual this young.

Feature 15

Age: adult
Sex: male

Feature 15, the burial of an adult male, was disturbed, with excellent preservation of the elements present. Missing elements were the right zygomatic, left mandible, left scapula, right clavicle, pubis, right patella, cervical vertebrae, four indeterminate thoracic vertebrae between the second and the ninth, and the majority of the bones of the hands and feet.

Gender determination was based on characteristics of the pelvis and cranium. The pelvis had a narrow sciatic notch, a very narrow superior inlet, a flat auricular surface, and no pre-auricular sulcus. The sacral body was larger than its ala. The cranium had pronounced supraorbital ridges, blunt superior orbit borders, medium-sized mastoid processes, and a developed suprameatal crest. The overall muscular development was relatively robust and consistent with male morphology.

Age at time of death was determined by epiphyseal fusion. All present epiphyses were fused, and the medial end of the clavicle was not present (18+ years). Dental wear was slight to moderate. The teeth from the left maxillary P2 to the right C were lost postmortem. The maxillary R:P1, P2, M3, and L:M3 and both M1s and M2s exhibited moderate wear. This wear pattern is consistent with adult dentition.

The dentition exhibited pathological conditions. The maxillary right deciduous canine was still present, indicating either super-eruption of the canine or retention of the deciduous tooth. All dentition displayed one enamel hypoplasia line. Pathological conditions were also present on the cranium, vertebrae, and tibia. The frontal bossing of the cranium had extensive porotic pitting that extended into the parietals. The most extensive remodeling was on the anterior of the parietal and the posterior of the frontal. The first sacral vertebra exhibited slight marginal lipping. The right tibia appeared to have well-healed periosteal lesions 8 to 13 cm from the distal end. The infection appeared to be local, with no evidence of breakage, but trauma was possible, since the surface was irregularly healed.

Feature 16

Age: 18–23 years
Sex: indeterminate

Feature 16 was the very incomplete but well-preserved remains of a young adult. The fragments present con-sisted of portions of the right parietal, left ischium, left tibia, fibulae, femoral shaft, left triquetral, left trapezium, left cuboid, right third cuneiform, and left first metatarsal. The only complete elements were the left talus and the right tibia.

Gender designation for this individual was not possible because of the incompleteness of the remains. Age at death was determined by epiphyseal fusion. The distal tibia, fibula, and calcaneus were all fused (17–20 years). The proximal tibia still had a line of fusion (18–23 years). The closest approximation to the age of Feature 16 at the time of death is 18–23 years.

Mild but abundant porotic pinhole pitting was present in the parietal region. The superior portion of the anterior crest of both tibias exhibited moderate rodent gnawing, as did the midshaft portion of the left fibula.

References

Abbott, David R.
1994   Detailed Analysis of Sherds. In *The Pueblo Grande Project: Ceramics and the Production and Exchange of Pottery in the Central Phoenix Basin*, edited by David R. Abbott, pp. 261–370. Soil Systems Publications in Archaeology No. 20, Vol. 3, Pt. 1. Phoenix.

Adams, Jenny L.
1979   Part I: Stone Implements, Miscellaneous Ground Stone, Miscellaneous Stone Artifacts, and Natural Objects. In *Walpi Archaeological Project Phase II, Volume IV: Stone Artifacts*, by Jenny L. Adams and David Greenwald, pp. 1–220. Museum of Northern Arizona, Flagstaff.

Ahlstrom, Richard V. N.
1985   *The Interpretation of Tree-ring Dates*. Ph.D. dissertation, Department of Anthropology, University of Arizona, Tucson.

1992   *A Class III Archaeological Survey on the Yavapai-Prescott Reservation, near Prescott, Yavapai County, Arizona*. SWCA Archaeological Report No. 92-21. Tucson.

Anderson, C. A., E. A. Scholz, and J. D. Strobell, Jr.
1955   *Geology and Ore Deposits of the Bagdad Area, Yavapai County, Arizona*. U.S. Geological Survey Professional Paper No. 278. Washington, D.C.

Anduze, Richard A., James M. Potter, and Thomas N. Motsinger
1999   *The Hassayampa Archaeological Project: Prehistory and History in West Prescott, Arizona*. SWCA Cultural Resources Report No. 98-10. Flagstaff.

Arriaza, Bernardo T., Charles F. Merbs, and Bruce M. Rothschild
1993   Diffuse Idiopathic Skeletal Hyperostosis in Meroitic Nubians from Semna South, Sudan. *American Journal of Physical Anthropology* 92:243–248.

Austin, Ken
2000   The Mountain Patayan People of West-central Arizona. Reprinted in *Archaeology in West-Central Arizona: Proceedings of the 1996 Arizona Archaeological Council Prescott Conference*, edited by Thomas N. Motsinger, Douglas R. Mitchell, and James M. McKie, pp. 63–74. Sharlot Hall Museum Press, Prescott.

Bannister, B., E. A. M. Gell, and J. W. Hannah
1966   *Tree-ring Dates from Arizona N–Q: Verde–Show Low–St. Johns Area*. Laboratory of Tree-Ring Research, University of Arizona, Tucson.

Barnett, Franklin
1970   *Matli Ranch Ruins: A Report of Excavation of Five Small Prehistoric Indian Ruins of the Prescott Culture in Arizona*. Museum of Northern Arizona Technical Series No. 10. Flagstaff.

1973a   *Lonesome Valley Ruin in Yavapai County, Arizona*. Museum of Northern Arizona Technical Series No. 13. Flagstaff.

1973b   *Dictionary of Prehistoric Indian Artifacts of the Southwest*. Northland Press, Flagstaff.

1974   *Excavation of Main Pueblo at Fitzmaurice Ruin: Prescott Culture in Yavapai County, Arizona*. Museum of Northern Arizona, Flagstaff.

1975   *Excavation of a Lower Room at Fitzmaurice Ruins (NA4031): A Prehistoric Prescott Culture Ruin in Yavapai County, Arizona*. Yavapai College, Prescott.

1978   *Las Vegas Ranch Ruin–East and Las Vegas Ranch Ruin–West: Two Small Prehistoric Prescott Indian Culture Ruins in West Central Arizona*. Museum of Northern Arizona Bulletin No. 51. Flagstaff.

1981   *These Were the Prehistoric Prescott Indians: A History of the Tenure of These Pioneers in Arizona*. Yavapai Chapter, Arizona Archaeological Society, Prescott.

Bass, William M.
1987   *Human Osteology: A Laboratory Field Manual.*
        3rd ed. Missouri Archaeological Society,
        Columbia.

Bayham, Frank E.
1977   Appendix E: Analysis of Faunal Remains and
        Animal Exploitation in Copper Basin. In
        *Archaeology in Copper Basin, Yavapai County,
        Arizona,* by Marvin D. Jeter, pp. 339–367. Ari-
        zona State University Archaeological Research
        Paper No. 11. Tempe.

Bernard-Shaw, Mary
1983   The Stone Tool Assemblage of the Salt-Gila
        Aqueduct Project Sites. In *Hohokam Archaeol-
        ogy along the Salt-Gila Aqueduct Central Ari-
        zona Project: Material Culture,* edited by Lynn
        S. Teague and Patricia L. Crown, pp. 373–443.
        Arizona State Museum Archaeological Series
        No. 150, Vol. 8. University of Arizona, Tucson.

1984   A Systematic and Comparative Study of
        Hohokam Tabular Tool Use. Paper presented at
        the 49th Annual Meeting of the Society for
        American Archaeology, Portland.

1985   MNA Tabular Knives Abstract. Ms. on file,
        SWCA Environmental Consultants, Flagstaff.

Black, T. K., III
1978   A New Method for Assessing the Sex of Frag-
        mentary Skeletal Remains: Femoral Shaft Cir-
        cumference. *American Journal of Physical
        Anthropology* 48:227–231.

Bradford, K.
1974   Conference on Central Arizona Plainwares. *Pot-
        tery Southwest* 1(3):2–3.

Brandes, Ray
1960   *Frontier Military Posts of Arizona.* Dale Stuart
        King, Globe.

Braun, David P., and Stephen Plog
1982   Evolution of "Tribal" Social Networks: Theory
        and Prehistoric North American Evidence.
        American Antiquity 47:504–525.

Breternitz, David A.
1960   *Excavations at Three Sites in the Verde Valley,
        Arizona.* Museum of Northern Arizona Bulletin
        No. 34. Flagstaff.

1966   *An Appraisal of Tree-Ring Dated Pottery in the
        Southwest.* University of Arizona Anthropologi-
        cal Papers No. 10. Tucson.

Brothwell, D. R.
1965   *Digging up Bones.* Cornell University Press,
        Ithaca.

Brown, David E., and Charles H. Lowe
1980   *Biotic Communities of the Southwest.* USDA
        Forest Service General Technical Report No.
        RM-78. Rocky Mountain Forest and Range
        Experiment Station, Fort Collins.

Bruggmann, Maximilien, and Sylvio Acatos
1990   *Pueblos: Prehistoric Indian Cultures of the
        Southwest.* Facts on File, New York.

Brusca, Richard C.
1980   *Common Intertidal Invertebrates of the Gulf of
        California.* 2nd ed. University of Arizona Press,
        Tucson.

Bubemyre, T., and Barbara J. Mills
1993   Clay Oxidation Analysis. In *Across the Colo-
        rado Plateau, Anthropological Studies for the
        Transwestern Pipeline Expansion Project:
        Interpretation of Ceramic Artifacts,* vol. 16,
        edited by Barbara J. Mills, Christine E. Goetze,
        and Maria Nieves Zedeño, pp. 235–277. Office
        of Contract Archeology and Maxwell Museum
        of Anthropology, University of New Mexico,
        Albuquerque.

Castetter, Edward F., Willis H. Bell, and Alvin R. Grove
1938   *Ethnobiological Studies in the American South-
        west: The Early Utilization and the Distribution
        of Agave in the American Southwest.* University
        of New Mexico Bulletin No. 6, Vol. 335. Albu-
        querque.

Caywood, Louis P.
1936   Fitzmaurice Ruin. In *Two Pueblo Ruins in West Central Arizona*, by Edward H. Spicer and Louis P. Caywood, pp. 87–115. University of Arizona Social Science Bulletin No. 10, Pt. 2. Tucson.

Caywood, Louis P., and Edward H. Spicer
1935   *Tuzigoot: The Excavation and Repair of a Ruin on the Verde River near Clarkdale, Arizona.* USDI National Park Service, Field Division of Education, Berkeley.

Chesterman, Charles W.
1978   *National Audubon Society Field Guide to North American Rocks and Minerals.* Alfred A. Knopf, New York.

Christenson, Andrew L.
1992   *Archaeological Overview of the City of Prescott.* City of Prescott, Arizona.

1995   Petrographic Analysis of Ceramics from the Neural and Sundown Sites. Ms. in possession of author, Prescott.

1996   Petrographic Analysis of Sands, Self-tempered Clays, and Prehistoric Ceramics in the Prescott Area. Paper presented at the Prescott Ceramics Conference, Prescott.

1997a   Identification of Mica in Prescott Area Ceramics. Ms. in possession of author.

1997b   Mean Ceramic Dating of Several Prescott Area Sites. In *The Neural Site, NA 20788*, edited by Joanne Grossman, pp. 69–75. Yavapai Chapter, Arizona Archaeological Society, Prescott.

2000   Petrographic Analysis of Sands, Self-tempered Clays, and Prehistoric Ceramics from the Prescott Area. In *Archaeology in West-Central Arizona: Proceedings of the 1996 Arizona Archaeological Council Prescott Conference*, edited by Thomas N. Motsinger, Douglas R. Mitchell, and James M. McKie, pp. 155–163. Sharlot Hall Museum Press, Prescott.

2001   Petrographic Analysis of Pottery from Five Prescott Culture Sites on or near the Yavapai-Prescott Indian Reservation. Report prepared for the Yavapai-Prescott Indian Tribe, Prescott.

2002   Ceramic Analysis. In *Archaeological Testing of Sites in Phase 2 of the StoneRidge Development, Prescott Valley, Yavapai County, Arizona*, by Banks L. Leonard, Mark R. Hackbarth, Aron J. Adams, Andrew L. Christenson, Phillip L. Condrey, and Brian E. Yunker, pp. 5.1–5.16. Soil Systems Technical Report No. 01-51. Phoenix.

ca. 2004   Two Amateur Archaeologists: George Langford and J. W. Simmons Encounter a Professionalizing Discipline. In preparation.

Chronic, Halka
1983   *Roadside Geology of Arizona.* Mountain Press, Missoula.

Cline, Joanne, and Earl Cline
1983   *The Storm Site, NA13,407: Excavations of Two Small Prescott Culture Ruins. The Arizona Archaeologist* No. 18. Arizona Archaeological Society, Phoenix.

Colton, Harold S.
1939a   *Prehistoric Culture Units and their Relationships in Northern Arizona.* Museum of Northern Arizona Bulletin No. 17. Flagstaff.

1939b   *An Archaeological Survey of Northwestern Arizona Including the Descriptions of Fifteen New Pottery Types.* Museum of Northern Arizona Bulletin No. 16. Flagstaff.

1941   *Winona and Ridge Ruin, Part II: Notes on the Technology and Taxonomy of the Pottery.* Museum of Northern Arizona Bulletin No. 19. Flagstaff

1955   *Check List of Southwestern Pottery Types.* Museum of Northern Arizona Ceramic Series No. 2. Flagstaff.

1958   *Pottery Types of the Southwest, Wares 14–18.* Museum of Northern Arizona Ceramic Series No. 3D. Flagstaff

1965   *Check List of Southwestern Pottery Types.* 2nd ed. Museum of Northern Arizona Ceramic Series No. 2. Flagstaff.

1974   Hopi History and Ethnobotany. In *Hopi Indians*, by Harold S. Colton, pp. 279–424. Garland, New York.

Colton, Harold S., and Lyndon L. Hargrave
1935   Naming Pottery Types and Rules of Priority. *Science* 82:462–463.

1937   *Handbook of Northern Arizona Pottery Wares.* Museum of Northern Arizona Bulletin No. 11. Flagstaff.

Cordell, Linda S.
1984   *Prehistory of the Southwest.* Academic Press, New York.

Crabtree, Don E.
1982   *An Introduction to Flintworking.* Idaho State University Museum Occasional Paper No. 28. Pocatello.

Crown, Patricia L.
1994   *Ceramics and Ideology.* University of New Mexico Press, Albuquerque.

Cummings, Linda Scott, Kathryn Puseman, and Thomas E. Moutoux
1999   Pollen and Macrofloral Analyses. In *The Hassayampa Archaeological Project: Prehistory and History in West Prescott, Arizona*, prepared by Richard A. Anduze, James M. Potter, and Thomas N. Motsinger, pp. 5.1–5.51. SWCA Cultural Resources Report No. 98-10. Flagstaff.

Deer, W. A., R. A. Howie, and J. Zussman
1962   *Rock Forming Minerals: Sheet Silicates.* vol. 3. Longman, London.

Dickinson, William R.
1970   Interpreting Detrital Modes of Greywacke and Arkose. *Journal of Sedimentary Petrology* 40: 695–707.

Di Peso, Charles C., John B. Rinaldo, and Gloria J. Fenner
1974   *Casas Grandes, A Fallen Center of the Gran Chichimeca: Stone and Metal.* Amerind Foundation Series No. 9, Vol. 7. Dragoon.

Dodd, Walter A., Jr.
1979   The Wear and Use of Battered Tools at Armijo Rockshelter. In *Lithic Use-Wear Analysis*, edited by Bryan Hayden, pp. 231–242. Academic Press, San Diego and Orlando.

Dosh, Deborah
1987   Ceramics. In *Archaeological Investigations, Iron Springs Land Exchange*, by Steven G. Dosh, pp. 12–15. Museum of Northern Arizona, Flagstaff.

Dosh, Steven G., and Carl D. Halbirt
1985   *The Mammoth Wash Project: Hunter-Gatherer Adaptation in the Mountain Region of West-Central Arizona.* Museum of Northern Arizona Research Paper No. 34. Flagstaff.

Downum, Christian E.
1988   *"One Grand History": A Critical Review of Flagstaff Archaeology, 1851–1988.* Ph.D. dissertation, Department of Anthropology, University of Arizona, Tucson.

Doyel, David E., and Mark D. Elson
1985   Ceramic Analysis. In *Hohokam Settlement and Economic Systems in the Central New River Drainage, Arizona*, edited by David E. Doyel and Mark D. Elson, pp. 437–519. Soil Systems Publications in Archaeology No. 4. Phoenix.

El-Najjar, M. Y., B. Lozoff, and D. J. Ryan
1975   The Paleoepidemiology of Porotic Hyperostosis in the American Southwest: Radiological and Ecological Considerations. *American Journal of Roentgenology, Radium Therapy, and Nuclear Medicine* 125:918–924.

Euler, Robert C.
1956   A Large Clay Figurine from Prescott, Arizona. *The Kiva* 22:4–7.

1958   *Walapai Culture History.* Ph.D. dissertation, University of New Mexico, Albuquerque.

1982 Ceramic Patterns of the Hakataya Tradition. In *Southwestern Ceramics: A Comparative Review*, edited by Albert H. Schroeder, pp. 53–69. *The Arizona Archaeologist* No. 10. Arizona Archaeological Society, Phoenix.

Euler, Robert C., and Henry F. Dobyns
1962 Excavations West of Prescott, Arizona. *Plateau* 34(3):69–84.

Everitt, B. S.
1977 *The Analysis of Contingency Tables*. Chapman and Hall, London.

Fairley, Helen C., and Phil R. Geib
1989 Data Gaps and Research Issues in Arizona Strip Prehistory. In *Man, Models and Management: An Overview of the Archaeology of the Arizona Strip and the Management of its Cultural Resources*, by Jeffrey H. Altschul and Helen C. Fairley, pp. 219–244. Statistical Research, Inc., Tucson.

Feinman, Gary M., Steadman Upham, and Kent Light-foot
1981 The Production Step Measure: An Ordinal Index of Labor Input in Ceramic Manufacture. *American Antiquity* 46:871–884.

Felger, Richard Stephen, and Mary Beck Moser
1991 *People of the Desert and Sea*. University of Arizona Press, Tucson.

Fewkes, Jesse W.
1912 Antiquities of the Upper Verde River and Walnut Creek Valleys, Arizona. In *Twenty-Eighth Annual Report of the Bureau of American Ethnology*, pp. 185–220. Smithsonian Institution, Washington, D.C.

Field, J. J.
1992 Petrographic Analysis of Ceramics. In *Archaeological Investigations at Lee Canyon: Kayenta Anasazi Farmsteads in the Upper Basin, Coconino County, Arizona*, edited by Stephanie M. Whittlesey, pp. 223–227. Statistical Research Technical Series No. 38. Tucson.

Fink, T. Michael
1986 Parasitism and Porotic Hyperostosis: A Study at Mt. Elden Pueblo. Paper presented at the 13th Annual Meeting of the Paleopathology Association, Albuquerque.

1989 The Human Skeletal Remains from the Grand Canal Ruins, AZ T:12:14 (ASU) and AZ T:12:16 (ASU). In *Archaeological Investigations at the Grand Canal Ruins: A Classic Period Site in Phoenix, Arizona*, edited by Douglas R. Mitchell, pp. 619–704. Soil Systems Publications in Archaeology No. 12. Phoenix.

Fish, Paul R., and Suzanne K. Fish
1977 *Verde Valley Archaeology: Review and Prospective*. Museum of Northern Arizona Research Paper No. 8. Flagstaff.

Fish, Suzanne K., Paul R. Fish, and John H. Madsen
1985 A Preliminary Analysis of Hohokam Settlement Pattern and Agriculture in the Northern Tucson Basin. In *Proceedings of the 1983 Hohokam Symposium*, edited by Alfred E. Dittert, Jr., and Donald E. Dove, pp. 75–106. Arizona Archaeological Society Occasional Papers No. 2, Pt. 1. Phoenix.

Fish, Suzanne K., Paul R. Fish, Charles Miksicek, and John Madsen
1985 Prehistoric Agave Cultivation in Southern Arizona. *Desert Plants* 7:107–112.

Formby, D. E.
1986 Pinto-Gypsum Complex Projectile Points from Arizona and New Mexico. *The Kiva* 51(2):99–127.

Fowler, M. G.
1934 Spectroscopic Examination of Potsherds: Potsherd Data. Ms. on file, Museum of Northern Arizona Ceramic Repository, Flagstaff.

1935 Spectrographic Examination of Potsherds. In *Tuzigoot: The Excavation and Repair of a Ruin on the Verde River near Clarkdale, Arizona*, by Louis P. Caywood and Edward H. Spicer, pp. 109–111. USDI National Park Service, Field Division of Education, Berkeley.

Frampton, F. P.
1978   Las Vegas Ranch Ruin–East: Analysis of Pot-
        sherds and Ceramic Wares. In *Las Vegas Ranch
        Ruin–East and Las Vegas Ranch Ruin–West:
        Two Small Prehistoric Prescott Indian Culture
        Ruins in West Central Arizona*, by Franklin Bar-
        nett, pp. 52–64. Museum of Northern Arizona
        Bulletin No. 51. Flagstaff.

1981   Comments on the Ceramics of the Prescott
        Region. In *These Were the Prehistoric Prescott
        Indians*, by Franklin Barnett, pp. 83–87. Yava-
        pai Chapter, Arizona Archaeological Society,
        Prescott.

Fryman, L. R.
1988   Ceramic Analysis. In *Archaeological Investiga-
        tions at Feature 40, AZ N:7:13 (ASM), at the
        U.S. Veterans Administration Medical Center,
        Prescott, Yavapai County, Arizona*, by D. G.
        Landis, pp. 28–33. Soil Systems Technical
        Report No. 88-5. Phoenix.

Gasser, Robert E.
1977   Appendix B. The Relationship of Plant Ecology
        and Plant Remains to Prehistoric Subsistence in
        Copper Basin. In *Archaeology in Copper Basin,
        Yavapai County, Arizona*, by Marvin D. Jeter,
        pp. 339–367. Arizona State University Archaeo-
        logical Research Paper No. 11. Tempe.

Genoves, S.
1967   Proportionality of Long Bones and their Rela-
        tion to Stature among Mesoamericans. *American
        Journal of Physical Anthropology* 26:67–78.

Gifford, E. W.
1936   *Northeastern and Western Yavapai*. University
        of California Publications in American Archae-
        ology and Ethnology Vol. 34, No. 4. Berkeley.

Gilbert, B. Miles
1980   *Mammalian Osteology*. Modern Printing for B.
        Miles Gilbert, Laramie.

Gilbert, B. Miles, Larry D. Martin, and Howard G. Sav-
age
1981   *Avian Osteology*. Modern Printing for B. Miles
        Gilbert, Laramie.

Gladwin, Harold S.
1934   *A Method for Designation of Cultures and Their
        Variations*. Medallion Papers No. 15. Gila
        Pueblo, Globe.

Gladwin, Winifred, and Harold S. Gladwin
1930a   *An Archaeological Survey of the Verde Valley*.
        Medallion Papers No. 6. Gila Pueblo, Globe.

1930b   *The Western Range of the Red-on-buff Culture*.
        Medallion Papers No. 5. Gila Pueblo, Globe.

Goodman, Alan H., G. J. Armelagos, and Jerome Rose
1984   The Chronological Distribution of Enamel Hypo-
        plasias from Prehistoric Dickson Mound Popula-
        tions. *American Journal of Anthropology*
        56:259–266.

Goodman, John D., II
1996   Faunal Remains from Areas 6 and 15, Pueblo
        Salado. In *Life on the Floodplain: Further
        Investigations at Pueblo Salado for Phoenix Sky
        Harbor International Airport*, edited by David
        H. Greenwald, Jean H. Ballagh, Douglas R.
        Mitchell, and Richard A. Anduze, pp. 245–277.
        Pueblo Grande Museum Anthropological Papers
        No. 4, Vol. 2. Phoenix.

Granger, Byrd H.
1960   *Will C. Barnes' Arizona Place Names*. Univer-
        sity of Arizona Press, Tucson.

Gratz, K., and D. C. Fiero
1974   *Agua Fria–Verde River Brownware Conference,
        16th Southwestern Ceramic Seminar*. Museum
        of Northern Arizona, Flagstaff.

Grayson, Donald K.
1984   *Quantitative Zooarchaeology: Topics in the
        Analysis of Archaeological Faunas*. Academic
        Press, New York.

Greenwald, Dawn M.
1988   Ground Stone. In *Hohokam Settlement along the
        Slopes of the Picacho Mountains: Material Cul-
        ture, Tucson Aqueduct Project*, edited by Martha
        M. Callahan, pp. 127–220. Museum of Northern
        Arizona Research Paper No. 35, Vol. 4. Flag-
        staff.

1990   *A Functional Evaluation of Hohokam Food Grinding Systems.* Master's thesis, Department of Anthropology, Northern Arizona University, Flagstaff.

1993   Ground Stone Artifacts from La Ciudad de los Hornos. In *In the Shadow of South Mountain: The Pre-Classic Hohokam of La Ciudad de los Hornos, 1991–1992 Excavations,* edited by Mark L. Chenault, Richard V. N. Ahlstrom, and Thomas N. Motsinger, pp. 317–358. SWCA Archaeological Report No. 93-30, Pt. 1. Tucson.

1994   Tabular Knives: Techno-Morphological Variation within a Tool Class. Paper presented at the 59th Annual Meeting of the Society for American Archaeology, Anaheim.

1996   Intraregional Comparisons of Flaked and Ground Stone Assemblages from Temporary and Permanently Occupied Sites. In *The Sky Harbor Project: Early Desert Farming and Irrigation Settlements. Archaeological Investigations in the Phoenix Sky Harbor Center: Special Studies, Synthesis, and Conclusions,* edited and compiled by David H. Greenwald and Jean H. Ballagh, pp. 193–215. SWCA Anthropological Research Paper No. 4, Vol. 4. Flagstaff and Tucson.

Grossman, Robert E.
2000   The Neural Site: A Late Prescott Area Site. In *Archaeology in West-Central Arizona: Proceedings of the 1996 Arizona Archaeological Council Prescott Conference,* edited by Thomas N. Motsinger, Douglas R. Mitchell, and James M. McKie, pp. 81–90. Sharlot Hall Museum Press, Prescott.

Gumerman, George J., John B. Thrift, and Robert H. Miller
1973   An Inventory and Assessment of the Archaeological Inventory of Phelps Dodge Selected and Offered Lands: Copper Basin and Parts of the Verde Drainage System. Ms. on file, USDA Prescott National Forest, Supervisor's Office, Prescott.

Gustafson, G., and G. Koch
1974   Age Estimation up to 16 Years of Age Based on Dental Development. *Odontologisk Revy* 25:297–306.

Hargrave, Lyndon L.
1932   *Guide to Forty Pottery Types from the Hopi Country and the San Francisco Mountains, Arizona.* Museum of Northern Arizona Bulletin No. 1. Flagstaff.

Harrington, James F.
1972   Seed Storage and Longevity. In *Seed Biology,* vol. 3, edited by T. T. Kozlowski, pp. 145–240. Academic Press, New York.

Haury, Emil W.
1937a   Figurines and Miscellaneous Clay Objects. In *Excavations at Snaketown: Material Culture,* by Harold S. Gladwin, Emil W. Haury, E. B. Sayles, and Nora Gladwin, pp. 233–245. Medallion Papers No. 25. Gila Pueblo, Globe.

1937b   Shell. In *Excavations at Snaketown: Material Culture,* edited by Harold S. Gladwin, Emil W. Haury, E. B. Sayles, and Nora Gladwin, pp. 135–153. Medallion Papers No. 25. Gila Pueblo, Globe.

Hawley, Florence M.
1936   *Field Manual of Prehistoric Southwestern Pottery Types.* University of New Mexico Bulletin No. 291, Anthropological Series No. 1, Vol. 4. Albuquerque.

1938   Classification of Black Pottery Pigments and Paint Areas. *University of New Mexico Bulletin* No. 321, *Anthropological Series* 2(4):3–14.

Hays-Gilpin, Kelley, and Mary-Ellen Walsh-Anduze
1997   Prescott Ceramic Conference Results. *Arizona Archaeological Council Newsletter* 21(1):2–3.

Higgins, Elisabeth S. (Betty)
1997   Analysis of the Ceramic Collection. In *The Neural Site, NA 20788,* edited by Joanne Grossman, pp. 19–53. Yavapai Chapter, Arizona Archaeological Society, Prescott.

2000   The Neural Site: A New Look at Prescott Tradition Ceramics. In *Archaeology in West-Central Arizona: Proceedings of the 1996 Arizona Archaeogical Council Prescott Conference,* edited by Thomas N. Motsinger, Douglas R. Mitchell, and James M. McKie, pp. 165–176. Sharlot Hall Museum Press, Prescott.

Hoffman, J. M.
1979   Age Estimation from Diaphyseal Lengths: Two
        Months to Twelve Years. *Journal of Forensic
        Sciences* 24(2):461–469.

Horton, Sarah
1994a   *Excavation of Lynx Creek Ruin: A Study of
        Architectural Differentiation.* Master's thesis,
        Department of Anthropology, Northern Arizona
        University, Flagstaff.

1994b   Ceramic Analysis. In *Archaeological Excava-
        tions of the Campground Site, AR-03-09-03-
        276, Granite Basin, Prescott National Forest,*
        by Noel Logan and Sarah Horton, pp. 19–28.
        Southwestern Environmental Consultants, Inc.,
        Sedona.

Horton, Sarah, and Noel Logan
1992   *Cultural Resource Survey of the Maverick Inte-
        grated Resource Management Area, Bradshaw
        Ranger District, Prescott National Forest.*
        Southwestern Environmental Consultants, Inc.,
        Sedona.

1993   *Archaeological Data Recovery for an Archaic
        Site near Glassford Hill, Prescott Valley, Ari-
        zona.* Southwest Environmental Consultants,
        Inc., Sedona.

1994   *Testing Excavations at Three Sites for Lynx
        Creek Ranch Estates, Prescott Valley, Arizona.*
        Southwest Environmental Consultants, Inc.,
        Sedona.

1995   *Cultural Resource Survey of the Crooks Canyon/
        Maverick Ecosystem Management Area, Brad-
        shaw Ranger District, Prescott National Forest,
        Arizona.* Rincon Archaeology, Williams.

1996   *Heritage Resource Inventory for the Prescott
        Basin Ecosystem Management Area, Bradshaw
        Ranger District, Prescott National Forest, Ari-
        zona.* Rincon Archaeology, Sedona.

Hudgens, B. R.
1975   *The Archaeology of Exhausted Cave: A Study of
        Prehistoric Cultural Ecology on the Coconino
        National Forest, Arizona.* Archeological Report
        No. 8. USDA Forest Service, Southwestern
        Region, Flagstaff.

Hurlbut, Cornelius S., Jr.
1970   *Minerals and Man.* Random House, New York.

Iscan, M. Y., and S. R. Loth
1986   Estimation of Age and Determination of Sex
        from the Sternal Rib. In *Forensic Osteology:
        Advances in the Identification of Human
        Remains,* edited by K. J. Reichs, pp. 68–89.
        C. C. Thomas, Springfield.

James, K. G.
1973   Ceramic Analysis. In *Lonesome Valley Ruin in
        Yavapai County, Arizona,* by Franklin Barnett,
        pp. 17–21. Museum of Northern Arizona Tech-
        nical Series No. 13. Flagstaff.

1974   Analysis of the Ceramic Collection. In *Excava-
        tion of Main Pueblo at Fitzmaurice Ruin,* by
        Franklin Barnett, pp. 106–129. Museum of
        Northern Arizona, Flagstaff.

Jeter, Marvin D.
1977   *Archaeology in Copper Basin, Yavapai County,
        Arizona: Model Building for the Prehistory of
        the Prescott Region.* Arizona State University
        Anthropological Research Paper No. 11. Tempe.

Justice, Oren L., and Louis N. Bass
1978   *Principles and Practices of Seed Storage.* U.S.
        Department of Agriculture Handbook No. 506.
        Washington, D.C.

Katz, Darryl, and Judy M. Suchey
1986   Age Determination of the Male *Os pubis.* *Amer-
        ican Journal of Physical Anthropology* 69:427–
        435.

Keller, Donald R.
1993   Prescott Gray Ware. In *Across the Colorado
        Plateau, Anthropological Studies for the Tran-
        swestern Pipeline Expansion Project: Interpre-
        tation of Ceramic Artifacts,* vol. 16, edited by
        Barbara J. Mills, Christine E. Goetze, and Maria
        Nieves Zedeño, pp. 66–69. Office of Contract
        Archeology and Maxwell Museum of Anthro-
        pology, University of New Mexico, Albuquer-
        que.

Keller, Donald R., and Pat H. Stein
1985 Archaeological Study at Three Twentieth Century Yavapai Wickiup Sites, Prescott, Arizona. Ms. on file, Museum of Northern Arizona, Flagstaff.

Kent, Susan
1987 The Influence of Sedentism and Aggregation on Porotic Hyperostosis and Anaemia: A Case Study. *Man* 21:605–636.

Khera, Sigrid, and Patricia S. Mariella
1983 Yavapai. In *Southwest*, edited by Alfonso Ortiz, pp. 38–54. Handbook of North American Indians, Vol. 10, William C. Sturtevant, general editor. Smithsonian Institution, Washington, D.C.

Krieger, M. H.
1965 *Geology of the Prescott and Paulden Quadrangles, Arizona.* USGS Professional Paper No. 467. Washington, D.C.

Krogman, W. M., and M. Y. Iscan
1986 *The Human Skeleton in Forensic Medicine.* C. C. Thomas, Springfield.

Lerner, Shereen
1976 A Comparative Study of Verde Brown Ceramics from Copper Basin, Perkinsville, and the Orme-Dugas Site in Central Arizona. Ms. on file, Department of Anthropology, Arizona State University, Tempe.

Lin, Mary
1995 Early Prescott People Made Figurines—But Why? *Prescott Courier* 22 January:6A. Prescott.

Linford, L. D.
1979 *Archaeological Investigations in West-Central Arizona: The Cyprus-Bagdad Project.* Arizona State Museum Archaeological Series No. 136. University of Arizona, Tucson.

Logan, Noel, and Sarah Horton
1994 *Archaeological Excavations of the Campground Site, AR-03-09-0276, Granite Basin, Prescott National Forest.* Southwest Environmental Consultants, Inc., Sedona.

Lombard, J. P.
1987 Provenance of Sand Temper in Hohokam Ceramics, Arizona. *Geoarchaeology* 2:91–119.

Lundin, R. J.
1995 Microscopic and Electron Microprobe Analysis of Sand and Ceramic Samples from the Neural Site (NA 20788). Ms. in possession of author.

Macnider, Barbara S., Richard W. Effland, Jr., and George Ford
1989 *Cultural Resources Overview: The Prescott National Forest.* Prescott National Forest Cultural Resource Inventory Report No. 89-062, Prescott, and Archaeological Consulting Services Cultural Resource Report No. 50, Tempe.

Martin, Alexander C., and William D. Barkley
1973 *Seed Identification Manual.* University of California Press, Berkeley.

Matthews, Meredith H.
1979 Appendix B. Soil Sample Analysis of 5MT2148, Dominguez Ruin, Dolores, Colorado. In *The Dominguez Ruin: A McElmo Phase Pueblo in Southwestern Colorado*, by Alan D. Reed, pp 173–194. USDI Bureau of Land Management Cultural Resource Series No. 7. Denver.

McKern, Thomas W., and T. D. Stewart
1957 *Skeletal Age Changes in Young American Males.* U.S. Army Quartermaster Research and Development Command Technical Report No. EP-45. U.S. Government Printing Office, Washington, D.C.

McKusick, Charmion Randolph
1976 Avifauna. In *The Hohokam, Desert Farmers and Craftsmen: Excavations at Snaketown, 1964–1965*, edited by Emil W. Haury, pp. 347–377. University of Arizona Press, Tucson.

Mensforth, R. P., C. O. Lovejoy, J. W. Lallo, and George J. Armelagos
1978 The Role of Constitutional Factors, Diet, and Infectious Disease in the Etiology of Porotic Hyperostosis and Periosteal Reactions in Prehistoric Infants and Children. *American Journal of Physical Anthropology* 68:79–85.

Miksa, Elizabeth
1992   Petrographic Evaluation of Sand and Sherd
        Samples: Methodology for the Quantitative and
        Qualitative Analysis. In *The Rye Creek Project:
        Archaeology in the Upper Tonto Basin, Synthe-
        sis and Conclusions*, by Mark D. Elson and D.
        Craig, pp. 158–185. Center for Desert Archaeol-
        ogy Anthropological Papers No. 11, Vol. 3. Tuc-
        son.

Miksa, Elizabeth, and J. M. Heidke
1995   Drawing a Line in the Sands: Models of
        Ceramic Temper Provenience. In *The Roosevelt
        Community Development Study: Ceramic Chro-
        nology, Technology, and Economics*, edited by J.
        M. Heidke and M. T. Stark, pp. 133–205. Center
        for Desert Archaeology Anthropological Papers
        No. 14, Vol. 2. Tucson.

Minnis, Paul E.
1981   Seeds in Archaeological Sites: Sources and
        Some Interpretive Problems. *American Antiq-
        uity* 46:143–152.

Mitchell, Douglas R., Thomas N. Motsinger, and Mark
C. Slaughter
2000   Settlement and Land Use in the Northern Black
        Hills between Chino Valley and Clarkdale. In
        *Archaeology in West-Central Arizona: Proceed-
        ings of the 1996 Arizona Archaeological Coun-
        cil Prescott Conference*, edited by Thomas N.
        Motsinger, Douglas R. Mitchell, and James M.
        McKie, pp. 17–26. Sharlot Hall Museum Press,
        Prescott.

Morris, Earl H.
1939   *Archaeological Studies in the La Plata District:
        Southwestern Colorado and Northwestern New
        Mexico.* Carnegie Institute, Washington, D.C.

Morris, Percy A.
1966   *A Field Guide to the Shell of the Pacific Coast
        and Hawaii.* 2nd ed. Houghton Mifflin, Boston.

Motsinger, Thomas N.
1995   *Archaeological Research Design and Plan of
        Work for Sites on the Hassayampa Country Club
        Property in Prescott, Yavapai County, Arizona.*
        SWCA Environmental Consultants, Tucson.

2000   Ceramic Figurines at the Hassayampa Ruin and
        Simmons' "Groom Creek Effigy Culture." In
        *Archaeology in West-Central Arizona: Proceed-
        ings of the 1996 Arizona Archaeological Coun-
        cil Prescott Conference*, edited by Thomas N.
        Motsinger, Douglas R. Mitchell, and James M.
        McKie, pp. 145–154. Sharlot Hall Museum
        Press, Prescott.

Motsinger, Thomas N., and Douglas R. Mitchell
1994   *The Clarkdale Pipeline Archaeological Project:
        Data Recovery at Ten Sites in the Northern
        Black Hills, Yavapai County, Arizona.* SWCA
        Archaeological Report No. 94-101. Tucson.

Motsinger, Thomas N., Douglas R. Mitchell, and James
M. McKie (editors)
2000   *Archaeology in West-Central Arizona: Proceed-
        ings of the 1996 Arizona Archaeological Coun-
        cil Prescott Conference.* Sharlot Hall Museum
        Press, Prescott.

Mueller, J. W., and D. Schecter
1970   Analysis of Ceramic Wares. In *Matli Ranch
        Ruins: A Report of Excavation of Five Small
        Prehistoric Indian Ruins of the Prescott Culture
        in Arizona*, by Franklin Barnett, pp. 80–89.
        Museum of Northern Arizona Technical Series
        No. 10. Flagstaff.

Musil, Albina F.
1978   *Identification of Crop and Weed Seeds.* Hand-
        book No. 219. U.S. Department of Agriculture,
        Washington, D.C.

Neusius, Phillip D.
1988   Functional Analysis of Selected Flaked Lithic
        Assemblages from the Dolores River Valley: A
        Low-Power Microwear Approach. In *Dolores
        Archaeological Program Supporting Studies:
        Additive and Reductive Technologies*, edited by
        Eric Blinman, Carl J. Phagan, and Richard H.
        Wilshusen, pp. 209–282. U.S. Department of the
        Interior, Washington, D.C.

O'Connor, Lucille
1981   Indian Ruin in Groom Creek: Human Figurines
        Were Crude, While Animals Showed Creative
        Detail. *Prescott Courier Westward Magazine*
        71(April):4–5.

Ogg, Jack L.
1973a Prehistoric Indian Sites of West Prescott. Ms. on file, Sharlot Hall Museum, Prescott.

1973b Letter to Mr. and Mrs. Franklin Barnett. 23 February. Copy on file, SWCA Environmental Consultants, Tucson.

Olsen, Stanley J.
1964   *Mammal Remains from Archaeological Sites, Southeastern and Southwestern United States.* Papers of the Peabody Museum of Archaeology and Ethnology Vol. 56, No. 1. Harvard University, Cambridge.

1968   *Fish, Amphibian, and Reptile Remains from Archaeological Sites.* Papers of the Peabody Museum of Archaeology and Ethnology Vol. 56, No. 2. Harvard University, Cambridge.

1979   *North American Birds.* Papers of the Peabody Museum of Archaeology and Ethnology Vol. 56, Nos. 4 and 5. Harvard University, Cambridge.

Ortner, Donald J., and Walter G. J. Putschar
1985   *Identification of Pathological Conditions in Human Skeletal Remains.* Contributions to Anthropology No. 28. Smithsonian Institution, Washington, D.C.

Page, Robert
1970   Primitive Warfare in the Prescott Area. *The Arizona Archaeologist* 5:47–56. Arizona Archaeological Society, Phoenix.

Palcovich, Ann M.
1980   *Pueblo Population and Society: The Arroyo Hondo Skeletal and Mortuary Remains.* Arroyo Hondo Archaeological Series Vol. 3. School of American Research Press, Santa Fe.

Parry, William J., and Robert L. Kelly
1987   Expedient Core Technology and Sedentism. In *The Organization of Core Technology*, edited by Jay K. Johnson and Carol A. Morrow, pp. 285–304. Special Studies in Archaeological Research, Westview Press, Boulder.

Patterson, L. W.
1982   The Importance of Flake Size Distribution. *Contract Abstracts and Cultural Resource Management Archaeology* 3(1):70–72.

Pettijohn, F. J., P. E. Potter, and R. Siever
1972   *Sand and Sandstone.* Springer-Verlag, New York.

Phagan, Carl
1976   Technology: Flake Analysis. In *Prehistory of the Ayacucho Basin, Peru*, vol. 3, edited by Richard S. MacNeish, Robert K. Vierra, Antoinette Nelkin-Terner, and Carl J. Phagan, pp. 233–281. University of Michigan Press, Ann Arbor.

Phenice, T. W.
1969   A Newly Developed Visual Method of Sexing the *Os pubis. American Journal of Physical Anthropology* 30:297–302.

Pilles, Peter J., Jr.
1981a The Southern Sinagua. *Plateau* 53(1):6–17.

1981b A Review of Yavapai Archaeology. In *The Protohistoric Period in the North American Southwest, A.D. 1450–1700*, edited by David R. Wilcox and W. Bruce Masse, pp. 163–182. Arizona State University Anthropological Research Paper No. 24. Tempe.

Pilles, Peter J., Jr., and Joseph F. Katich
1967   The Excavation of Olla Negra, A Rock Shelter Site in Central Arizona, ASU O:13:3. Ms. on file, Department of Anthropology, Arizona State University, Tempe.

Potter, James M.
1995   The Effects of Sedentism on the Processing of Hunted Carcasses in the American Southwest: A Comparison of Two Pueblo IV Sites in Central New Mexico. *Kiva* 60(3):411–428.

1997   Communal Ritual and Faunal Remains: An Example from the Dolores Anasazi. *Journal of Field Archaeology* 24(3):353–364.

1999   Faunal Remains. In *Early Formative Period Occupation above the Mogollon Rim: Results of Archaeological Testing and Phase I and II Data Recovery within the Starlight Pines Land*

Exchange, Coconino National Forest, Blue Ridge Ranger District, Arizona, edited by Randal R. Fox and Lynn A. Neal, pp. 134–138. SWCA Cultural Resources Report No. 98-16. Flagstaff.

Punzmann, Walter R.
2000   Changing Adaptations along Big Bug Creek in the Early Prehistoric Period. In *Archaeology in West-Central Arizona: Proceedings of the 1996 Prescott Archaeology Conference*, edited by Thomas N. Motsinger, Douglas R. Mitchell, and James M. McKie, pp. 47–62. Sharlot Hall Museum Press, Prescott.

Punzmann, Walter R., Margerie Green, Lourdes Aguila, and Amy Phillips
1998   Life along Big Bug Creek in the Early Years: The SR 69 Cordes Junction to Mayer Archaeological Project. Archaeological Consulting Services Cultural Resources Report No. 105. Tempe.

Quick, Clarence R.
1961   How Long Can a Seed Remain Alive? In *Seeds, The Yearbook of Agriculture*, edited by A. Stefferud, pp. 94–99. U.S. Government Printing Office, Washington, D.C.

Quirt-Booth, Tina, and Kathryn Cruz-Uribe
1997   Analysis of Leporid Remains from Prehistoric Sinagua Sites, Northern Arizona. *Journal of Archaeological Science* 24:945–960.

Reed, E. K.
1939   Preliminary Study of Pottery, Room 7, Wupatki Pueblo. *Southwestern Monuments Monthly Reports Supplement* March:209–237.

Rice, Prudence M.
1976   Rethinking the Ware Concept. *American Antiquity* 41:538–543.

1987   *Pottery Analysis: A Sourcebook*. University of Chicago Press, Chicago.

Rodgers, James B.
1977   *Archaeological Investigation of the Granite Reef Aqueduct, Cave Creek Archaeological District, Arizona*. Arizona State University Archaeological Papers No. 12. Tempe.

Rodgers, James B., and Donald E. Weaver, Jr.
1990   Preliminary Testing Report and Data Recovery Research Plan for Six Archaeological Sites along State Route 69 near Dewey in Yavapai County, Arizona. Ms. on file, Arizona Department of Transportation, Phoenix.

Rogers, Malcolm J.
1939   *Early Lithic Industries of the Lower Colorado River and Adjacent Desert Areas*. San Diego Museum Papers No. 3. San Diego.

Ruskin, Fred
1993   A Short History of the Cienega Ranch, Yavapai County, Arizona. Ms. in possession of Paul V. Long, Prescott.

Russell, Frank
1975   *The Pima Indians*. Annual Report of the Bureau of American Ethnology No. 26. Reprinted. University of Arizona Press, Tucson. Originally published 1908, Smithsonian Institution, Washington, D.C.

Ryan, Denise
1992   Review of Archaic Sites on Big Chino Wash, Yavapai County, Arizona. Paper presented at the 66th Pecos Conference, Casa Malpais, Arizona.

Salls, Roy A.
1985   The Scraper Plane: A Functional Interpretation. *Journal of Field Archaeology* 12(1):99–106.

Samples, Terry, and David R. Wilcox
1991   Permit Report to Kaibab National Forest on Work of the 1990 MNA/NAU/Oberlin Archaeological Field School and Subsequent Studies during 1991. Draft.

Sayles, E. B.
1965   Stone Implements and Bowls. In *Excavations at Snaketown: Material Culture*, by Harold S. Gladwin, Emil W. Haury, E. B. Sayles, and Nora Gladwin, pp. 101–120. University of Arizona Press, Tucson.

Schaller, David M.
1994   Geographic Sources of Phoenix Basin Hohokam Plainware Based on Petrographic Analysis. In *The Pueblo Grande Project: Ceramics and the Production and Exchange of Pottery in the Cen-*

tral Phoenix Basin, edited by David R. Abbott, pp. 17–90. Soil Systems Publications in Archaeology No. 20, Vol. 3, Pt. 1. Phoenix.

Schopmeyer, C. S.
1974   *Seeds of Woody Plants in the United States.* USDA Forest Service Handbook No. 450. Washington, D.C.

Schroeder, Albert H.
1957   The Hakataya Cultural Tradition. *American Antiquity* 23(2):176–178.

1960   *The Hohokam, Sinagua and the Hakataya.* Archives of Archaeology No. 5. Madison.

1974   *The Hohokam, Sinagua and the Hakataya.* Imperial Valley College Museum Occasional Papers No. 3. Imperial.

1991   *The Hakataya Concept and Origin of Its Groups.* Office of Archaeological Studies Archeological Notes No. 47. Museum of New Mexico, Santa Fe.

Scott, Stuart D.
1960   Pottery Figurines from Central Arizona. *The Kiva* 26:11–26.

Shepard, Anna O.
1980   *Ceramics for the Archaeologist.* Carnegie Institute of Washington Publication No. 609. Washington, D.C. Originally published 1956.

Shepard, Kristopher S., and J. Simon Bruder
1996   *Spanning Forgotten Moments: Archaeological Data Recovery and Archival Research for the Yavapai Substation and Transmission Line Facilities Project, Yavapai County, Arizona.* Dames & Moore Intermountain Cultural Resource Services Research Paper No. 34. Phoenix.

1997   *A Glimpse at Projectile Point Assemblages from Five Archaeological Sites Situated along the Eastern Periphery of Lonesome Valley, Arizona.* Dames & Moore, Phoenix.

Simmons, J. W.
n.d.   J. W. Simmons Collection. On file, Arizona State Museum Archives, Tucson.

1931a   The Black on Grey Culture of Western Yavapai County. *Yavapai Magazine* 21(10):12–13, 16.

1931b   The Fitzmaurice Ruin. Compiled for Federal Works Project 41569. (cited by Barnett 1974)

Simonis, Donald E.
2000   Western Prescott and Cohonina Traditions. In *Archaeology in West-Central Arizona: Proceedings of the 1996 Arizona Archaeological Council Prescott Conference*, edited by Thomas N. Motsinger, Douglas R. Mitchell, and James M. McKie, pp. 195–203. Sharlot Hall Museum Press, Prescott.

Smith, Randall M., Christine Hanson, R. Linda Wheeler, and Charles Merbs
1977   Human Remains from Copper Basin, Arizona. In *Archaeology of Copper Basin, Yavapai County, Arizona: Model Building for the Prehistory of the Prescott Region*, edited by Marvin D. Jeter, pp. 368–375. Arizona State University Anthropological Research Paper No. 11. Tempe.

Spicer, Edward H.
1933   *The Prescott Black-on-grey Culture, Its Nature and Relations, as Exemplified in King's Ruin, Arizona.* Master's thesis, University of Arizona, Tucson.

1936   King's Ruin. In *Two Pueblo Ruins in West Central Arizona*, by Edward H. Spicer and Louis P. Caywood, pp. 5–85. University of Arizona Social Science Bulletin No. 10, Pt. 1. Tucson.

Spicer, Edward H., and Louis P. Caywood
1936   *Two Pueblo Ruins in West Central Arizona.* University of Arizona Social Science Bulletin No. 10. Tucson.

Spoerl, Patricia M., John C. Ravesloot, and George J. Gumerman
1984   Cultural History and Chronology. In *Prehistoric Cultural Development in Central Arizona: Archaeology of the Upper New River Region*, edited by Patricia M. Spoerl and George J. Gumerman, pp. 163–181. Center for Archaeological Investigations Occasional Paper No. 5. Southern Illinois University, Carbondale.

Steele, D. G.
1970   Estimation of Stature from Fragments of Long
        Bones. In *Personal Identification in Mass
        Disasters*, edited by T. D. Stewart, pp. 85–97.
        National Museum of Natural History, Smith-
        sonian Institution, Washington, D.C.

Steele, D. G., and C. A. Bramblett
1988   *The Anatomy and Biology of the Human Skele-
        ton*. Texas A&M University Press, College Sta-
        tion.

Stenholm, Nancy A.
1994   Paleoethnobotanical Analysis of Archaeologi-
        cal Samples Recovered in the Fort Rock Basin.
        In *Archaeological Researches in the Northern
        Great Basin: Fort Rock Archaeology since
        Cressman*, edited by C. M. Aikens and D. L.
        Jenkins, pp. 531–559. University of Oregon
        Anthropological Papers No. 50. Department of
        Anthropology and State Museum of Anthropol-
        ogy, University of Oregon, Eugene.

Stewart, T. D.
1979   *Essentials of Forensic Anthropology*.
        C. C. Thomas, Springfield.

Stone, Connie L.
1982   An Examination of Ceramic Variability in West-
        Central Arizona. In *Granite Reef: A Study in
        Desert Archaeology*, edited by Patricia Eyring
        Brown and Connie Lynn Stone, pp. 99–131. Ari-
        zona State University Anthropological Field
        Studies No. 3. Tempe.

1986   *Deceptive Desolation: Prehistory of the Sono-
        ran Desert in West Central Arizona*. USDI
        Bureau of Land Management Cultural Resource
        Series No. 1. USDI BLM, Arizona State Office,
        Phoenix.

1987   *People of the Desert, Canyons and Pines: Pre-
        history of the Patayan Country in West Central
        Arizona*. USDI Bureau of Land Management
        Cultural Resource Series No. 5. USDI BLM,
        Phoenix.

Stuart-Macadam, Patty
1987   Porotic Hyperostosis: New Evidence to Support
        the Anemia Theory. *American Journal of Physi-
        cal Anthropology* 74:521–526.

Suchey, Judy M., Sheilagh T. Brooks, and Darryl Katz
1988   Instructional materials accompanying female
        pubic symphyseal models of the Suchey-Brooks
        system. France Casting, Fort Collins.

Suchey, Judy M., Wiseley, Dean V., and Darryl Katz
1986   Evaluation of the Todd and McKern-Stewart
        Methods for Aging the Male *Os pubis*. In *Foren-
        sic Osteology: Advances in the Identification of
        Human Remains*, edited by K. J. Reichs, pp. 33–
        67. C. C. Thomas, Springfield.

Sullivan, Alan P., III, and Kenneth C. Rozen
1985   Debitage Analysis and Archaeological Interpre-
        tation. *American Antiquity* 50:755–779.

Terzis, Lee, John D. Goodman II, and Kevin (Lex)
Palmer
1996   *A Class III Cultural Resource Inventory of
        Approximately 1,300 Acres in the Regent Mining
        District, Mineral County, Nevada*. SWCA
        Archaeological Report No. 95-195. Tucson.

Terzis, Lee A., and Thomas N. Motsinger
1995   *Class III Cultural Resource Survey of 435 Acres
        on the Hassayampa Country Club Property in
        Prescott, Yavapai County, Arizona*. SWCA
        Archaeological Report No. 95-84. Tucson.

Todd, T. W.
1920   Age Changes in the Pubic Bone I: The White
        Male Pubis. *American Journal of Physical
        Anthropology* 3:285–234.

Trotter, M., and G. C. Gleser
1952   Estimation of Stature for Long Bones of Ameri-
        can Whites and Negroes. *American Journal of
        Physical Anthropology* 10:463–514.

Ubelacker, D. H.
1989   *Human Skeletal Remains: Excavation, Analysis,
        Interpretation*. 2nd ed. Taraxacum, Washington,
        D.C.

Walker, P. L.
1986   Porotic Hyperostosis in a Marine-dependent
        California Indian Population. *American Journal
        of Physical Anthropology* 69:345–354.

Walsh-Anduze, Mary-Ellen

1994   The Pueblo Grande Whole Vessel Study: An Analysis of Production and Short-Distance Exchange. In *The Pueblo Grande Project: Ceramics and the Production and Exchange of Pottery in the Central Phoenix Basin*, edited by David R. Abbott, pp. 249–260. Soil Systems Publications in Archaeology No. 20. Phoenix.

1996   Defining the Range of Variability in Prescott Gray Ceramics. Paper presented at the Spring Meeting of the Arizona Archaeological Council, Smoki Museum, Prescott.

Ward, Albert E.

1975   The PC Ruin: Archaeological Investigations in the Prescott Tradition. *The Kiva* 40(3):131–164.

Weaver, Donald E., Jr.

1996   Early Prescott Culture Settlements in the Dewey Area. Paper presented at the 1996 Arizona Archaeological Council Prescott Conference, Smoki Museum, Prescott.

Webb, P. A. O., and Judy M. Suchey.

1985   Epiphyseal Union of the Anterior Iliac Crest and Medial Clavicle in a Modern Multiracial Sample of American Males and Females. *American Journal of Physical Anthropology* 68:457–466.

Weed, Carol S.

1973   A Model for Centralized Redistribution. Paper presented at the Annual Meeting of the Society for American Archaeology, New Orleans.

Weed, Carol S., and Albert E. Ward

1970   The Henderson Site: Colonial Hohokam in North Central Arizona: A Preliminary Report. *The Kiva* 36(2):1–12.

Westfall, Deborah, and Marvin D. Jeter

1977   The Ceramics of Copper Basin. In *Archaeology in Copper Basin, Yavapai County, Arizona: Model Building for the Prehistory of the Prescott Region*, by Marvin D. Jeter, pp. 376–389. Arizona State University Anthropological Research Paper No. 11. Tempe.

White, Tim D.

1991   *Human Osteology.* Academic Press, San Diego.

Wiessner, Polly

1983   Style and Social Information in Kalahari San Projectile Points. *American Antiquity* 49:253–276.

Wobst, H. Martin

1977   Stylistic Behavior and Information Exchange. In *For the Director: Research Essays in Honor of James B. Griffen*, edited by Charles Cleland, pp. 317–342. Museum of Anthropology Anthropological Papers No. 61. University of Michigan, Ann Arbor.

Wood, J. Scott

1978   *An Archaeological Survey of the Battle Flat Watershed Experimental Chaparral Conversion Project, Crown King Ranger District Prescott National Forest: Culture History and Prehistoric Land Use in the Bradshaw Mountains of Central Arizona.* USDA Forest Service Cultural Resources Report No. 24. Southwestern Region, Albuquerque.

1980   The Prehistoric Resources of the Skull Valley Planning Unit (BLM) Northern Section (Kirkland Creek). Ms. on file, USDI Bureau of Land Management, Phoenix.

Wood, John S.

1987   *Checklist of Pottery Types for the Tonto National Forest.* Arizona Archaeologist No. 21. Phoenix.

Woodbury, Richard B.

1954   *Prehistoric Stone Implements of Northeastern Arizona.* Reports of the Awatovi Expedition No. 6 and Papers of the Peabody Museum of American Archaeology and Ethnology No. 24. Harvard University, Cambridge.

Zedeño, Maria Nieves, J. Busman, J. Burton, and Barbara J. Mills

1993   Ceramic Compositional Analysis. In *Across the Colorado Plateau, Anthropological Studies for the Transwestern Pipeline Expansion Project: Interpretation of Ceramic Artifacts*, vol. 16, edited by Barbara J. Mills, Christine E. Goetze, and Maria Nieves Zedeño, pp. 187–234. Office of Contract Archeology and Maxwell Museum of Anthropology, University of New Mexico, Albuquerque.